RISK AND LIQUIDITY

Risk and Liquidity

HYUN SONG SHIN

OXFORD

UNIVERSITY PRESS

OXFORD
UNIVERSITY PRESS

Great Clarendon Street, Oxford OX2 6DP

Oxford University Press is a department of the University of Oxford.
It furthers the University's objective of excellence in research, scholarship,
and education by publishing worldwide in

Oxford New York

Auckland Cape Town Dar es Salaam Hong Kong Karachi
Kuala Lumpur Madrid Melbourne Mexico City Nairobi
New Delhi Shanghai Taipei Toronto

With offices in

Argentina Austria Brazil Chile Czech Republic France Greece
Guatemala Hungary Italy Japan Poland Portugal Singapore
South Korea Switzerland Thailand Turkey Ukraine Vietnam

Oxford is a registered trade mark of Oxford University Press
in the UK and in certain other countries

Published in the United States
by Oxford University Press Inc., New York

© Hyun Song Shin 2010

appear by permission of their original publishers as cited in text

The moral rights of the authors have been asserted
Database right Oxford University Press (maker)

First published 2010

All rights reserved. No part of this publication may be reproduced,
stored in a retrieval system, or transmitted, in any form or by any means,
without the prior permission in writing of Oxford University Press,
or as expressly permitted by law, or under terms agreed with the appropriate
reprographics rights organization. Enquiries concerning reproduction
outside the scope of the above should be sent to the Rights Department,
Oxford University Press, at the address above

You must not circulate this book in any other binding or cover
and you must impose the same condition on any acquirer

British Library Cataloguing in Publication Data

Data available

Library of Congress Cataloging in Publication Data
Library of Congress Control Number: 2010925610

Typeset by SPI Publisher Services, Pondicherry, India
Printed in Great Britain
on acid-free paper by
Clays Ltd, St Ives plc

ISBN 978–0–19–954636–7

1 3 5 7 9 10 8 6 4 2

Acknowledgments

These lectures draw on the many insights of my collaborators, Viral Acharya, Tobias Adrian, Gara Afonso, Franklin Allen, Jon Danielsson, Prasanna Gai, Charles Goodhart, Masazumi Hattori, Anil Kashyap, Se-Jik Kim, Stephen Morris, Guillaume Plantin, Haresh Sapra, Tanju Yorulmazer, and Jean-Pierre Zigrand, who have shaped my views and patiently tolerated my errors. I am especially grateful to Tobias Adrian and Stephen Morris for allowing me to draw on our on-going research and to Gara Afonso, Huijia Wu, and Juan Ortner for detailed comments during the preparation of the manuscript. The material in these lectures was exposed to several cohorts of students at the London School of Economics and at Princeton, and I have benefited from their feedback. Delivering the Clarendon Lectures in front of my teachers and former colleagues at Oxford was a rare privilege. I thank my former colleagues at Oxford for their hospitality and Sarah Caro and Aimee Wright at Oxford University Press for guiding this manuscript through its various stages.

Contents

List of Figures

List of Tables

1

Nature of Financial Risk

The value added of a good risk management system is that you can take more risks.

(Anonymous risk manager, Spring 2007)

One of the paradoxes of the recent global financial crisis is that the crisis erupted in an era when risk management was at the heart of the management of the largest and most sophisticated financial institutions. For institutions who see their role as making money by taking judicious risks, the management of those risks is pivotal in their daily operations. The risk manager quoted above was merely re-affirming the firm's goals. The risk manager's task is to enable the firm to fulfill its purpose by providing the framework for measuring risks accurately, enabling the firm to take advantage of greater precision so as to extract the last ounce of return from the firm's portfolio.

Financial risk is endogenous due in large part to the reasoning embedded in the opening quote. Endogenous risk refers to risks that are generated and amplified within the financial system, rather than risks from shocks that arrive from outside the financial system. The precondition for endogenous risk is the conjunction of circumstances where individual actors react to changes in their environment and where those individuals' actions *affect* their environment. As we will see in the course of this book, the financial system is the supreme example of an environment where individuals react to what's happening around them and where their actions drive the realized outcomes themselves.

Underpinning this two-way flow is the galvanizing role of market prices which serves to synchronize and amplify the feedback process. In an era where loans are packaged into securities and balance sheets are continuously marked to market, the galvanizing role of market prices reaches into every nook and cranny of the financial system. It will be a central thesis in this book that the severity of the global financial crisis is explained in large part by financial development that put marketable assets at the heart of the financial system, and the increased sophistication of financial institutions that held and traded the assets.

Millennium Bridge

But before we deal with the financial system, it is instructive to study the potency of synchronized feedback from an example from outside economics or finance. The saga of the Millennium Bridge in London is a revealing lesson on market failure from outside economics. Many readers will be familiar with the Millennium Bridge. As the name suggests, the bridge was part of the Millennium celebrations in the year 2000. It was the first new crossing over the Thames for over a hundred years, constructed at a cost of £18 million. The sleek 325 meter-long structure used an innovative "lateral suspension" design, built without the tall supporting columns that are more familiar with other suspension bridges. The vision was of a "blade of light" across the river, connecting St Paul's with the new Tate Modern gallery. The bridge was opened by the Queen on a sunny day in June, and the press was there in force. Many thousands of people turned up after the tape was cut and crowded on to the bridge to savor the occasion. However, within moments of the bridge's opening, it began to shake violently. The shaking was so severe that many pedestrians clung on to the side-rails. The BBC's website has a page dedicated to the episode and posts some dramatic video news clips of the opening day.[1] The bridge was closed shortly after the opening and was to remain closed for 18 months.

When engineers used shaking machines to send vibrations through the bridge, they found that horizontal shaking at 1 hertz (that is, at one cycle per second) set off the wobble seen on the opening day. Now, this was an important clue, since normal walking pace is around two strides per second, which means that we're on our left foot every second and on our right foot every second. Walking produces a vertical force (depending on our body mass) of around 750 Newtons or 165 pounds at 2 hertz. However, there is also a small sideways force caused by the sway of our body mass due to the fact that our legs are slightly apart. Anyone who has been on a rope bridge should be well aware of the existence of this sideways force. This force (around 25 Newtons or 5.5 pounds) is directed to the left when we are on our left foot, and to the right when we are on our right foot. This force occurs at half the frequency (or at 1 hertz). This was the frequency that was causing the problems.

But why should this be a problem? We know that soldiers should break step before crossing a bridge. For thousands of pedestrians walking at random, one person's sway to the left should be cancelled out by another's sway to the right. If anything, the principle of diversification suggests that having lots of people on the bridge is the best way of cancelling out the sideways forces on the bridge.

Or, to put it another way, what is the probability that a thousand people walking at random will end up walking exactly in step, and remain in lock-step thereafter? It is tempting to say "close to zero". After all, if each person's step is an independent event, then the probability of everyone walking in step would be the product of many small numbers—giving us a probability close to zero.

---

[1] <http://news.bbc.co.uk/hi/english/static/in_depth/uk/2000/millennium_bridge/default.stm>.

Figure 1.1: Millennium Bridge feedback

However, we have to take into account the way that people react to their environment. Pedestrians on the bridge react to how the bridge is moving. When the bridge moves from under your feet, it is a natural reaction to adjust your stance to regain balance. But here is the catch. When the bridge moves, everyone adjusts his or her stance *at the same time.* This synchronized movement pushes the bridge that the people are standing on, and makes the bridge move even more. This, in turn, makes the pedestrians adjust their stance more drastically, and so on. In other words, the wobble of the bridge feeds on itself. When the bridge wobbles, everyone adjusts their stance, which makes the wobble even worse. So, the wobble will continue and get stronger even though the initial shock (say, a small gust of wind) has long passed, as depicted in Figure 1.1.

Arup, the bridge's engineers, found that the critical threshold for the number of pedestrians that started the wobble was 156. Up to that number, the movement increased only slightly as more people came on the bridge. However, with ten more people, the wobble increased at a sharply higher rate.[2]

The wobble is an example of a shock that is generated and amplified *within* the system. It is very different from a shock that comes from a storm or an earthquake which come from outside the system. Stress testing on the computer that looks only at storms, earthquakes, and heavy loads on the bridge would regard the events on the opening day as a "perfect storm". But this is a perfect storm that is guaranteed to come every day.

Dual Role of Prices

What does all this have to do with financial markets? Financial markets are the supreme example of an environment where individuals react to what's happening around them, and where individuals' actions affect the outcomes themselves. The pedestrians on the Millennium Bridge are rather like modern banks that react to price changes, and the movements in the bridge itself are rather like price changes in the market. So, under the right conditions, price changes will elicit reactions from the banks, which move prices, which elicit further reactions, and so on.

Financial development has meant that banks and other financial institutions are now at the cutting edge of price-sensitive incentive schemes and price-sensitive risk-management systems. Mark-to-market accounting ensures that any price change shows up immediately on the balance sheet. So, when

---

[2] <http://www.arup.com/millenniumbridge/challenge/results.html>.

the bridge moves, banks adjust their stance more than they used to, and marking to market ensures that they all do so *at the same time*.

The Millennium Bridge example serves to highlight the dual role of prices. Prices play two roles. Not only are they a reflection of the underlying economic fundamentals, they are also an imperative to action. That is, prices induce actions on the part of the economic agents. Some actions induced by price changes are desirable, not only from the point of view of the individual, but from a system perspective, too. However, some actions borne out of binding constraints or actions that exert harmful spillover effects on others are undesirable when viewed from the perspective of the group. It is when the action-inducing nature of price changes elicits harmful spillover effects that the double-edged nature of prices takes on its maximum potency. The problem comes when the *reliance* on market prices *distorts* those same market prices. The more weight is given to prices in making decisions, the greater are the spillover effects that ultimately undermine the integrity of those prices. When prices are so distorted, their allocational role is severely impaired. Far from promoting efficiency, contaminated prices undermine their allocational role.

Financial crises could almost be defined as episodes where the allocational role of prices break down. The action-inducing role of price changes introduces distortions and causes an amplified spiral of price changes and actions that can cause great damage along the way. Financial crises are often accompanied by large price changes, but large price changes by themselves do not constitute a crisis. Public announcements of important macroeconomic statistics, such as the US employment report, are sometimes marked by large, discrete price changes at the time of announcement. However, such price changes are arguably the signs of a smoothly functioning market that is able to incorporate new information quickly. The market typically finds composure quite rapidly after such discrete price changes.

In contrast, the distinguishing feature of crisis episodes is that they seem to gather momentum from the endogenous responses of the market participants themselves. Rather like a tropical storm over a warm sea, they appear to gather more energy as they develop. As financial conditions worsen, the willingness of market participants to bear risk seemingly evaporates. Such episodes have been

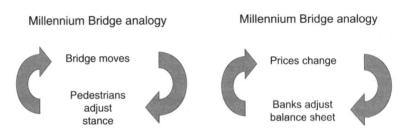

Figure 1.2: Feedback in financial systems

dubbed "liquidity black holes". The terminology is perhaps overly dramatic, but it conveys the sense of free-fall. As prices fall or measured risks rise or previous correlations break down (or some combination of the three), previously over-stretched market participants respond by cutting back, giving a further push to the downward spiral. The global financial crisis that erupted in 2007 has served as a live laboratory for many such distress episodes.

Imagine an emerging market country defending a currency peg in adverse circumstances in the face of deteriorating macroeconomic conditions and hostile capital markets. Similar forces operate in more recent crises, including the events surrounding the runs on Bear Stearns and Lehman Brothers in the crisis of 2008. Defending the peg is often dictated by political goals more than economic ones, such as eventual accession to the European Union, the adoption of the euro, or keeping the peg in tact in order to shield domestic borrowers who have borrowed in dollars or euros.

However, defending the currency also entails raising interest rates and keeping them high. The costs of defending the currency bear many depressingly familiar symptoms—collapsing asset values and a weakened domestic banking system that chokes off credit to the rest of the economy. Whatever the perceived political benefits of maintaining a currency peg, and whatever their official pronounce-ments, all governments and their monetary authorities have a pain threshold at which the costs of defending the peg outweighs the benefits of doing so. Specu-lators understand well that their job is almost done when the finance minister of the stricken country appears on evening television vowing never to devalue the currency. Understanding the source and the severity of this pain is a key to understanding the onset of currency attacks.

Facing the monetary authority is an array of diverse private sector actors, both domestic and foreign, whose interests are affected by the actions of the other members of this group, and by the actions of the monetary authority and government. The main actors are domestic companies and households, domestic banks and their depositors, foreign creditor banks, and outright speculators—whether in the form of hedge funds or the proprietary trading desks of the international banks. Two features stand out, and deserve emphasis.

First, each of these diverse actors faces a choice between actions which exacer-bate the pain of maintaining the peg and actions which are more benign. Second, the more prevalent are the actions which increase the pain of holding the peg, the greater is the incentive for an individual actor to adopt the action which increases the pain. In other words, the actions which tend to undermine the currency peg are mutually reinforcing.

Imagine that we are in Thailand in the early summer of 1997 just prior to the onset of the Asian financial crisis. For domestic financial institutions or com-panies which had borrowed dollars to finance their operations, they can either attempt to reduce their dollar exposures or not. The action to reduce their exposure—of selling Baht assets to buy dollars in order to repay their dollar loans, for example, is identical in its mechanics (if not in its intention) to the action of a hedge fund which takes a net short position in Baht in the forward

market. For domestic banks and finance companies which have facilitated such
dollar loans to local firms, they can either attempt to hedge the dollar exposure on
their balance sheets by selling Baht in the capital markets, or sit tight and tough it
out. Again, the former action is identical in its consequence to a hedge fund
short-selling Baht. As a greater proportion of these actors adopt the action of
selling the domestic currency, the greater is the domestic economic distress, and
hence the greater is the likelihood of abandonment of the peg. Everyone under-
stands this, especially the more sophisticated market players that have access to
hedging tools. As the pain of holding on to the peg reaches the critical threshold,
the argument for selling Baht becomes overwhelming. In this sense, the actions
which undermine the currency peg are mutually reinforcing.

The action-inducing nature of price changes turns up in this scenario
through balance sheet stress in the twin crisis that combines a banking crisis
with a currency crisis. The precipitous decline in the exchange rate means that
the Baht value of foreign currency debts balloons past the value of Baht assets
that have been financed with such loans. At the same time, the higher domestic
interest rates put in place to defend the currency undermine the Baht value of
those assets. Assets decline and liabilities increase. Equity is squeezed from both
directions. As the Thai Baht collapses, the mutually reinforcing nature of price
changes and distressed actions gathers momentum. As domestic firms with
dollar liabilities experience difficulties in servicing their debt, the banks which
have facilitated such dollar loans attempt to cover their foreign currency losses
and improve their balance sheet by a contraction of credit. For foreign creditor
banks with short-term exposure, this is normally a cue to cut off credit lines, or
to refuse to roll over short-term debt. Even for firms with no foreign currency
exposure, the general contraction of credit increases corporate distress. Such
deterioration in the domestic economic environment exacerbates the pain of
maintaining the peg, thereby serving to reinforce the actions which tend to
undermine it. To make matters worse still, the belated hedging activity by banks
is usually accompanied by a run on their deposits, as depositors scramble to
withdraw their money.

To be sure, the actual *motives* behind these actions are as diverse as the actors
themselves. A currency speculator rubbing his hands and looking on in glee as his
target country descends into economic chaos has very different motives from a
desperate owner of a firm in that country trying frantically to salvage what he can,
or a depositor queuing to salvage her meagre life savings. However, whatever the
motives underlying these actions, they are identical in their consequences. They
all lead to greater pains of holding to the peg, and hence hasten its demise.

Booms

The action-inducing nature of market prices is at its most dramatic during
crisis episodes, but arguably it is at its most damaging in boom times when

it operates away from the glare of the television cameras. Financial crises don't happen out of the blue. They invariably follow booms. As Andrew Crockett (2000) has put it,

The received wisdom is that risk increases in recessions and falls in booms. In contrast, it may be more helpful to think of risk as *increasing* during upswings, as financial imbalances build up, and *materialising* in recessions.

To fully grasp this point, recall the opening quote from the anonymous risk manager who insisted that the value-added of a good risk management system is that one can take more risks. The risk manager was re-affirming the importance of a framework for measuring risks accurately, thereby enabling the bank to deploy its scarce capital in the most efficient way. During a boom, the action-inducing nature of market prices do their work through the increased capacity of banks to lend. When asset prices rise or measured risks fall, less capital is needed to act as a loss buffer for a given pool of loans or securities. At the same time, higher bank profits also add to the bank's capital. In boom times, banks have surplus capital.

When balance sheets are marked to market, the surplus capital becomes even more apparent. In the eyes of the bank's top management, a bank with surplus capital is like a manufacturing plant with idle capacity. Just as good managers of the manufacturing plant will utilize surplus capacity to expand their business, so the bank's top management will expand its business. If they fail to expand their business, they know that the ranks of bank equity analysts will start to castigate them for failing to achieve the 20% return on equity achieved by some of their peers.

For a bank, expanding its business means expanding its balance sheet by purchasing more securities or increasing its lending. But expanding assets means finding new borrowers. *Someone* has to be on the receiving end of new loans. When all the good borrowers already have a mortgage, the bank has to lower its lending standards in order to lend to new borrowers. The new borrowers are those who were previously shut out of the credit market, but who suddenly find themselves showered with credit. The ballooning of subprime mortgage lending could be seen through this lens.

The pressure on the bank's managers to expand lending reveals an important feature of the capital constraint facing banks. As with any meaningful economic constraint, the capital constraint binds all the time—in booms as well as in busts. Binding capital constraints during bust phase is well understood. However, less appreciated is the binding nature of the capital constraint in boom times. In boom times, the constraint operates through channels that appear more benign, such as the pursuit of shareholder value by raising return on equity.

The action-inducing effects of market prices derive their potency from the apparently tangible nature of the wealth generated when asset prices appreciate. Consider the following passage from a commentary published in the *Wall*

Street Journal in May 2005, at the height of the housing boom in the United States.[3]

While many believe that irresponsible borrowing is creating a bubble in housing, this is not necessarily true. At the end of 2004, U.S. households owned $17.2 trillion in housing assets, an increase of 18.1% (or $2.6 trillion) from the third quarter of 2003. Over the same five quarters, mortgage debt (including home equity lines) rose $1.1 trillion to $7.5 trillion. The result: a $1.5 trillion increase in net housing equity over the past 15 months.

The argument is that when the whole US housing stock is valued at the current marginal transactions price, the total value is $17.2 trillion (although it was to rise much more subsequently). Although household debt had increased by over a trillion dollars in the meantime, this still left them an increase in net worth of $1.5 trillion.

One can question how tangible this increase in housing wealth is in the face of a possible downturn. But for banks and other financial institutions who mark their balance sheets to market continuously, the increase in marked-to-market equity is very tangible indeed. The surplus capital generated by asset price appreciation and greater profits weighs on the bank's top management, and induces them to take on additional exposure. Risk spreads fall, and borrowers who did not meet the necessary hurdle begin to receive credit. The seeds of the subsequent downturn are thus sown.

The action-inducing nature of asset price booms is strongest for leveraged institutions such as banks and securities firms since leverage magnifies the increase in marked-to-market equity. Thus, the reasoning quoted above in the *Wall Street Journal* commentary ripples through the financial system through the actions of leveraged financial institutions.

The classic signs of the late stages of a boom are the compression of risk spreads and the erosion of the price of risk. The phenomenon of "search for yield" often appears in the late stages of a boom as investors migrate down the asset quality curve as risk spreads are compressed. The following commentary from the Bank of England's *Financial Stability Review* of December 2004 describes the classic symptoms.

Financial intermediaries and investors appear to have continued their "search for yield" in a wide range of markets, holding positions that could leave them vulnerable to instability in the pattern of global capital flows and exchange rates, credit events or sharper-than-expected interest rate rises. A number of market participants have also discussed the possibility that risk is being underpriced. In the event of an adverse shock, any over-accumulation of exposures from the mis-pricing of assets may result in an abrupt, and costly, adjustment of balance sheets.   (Bank of England 2004: 49)

In Chapter 3, we examine a general equilibrium model of the credit sector that plays the role of the engine of the boom-bust cycle. We will see that the double-edged nature of price changes operates in booms as well as in busts, but arguably

---

[3] "Mr. Greenspan's Cappuccino", Commentary by Brian S. Wesbury, *Wall Street Journal*, May 31, 2005. The title makes reference to Alan Greenspan's comments on the "froth" in the US housing market.

the biggest damage is done in the boom phase of the financial cycle when the outward signs are benign. The apparent "underpricing of risk" arises as an integral part of a general equilibrium of the economy where financial intermediaries use Value-at-Risk to deploy capital in the most efficient way. In this way, the biggest damage is done in booms, because that is when the worst quality loans are made.

The action-inducing nature of market prices during booms operates away from the glare of the television cameras, and without the chorus of politicians complaining about the effects of mark-to-market accounting rules. But the insidious effects of mark-to-market accounting are at their most potent during the booms. Andrew Crockett's statement that risks *increase* in booms and *materialize* in busts is an important lesson that is relearnt after each financial crisis. The challenge for policy makers is to reduce the frequency with which we undergo the re-education.

Marking to Market

The double-edged nature of market prices raises important issues for accounting, especially on the role of mark-to-market accounting rules. Some proponents of marking to market like to pose the issues in black and white terms, asking rhetorically, "Do you want the truth, or do you want a lie?"

The unstated assumption behind this rhetorical question is that accounting is just a measurement issue, leaving what is measured completely undisturbed. The assumption is that accounting is just a veil that merely obscures the true economic fundamentals, and that the role of accounting is to shine a bright light into the dark corners of a firm's accounts to illuminate the true state of that firm. In the context of completely frictionless markets, where decision making is done without distorting constraints or inefficient spillover effects, such a world view would be entirely justified.

On the other hand, in such a perfect world, accounting would be irrelevant since reliable market prices would be readily available to all, and it would simply be a matter of reading off the available prices. Just as accounting is irrelevant in such a world, so would any talk of establishing and enforcing accounting standards.

To state the proposition the other way round, accounting is relevant *only because* we live in an imperfect world, where actions may reflect distorted incentives or self-defeating constraints as well as the hypothetical economic fundamentals. In such an imperfect world, transaction prices may not always be readily available. Even those prices that are available may not correspond to the hypothetical fundamental prices that would prevail in frictionless perfect markets. Therefore, when we debate issues regarding accounting, it is important to be clear on the nature and consequences of the imperfections.

The key to the debate on marking to market is whether mark-to-market accounting injects artificial volatility into transactions prices—an additional, endogenous source of volatility that is purely a consequence of the accounting norm, rather than something that reflects the underlying fundamentals. Real decisions would then be distorted due to the measurement regime. As we have seen from the subprime crisis, distortions to real decisions can sometimes exact very large economic costs.

It is important here to distinguish volatility of prices that merely reflect the volatility of the underlying fundamentals from volatility that cannot be justified by these fundamentals. If the fundamentals themselves are volatile, then market prices will merely reflect the underlying reality. However, the "artificial" nature of the volatility refers to something more pernicious. When the decision horizons of market participants are shortened due to short-term incentives, binding constraints, or other market imperfections, then short-term price fluctuations affect the interests of these market participants, and hence will influence their actions. There is then the possibility of a feedback loop, where anticipation of short-term price movements will induce market participants to act in such a way as to amplify these price movements. When such feedback effects are strong, then banks' decisions are based on the second-guessing of others' decisions rather than on the basis of perceived fundamentals. In this sense, there is the danger of the emergence of an additional, endogenous source of volatility that is purely a consequence of the accounting norm, rather than something that reflects the underlying fundamentals.

Ultimately, it is important to be clear on the ultimate objectives of the accounting regime. What is the purpose of accounting standards? Whom should they serve? Should they serve the interests of equity investors? Should they serve the interests of a wider class of investors? Or, should we look beyond investors per se to the wider public interest, as for any other public policy issue?

Of course, in practice, we may expect wide overlaps between the interests of equity investors, creditors, and the wider public interest. However, they are logically distinct, and sometimes lead to very different policy prescriptions. Traditionally, accounting standard setters have not seen their remit extending as far as to take account of the broader public interest. In this respect, accounting may be too important to be left solely to the accountants.

Upward-Sloping Demand Responses

We will see in Chapter 3 that in a boom phase, we can characterize the decisions of a leveraged financial institution as if coming from a decision maker who has become less risk averse, even though the underlying preferences of that institution have remained unchanged. The shift in the "as if" preferences flow from the capital gains of the institution which feeds into an increased capacity to bear risk. To an outside observer, all the outward signs are that the decisions emanate from someone who has become less risk averse. The upshot is that demand responses to price changes are upward-sloping. When the price of the risky asset rises, the leveraged financial institution purchases more of the risky asset. The apparent increase in risk appetite induced by the price rise results in a desired holding of the asset that is larger than before the price increase. But then, the additional purchases of risky assets that result from such increased risk appetite fuel the asset price boom further, giving further impetus to the boom. The upward-sloping demand response has a mirror image in the downward phase of the financial cycle. When price falls, the risk appetite of the leveraged institution falls so much that, in spite of the fall in the price, the desired holding of the risky asset falls. The supply response is downward-sloping. As price falls, more of the asset is dumped on the market, depressing the price further.

The theme of upward-sloping demand response and the downward-sloping supply response goes hand in hand with the dual role of prices as both the reflection of fundamentals and the imperative for action. In Chapter 4, we see this theme being played out in the market-wide impact of dynamic hedging of options that lay behind the stock market crash of October 1987.

The Presidential Commission appointed to investigate the circumstances of the crash (and chaired by the future Treasury Secretary Nicholas Brady) identified dynamic trading strategies by portfolio insurers as one of the main contributing factors in the crash (Brady 1988). Dynamic hedging attempts to position one's portfolio in reaction to price changes in order to mimic the payoffs from a put option. Since put options pay out when prices are low, this means maintaining a short position in the asset that becomes steeper as the price falls. In other words, dynamic hedging dictates that when the price falls, you sell more of the asset. This is a strategy that induces upward-sloping demand responses and downward-sloping supply responses—exactly the type of portfolio rebalancing responses that tend to amplify price changes. Just as with the leveraged financial institutions with apparently shifting risk appetite, the portfolio insurers who relied on dynamic hedging were an illustration of the principle that prices play a dual role—both as a reflection of actions (prices fell when they sold) as well as an imperative for actions (they sold when prices fell). Once locked into this loop, the feedback effect gained momentum.

Dynamic hedging relies on liquid markets—on there being others who will buy when I sell. But liquidity is a public good that comes from the diversity of trading positions. When a large segment of the market is engaged in such trading strategies, they become consumers of liquidity rather than providers of liquidity. But when price goes down, dynamic hedging dictates even larger sales. And as the market adage goes, one should never try to catch a falling knife, and so potential buyers stand on the sidelines until the knife drops to the ground.

Indeed, upward-sloping demands and downward-sloping supplies turn out to be much more pervasive when we look around the key players in financial markets. Many hedging strategies that attempt to rebalance assets and liabilities to shifts in market prices turn out, on closer inspection, to be variations of the dynamic hedging strategy described above. Market participants who pursue such strategies are consumers of liquidity rather than providers of liquidity. The demand and supply responses that such hedging strategies give rise to are often reinforced by regulations. Such regulations, although sensible in isolation, tend to promote instability in aggregate. The matching of asset and liability durations by pension funds is a good example, and is examined in Chapter 5.

The marking to market of pension fund liabilities is a practise adopted by pension regulators motivated by the desire to ensure the solvency of pension funds and to guide them toward better risk management practises in matching their assets to their future commitments. Accounting standards combined with solvency regulation have been important spurs to the adoption of asset-liability hedging strategies by pension funds who mark their liabilities to market and then hold an asset portfolio that shifts in line with the value of its liabilities. But as we will see in Chapter 5, such hedging techniques give rise to exactly the type of perverse demand and supply responses that tend to amplify the financial cycle. Once again, there is a divergence between what is prudent from the point of view of an individual actor and what promotes a resilient financial system.

Above all, the boom-bust financial cycle owes itself to the way that the individual motives interact with the aggregate outcome in the financial system. One of the characteristic features of the financial system in the run-up to the global financial crisis of 2007 and 2008 has been the increased cross-exposures between financial institutions, whereby balance sheets of financial institutions, have become more intertwined.

We construct a framework for analysis in Chapters 6 and 9 that delves deeper into the structural features of interconnected markets. The organizing framework is the aggregate balance sheet of the banking and intermediary sector as a whole, where the assets are summed across individual institutions and the liabilities are also summed across. Every liability that a bank has to another bank is an asset when viewed from the point of view of the lending bank. One asset cancels out another equal and opposite liability. In aggregate, all the claims and obligations across banks cancel out. Thus, in aggregate, the assets of the banking sector as a whole against other sectors of the economy consist of the lending to non-bank borrowers. This lending must be met by two sources—the total equity of the banking system, and the liabilities that banks have to lenders *outside* the banking system.

In a boom scenario where the marked-to-market equity of the banks is healthy and the measured risks are low, banks attempt to increase their balance sheets— sometimes quite substantially. The fluctuations in financial intermediary balance sheets in aggregate tend to be much larger in scale compared to the available funding that is available from ultimate creditors (such as retail depositors) from outside the banking sector. Aggregate balance sheets can then grow only by the banks lending and borrowing more from each other. The desired risk-taking profiles and desired high leverage mean that banks take on more of each other's debts, and the intertwining of claims and liabilities become more far-reaching. As a consequence, the balance sheet trail from ultimate lender to ultimate borrower grows longer, and more tenuous.

The image is of an increasingly elaborate edifice built on the same narrow foundation, so that the structure becomes more and more precarious. The systemic risks therefore increase during the boom scenario.

The shortening of maturities is a natural companion to the lengthening of intermediation chains. In order for each link in the chain to be a profitable leveraged transaction, the funding leg of the transaction must be at a lower interest rate. When the yield curve is upward-sloping, this entails funding with shorter and shorter maturities at each step in the chain. The prevalence of the overnight repo as the dominant funding choice for securities firms before the current crisis can be understood in this context. The use of ultra-short-term debt is part and parcel of long intermediation chains, as is the importance of short-term interest rates in determining the rate of growth of the financial sector balance sheets that fuel the boom.

Eventually, when the boom scenario gives way to the bust, all the processes that were involved in the boom then go into reverse in the bust. Leverage and risk spreads reverse leading to smaller balance sheets. Just as expanding balance sheets entail greater intertwining of bank balance sheets, so the contraction of balance sheets entails the withdrawal of the funds that banks had granted to each other. This is a classic run scenario where banks run on other banks. The runs on Northern Rock, Bear Stearns, and Lehman Brothers are all instances of such a run. Chapter 8 is a case study of Northern Rock—the UK mortgage bank that failed in 2007, thereby heralding the global financial crisis that followed.

This brings us back full circle to the opening quote by the anonymous risk manager. Risk management is an essential part of the operation of a financial institution, and the value-added of a good risk management system can indeed be substantial. But there may be a divergence of interests between an individual firm and the system as a whole. Exploring exactly how the divergence of interests plays out in the economy is an urgent modeling task for economists. As a first step, putting Value-at-Risk into a general equilibrium context is an important conceptual task that has barely begun. More needs to be done.

As well as the intellectual endeavors, there is also a need for a clear identification of the policy priorities. Academics, policy makers, and market participants have pondered the lessons from the financial crisis, and are beginning to arrive at a consensus on the need for tougher regulatory oversight of financial institutions. However, as desirable as such regulatory changes are, they are almost certainly inadequate by themselves in meeting the challenge of the next boom-bust cycle. As the following chapter will hope to demonstrate, boom-bust cycles are driven by the fluctuations in the price of risk. Even if a new set of regulatory rules can be put in place that would have been effective at preventing yesterday's crisis, there is little guarantee that they will continue to be effective against new crises, riding on the back of as yet unimagined innovations designed to circumvent the rules.

Indeed, the greatest danger of the newly found consensus on the need for tougher regulation arises not from the possible circumvention of the rules, but rather from the opportunities that the new consensus will present to central banks to repeat their mistakes in the conduct of monetary policy by giving them the all-clear to go back to business as usual, leaving the messy and unglamorous business of financial stability to others. As we will see in this book, financial stability has to do with fluctuations in the price of risk, and monetary policy must play its part in regulating the pricing of risk. Changes to financial regulation will be for nothing if the intellectual landscape at the institution at the core of the financial system (the central bank) does not change.

Notes on Further Reading

The discussion of the Millennium Bridge is drawn from Danielsson and Shin (2003), who coined the term "endogenous risk" in the context of financial market risk. The analogy cropped up again in Shin (2005b) at the 2005 Jackson Hole symposium in a discussion on increasing financial risks. The Millennium Bridge analogy is used to good effect by John Cassidy in his recent book (Cassidy 2009), which gives a panoramic account of the intellectual roots of the mainstream economic thinking that led to the recent financial crisis. Further details on the wobble of the Millennium Bridge can be obtained from "Bad Vibrations", *New Scientist*, 167 (2246), July 8, 2000. The webpage[4] set up by Arup, the contruction engineers of the bridge, is also a useful reference on the diagnosis of the problem and the remedies that were used.

Liquidity black holes were studied in Morris and Shin (2004), which drew on the global game analysis of currency crises in Morris and Shin (1998, 1999). The terminology stems from use by market practitioners, and was popularized by Persaud (2001). Crisis dynamics using competitive equilibrium were studied by Genotte and Leland (1990) and Geanakoplos (1997, 2009). Shleifer and Vishny's (1997) observation that margin constraints limit the ability of arbitrageurs to exploit price differences, as well as Holmstrom and Tirole's (1997) work on debt capacities brought ideas and tools from corporate finance into the study of financial market fluctuations. Building on these themes has been a large body of recent theoretical work. Amplification through wealth effects was studied by Xiong (2001) and Kyle and Xiong (2001). He and Krishnamurthy (2007) look at a dynamic asset pricing model, where the intermediaries' capital constraints enter into the asset pricing problem as a determinant of portfolio capacity. Balance sheet constraints enter in Gromb and Vayanos (2002) and Brunnermeier and Pedersen (2009), who coined the term "margin spiral". Incorporating balance sheet constraints on asset pricing problems has been examined by Adrian, Etula, and Shin (2009) for the foreign exchange market, Etula (2009) for the commodities market and by Adrian, Moench, and Shin (2009) for the interaction between macro and balance sheet variables. Garleanu and Pedersen (2009) derive an extension of the capital asset pricing model that incorporates balance sheet constraints.

---

[4] <http://www.arup.com/millenniumbridge/challenge/oscillation.html>.

The role of mark-to-market accounting in amplifying financial market fluctuations was examined in Plantin, Sapra, and Shin (2008), which describes the tradeoff between mark-to-market and historical cost accounting regimes. The link between marking to market and balance sheet management in financial booms was examined by Adrian and Shin (forthcoming), which provides a commentary on the fluctuating fortunes of the (then) five stand-alone US investment banks.

busines cycles driven by fluctuations in price risk

endogenous risk
vs.
exogenous risk
individuals react to this environment
change it + the full change
are changed by the environment
Synchronized feedback

prices - info + action to use

mark to market accounting
amplifying

Boom - banks delivering they
surplus capital
risk costs low
yet risk is greater in boom

2

Value-at-Risk and Capital

The concept of *Value-at-Risk* is motivated by the need to find an answer to the following question:

> *What (realistically) is the worst that could happen over one day,*
> *one week, or one year?*

We can imagine all kinds of bad outcomes that may conceivably happen, but running a firm or a bank with such worst-case scenarios in mind would be pretty debilitating. Instead, the important qualifier in the question above is that the worst-case outcome is something that we could realistically expect to happen. The question is how we should define "realistically". If we had some idea of the probabilities with which the possible outcomes transpire, we could try to put some numerical magnitudes on what we mean by "realistically". Value-at-Risk (VaR) is an answer to the question above where "realistically" is defined by finding an outcome that is so bad that anything worse is highly unlikely. More precisely, Value-at-Risk is the realistically worst-case outcome in the sense that anything worse only happens with probability less than some benchmark level.

Definition.   Let W be a random variable. The **Value-at-Risk** at confidence level α relative to base level W_0 is the smallest non-negative number denoted by VaR such that

$$\text{Prob}(W < W_0 - \text{VaR}) \leq 1 - \alpha$$

In other words, the Value-at-Risk is a quantile of the outcome distribution, where the outcome is measured relative to the base level W_0. Denoting by F the cumulative distribution function of W, the Value-at-Risk is defined as

$$\text{VaR} \equiv \inf\{V | F(W_0 - V) \leq 1 - \alpha\} \tag{2.1}$$

Notice that the definition of Value-at-Risk specifies three things. First, it specifies some random variable W. By specifying a random variable, we are already defining implicitly the *time horizon* over which we measure the potential loss, and the process governing the evolution of W over time. Second, we are specifying the base level W_0 from which final outcomes can be measured. Finally, we specify the confidence level α which gives concrete meaning to "realistically worst-case" outcome.

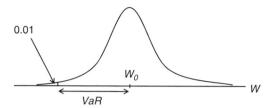

Figure 2.1: Outcome density and Value-at-Risk

Example. Suppose that the random variable W is the value of a portfolio in three months' time. Suppose that W has a known probability density, as depicted in Figure 2.1. The base level W_0 is today's value of the portfolio, and so outcomes are measured relative to today's value. The confidence level α is set at 99%. Then the Value-at-Risk relative to today's value at confidence level 99% is the distance indicated by the double arrow.

What is the rationale for Value-at-Risk? In what sense is it the right measure of risk? At a superficial level, Value-at-Risk could be used as a measure of potential extreme loss. But in some ways, VaR is not ideal as a measure of potential extreme loss. VaR is a quantile measure that disregards outcomes that have probability less than the benchmark level. However, if we are worried about the worst-case scenario, being able to say something about how bad things get conditional on something really bad happening would be very useful. Value-at-Risk is not good at giving that kind of measure.

Example. A bank is owed $1 million by firm A, and is owed $1 million by firm B. Both firms are creditworthy and will pay the $1 million with probability 0.995. However, when firm A defaults, the bank still recovers $0.5 million by selling the collateral put up by firm A. But when firm B defaults, the bank recovers nothing. The VaR relative to the face value of the loan of $1 million at the 99% confidence level is zero in both cases.

To see why the VaR is zero in both cases, let us go to the definition of Value-at-Risk. We want the smallest non-negative number x for which

$$\text{Prob(repayment} < \$1m - x) \le 0.01 \tag{2.2}$$

But since both firms will repay with probability 0.995, we can set $x = 0$, and still have

$$\text{Prob(repayment} < \$1m) = 0.005 \le 0.01$$

Thus, (2.2) holds with $x = 0$. Since there is no smaller non-negative number than zero, the Value-at-Risk is zero. This is true for both firm A and firm B. But intuitively, the answer seems to miss something important. The bank has more to lose when firm B defaults than when firm A defaults. Yet, Value-at-Risk does not capture this feature.

If what we care about is the size of the potential loss conditional on something really bad happening, then possibly a better measure for the potential loss would be the *conditional expected loss*, sometimes known as *tail loss*. The tail loss is defined as the expected loss conditional on the random variable W falling below some threshold point q.

$$\text{Tail loss} = E(W|W < q) = \frac{\int_{-\infty}^{q} W \, f(W) dW}{\int_{-\infty}^{q} f(W) dW} \tag{2.3}$$

However, there is a more important rationale for the concept of Value-at-Risk, which is in terms of the capital or net worth that a firm or bank must hold against possible failure. See Figure 2.2. Suppose W measures the value of total assets of the firm at some fixed date in the future, and W_0 is today's value of the firm's assets. If the firm has capital (net worth, or equity) indicated by the size of the double arrow, then the firm will remain solvent as long as W does not fall below W_0 minus the capital. So, the probability that the firm will go bankrupt is p. By holding larger capital, the probability of failure can be decreased further.

If the firm or bank has limited liability, then it does not matter whether the firm goes bust just marginally, or whether it goes bust spectacularly, leaving a big shortfall. In this sense, the tail loss is not a concern for equity holders. From the perspective of the owner of the firm with limited liability, the Value-at-Risk conveys a crucial piece of information. It indicates the amount of capital that it must hold so as to stave off default with a high probability.

Note that the interests of the creditors are not taken into account in this calculation, nor the interests of other claimholders in the wider economy such as taxpayers who are called on to bail out failing banks. For creditors, they would find the information on the tail loss very useful, since the tail loss conveys important information on recovery of claims in the face of default by the firm. However, such concerns are irrelevant for the equity holders, and it is the equity holders who control the firm. The divergent interests of debt holders and equity holders drive their differing attitudes to the usefulness of the Value-at-Risk measure.

As well as conveying information on the amount of capital needed to stave off default, Value-at-Risk will also give useful information on remedial actions that the owners will have to take if the firm or bank were to get into difficulties. If the bank gets into difficulties, it faces loss of value of its claims and faces the possibility of going bust. However, before the bank goes bust, it could raise

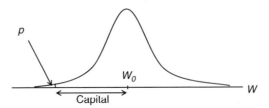

Figure 2.2: Value-at-Risk and capital

additional equity capital by inviting new owners to take a stake in the bank, or asking the existing owners to put up more money to recapitalize the bank. Provided that the situation does not deteriorate too rapidly, there may still be time to recover the situation by taking corrective action. Here is where the time horizon of Value-at-Risk comes into play. The fact that value at risk is measured with a fixed horizon means that the time dimension can be set in an appropriate way for the particular case under consideration. The idea is that the time horizon in the definition of VaR is long enough so that

- corrective measures can be taken to rectify the problem (e.g. through recapitalization, rescue, or reorganization)
- the horizon is also appropriate for the degree of illiquidity of the assets held by the firm
- confidence level is chosen based on ease with which potential investors can be recruited in the recapitalization

For these reasons, Value-at-Risk is a better measure of risk when it is interpreted as a buffer against possible failure, and has played an important role in the internal governance of banks and other financial firms, especially those that employ leverage. The concept of Value-at-Risk has been adopted widely, both by the private sector and regulators, and is the bedrock of the capital regulations adopted by the Basel regulations. The 1996 Market Risk Amendment of the original 1988 Basel Accord is based on the notion of value at risk, and the Basel II regulations have further built on the notion of value at risk.

2.1 PORTFOLIO CHOICE UNDER VaR CONSTRAINT

There are consequences for portfolio decisions when an investor uses Value-at-Risk to manage risk. What is notable is the way that the attitude to risk varies as underlying conditions vary. We first examine the portfolio decision taken in isolation, before looking into how such individual decisions impact on the overall price of risk, which is the topic of Chapter 3.

An investor forms a portfolio consisting of two assets—a risky security and cash. The price of the risky security at date t is denoted p_t, and the number of units of the risky security held by the investor is denoted by y_t. The holding of cash at date t is denoted by c_t. The price of the risky security next period (at date $t + 1$) is denoted by p_{t+1}, and is uncertain when viewed from date t. Denote by $\tilde{r}_{t+1}$ the return from date t to date $t + 1$ on the risky security. Then

$$p_{t+1} = (1 + \tilde{r}_{t+1})p_t \qquad (2.4)$$

Let us make the simplifying assumption for now that $\tilde{r}_{t+1}$ is independent across dates, and is identically distributed at all dates with mean $\mu > 0$ and variance σ^2.

The capital of the investor at date t is denoted by e_t. The capital is the investor's net worth or equity that is allocated to the two assets in the portfolio. We will use the terms *capital, net worth* and *equity* interchangeably in this book.

The investor is free to allocate his capital between the risky asset and the risk-free asset, but is not limited to holding positive quantities of both. For instance, the investor is free to borrow cash and use the proceeds to buy up more of the risky security. In that case, the holding of cash c_t will be a negative number, and the investor incurs a debt of $-c_t$ that needs to be repaid. For now, let us assume that the risk-free interest rate on cash is zero, and that the investor can borrow or lend any amount at this risk-free interest rate. We will comment later on how our conclusions are affected (if at all) if we relax these assumptions.

The investor who borrows in order to buy more of the risky asset has a balance sheet at date t which an be depicted as follows. The investor incurs debt of $-c_t > 0$ and buys risky securities worth the sum of his own capital e_t and the borrowed money $-c_t$.

Assets	Liabilities	
Securities $p_t y_t$	Equity e_t Debt $-c_t$	(2.5)

The investor is leveraged, in the sense that the total assets on the balance sheet is larger than the size of his capital. Leverage is defined as the ratio of total assets to equity. The leverage of this investor is given by

$$\frac{p_t y_t}{e_t} \qquad (2.6)$$

Such a balance sheet indicates the stance of an investor who is optimstic about the risky security. The greater is the borrowing $-c_t$, the more aggressive is the investor in backing the risky security.

In contrast, we could imagine an investor who is very pessimistic about the prospects of the risky security, and who takes a short position in it. In other words, the investor borrows some units of the risky security, sells it in the market, and keeps the proceeds of the sale in the form of cash. By having a short position in the risky security, the holding y_t is a negative number. The balance sheet of this pessimistic investor can be depicted as follows.

Assets	Liabilities	
Cash c_t	Equity e_t Securities $-p_t y_t$	(2.7)

This investor's short position in the risky securities enters on the liabilities side of the balance sheet, since the investor has incurred the liability of buying back the securities at a future date to redeem the short position. Since $y_t < 0$, the liability $-p_t y_t$ is recorded as a positive number on the liabilities side of the balance sheet. On the asset side, the investor holds cash only. Of course, even though the investor only holds cash on the asset side, this doesn't mean that the investor's position is risk free. The problem is that the investor's *liabilities* are uncertain, so that the investor's net worth e_t (which is ultimately what the investor cares about) is highly variable. The pessimistic investor is also leveraged, in the sense that the ratio of assets to equity is bigger than one. The leverage of the pessimistic investor with balance sheet (2.7) is

$$\frac{e_t - p_t y_t}{e_t} \qquad (2.8)$$

Finally, we can consider an investor who holds positive quantities of both the risky security and cash, and funds the positive holding of both from his capital. The balance sheet that corresponds to such a position is

Assets	Liabilities	
Cash c_t	Equity e_t	(2.9)
Securities $p_t y_t$		

Such an asset portfolio would be typical of a "long only" investor such as a pension fund or mutual fund who allocates a given amount of wealth e_t between cash and securities. Such an investor is not leveraged, in that the ratio of total assets to equity is 1.

We can see from (2.5), (2.7), and (2.9) that whatever form the balance sheet takes, the following balance sheet identity holds at every date t, which ties down the two sides of the balance sheet.

$$p_t y_t + c_t = e_t \qquad (2.10)$$

At the time that the investor chooses how much of the risky security y_t to hold, he knows the current price p_t, and his own equity e_t. Once y_t has been chosen, the new price p_{t+1} is drawn by Nature. If this new price is higher than the old price and $y_t > 0$, the investor makes a gain. If the new price is lower, the investor makes a loss. The value of equity that the investor takes into the next period's portfolio choice problem reflects the gain or loss. The new value of capital e_{t+1} is a function of the new realised price p_{t+1}, and satisfies:

$$e_{t+1} = p_{t+1}y_t + c_t$$
$$= p_{t+1}y_t + e_t - p_t y_t$$
$$= (p_{t+1} - p_t)y_t + e_t \qquad (2.11)$$
$$= [(1 + \tilde{r}_{t+1})p_t - p_t]y_t + e_t$$
$$= \tilde{r}_{t+1}p_t y_t + e_t$$

Since the interest rate on cash is zero in our set-up, the new equity value reflects any gains or losses on the holding of the risky security. Of course, when viewed from date t, this future capital value is uncertain, since $\tilde{r}_{t+1}$ is uncertain.

Let us now consider how risk management enters into portfolio choice by considering the decision problem of an investor who faces a Value-at-Risk constraint. The investor is risk-neutral otherwise. Consider the case where $\mu > 0$, so that the expected return on the risky security is higher than that on cash. For the risk-neutral investor, holding the risky security is preferred. Without any constraint on the size of the portfolio, the choice problem will be ill-defined, since the investor would wish to hold a larger and larger position in the risky security. However, the risk constraint will put a bound on the size of the risky security holding.

The investor has a period-by-period decision problem in which the objective at date t is to maximize the expected return on his capital from date t to date $t + 1$, subject only to the constraint that the risk is kept to some acceptable limit. The "acceptable" level of risk is expressed as a Value-at-Risk constraint on the probability of insolvency next period. The investor goes bust when the capital next period falls below zero. Let the confidence level associated with the VaR constraint be α. At each date, the investor must ensure that the probability that he will become insolvent next period is at most $1 - \alpha$.

The investor becomes insolvent if $e_{t+1} \leq 0$. From equation (2.11), this happens when the return on the risky security is sufficiently bad so that $\tilde{r}_{t+1}p_t y_t + e_t \leq 0$, or

$$\tilde{r}_{t+1} \leq -\frac{e_t}{p_t y_t} \qquad (2.12)$$

Figure 2.3 illustrates the argument. The smaller is the initial equity level e_t or the larger is the initial holding y_t, the greater is the chance of going bust. Let ϕ be defined as the constant for which we have

$$\text{Prob}(\tilde{r}_{t+1} \leq \mu - \phi\sigma) = 1 - \alpha \qquad (2.13)$$

In other words, $\phi\sigma$ is the Value-at-Risk for the risky return $\tilde{r}_{t+1}$ at the confidence level α relative to the mean return μ. Then, by choosing the size of the holding of the risky asset y_t, the investor can ensure that the probability of his becoming

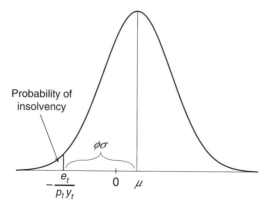

Figure 2.3: Probability density of $\bar{r}_{t+1}$

insolvent next period is at most $1 - \alpha$. From Figure 2.3 we see that the probability of insolvency is exactly $1 - \alpha$ when

$$\mu + \frac{e_t}{p_t y_t} = \phi \sigma \tag{2.14}$$

Solving for the dollar value of the risky security position, we have

$$p_t y_t = \frac{e_t}{\phi \sigma - \mu} \tag{2.15}$$

The investor cannot hold any more than this amount of the risky security, since then the probability of insolvency rises above the threshold value $1 - \alpha$, thereby violating his Value-at-Risk constraint.

Will the investor hold any less than the amount in (2.15)? No, since we are considering the case where $\mu > 0$, so that from (2.11), we have

$$E(e_{t+1}) = \mu p_t y_t + e_t \tag{2.16}$$

The expected equity value next period is strictly increasing in y_t, so that the investor wishes to hold as much of the risky security as is permitted by his Value-at-Risk constraint. This is a consequence of the fact that the return on the risky security is strictly higher than that on cash. The upshot is that the investor's holding of the risky security is given exactly by (2.15).

2.2 UPWARD-SLOPING DEMAND REACTIONS

Another perspective on the investor's decision is to consider the leverage maintained on the balance sheet. From equation (2.15) we see that the investor's leverage is given by

$$L = \frac{p_t y_t}{e_t} = \frac{1}{\phi \sigma - \mu} \tag{2.17}$$

Given our assumption of constant μ and σ, leverage is also constant. Therefore, one way we can characterize the investor's portfolio decision is one of maintaining constant leverage in the face of price changes. However, leveraging targeting entails upward-sloping demand responses and downward-sloping supply responses—that is, the investor will buy more of the risky security if its price rises, and sells some of the risky security if the price falls. Such price responses provide the preconditions for the amplification of shocks.

In order to appreciate the consequences of a leverage target on the demand and supply responses to price changes, let us first consider a simple numerical example of an investor who aims to maintain a *constant* leverage of 10. The initial balance sheet is as follows. The investor holds 100 dollars' worth of securities, and has funded this holding with debt worth 90.

Assets	Liabilities
Securities 100	Equity, 10
	Debt, 90

Assume that the price of debt is approximately constant for small changes in the price of the securities, so that the burden of adjustment falls on the equity. Suppose the price of securities increases by 1% so that the dollar holding of the securities rises to 101.

Assets	Liabilities
Securities, 101	Equity, 11
	Debt, 90

At this new higher price, the equity rises to 11, so that leverage then falls to 101/11 = 9.18. This is because the equity rises by a much larger percentage rate (10%) due to the leverage. At the higher level of equity, the investor can restore leverage by taking on additional debt of D to purchase D worth of securities on the asset side so that

$$\frac{\text{assets}}{\text{equity}} = \frac{101 + D}{11} = 10$$

The solution is $D = 9$. The investor takes on additional debt worth 9, and with this money purchases securities worth 9. Thus, an increase in the price of the security of 1 leads to an increased holding worth 9. The demand response is upward-sloping. After the purchase, leverage is now back up to 10.

Assets	Liabilities
Securities, 110	Equity, 11
	Debt, 99

The mechanism works in reverse, too. Suppose there is shock to the securities price so that the value of security holdings falls to 109. On the liabilities side, it is equity that bears the burden of adjustment, since the value of debt stays approximately constant.

Assets	Liabilities
Securities, 109	Equity, 10
	Debt, 99

Leverage is now too high ($109/10 = 10.9$). The investor can adjust down his leverage by selling securities worth 9, and paying down 9 worth of debt. Thus, a *fall* in the price of securities leads to *sales* of securities. The supply response is downward-sloping. The new balance sheet then looks as follows. The balance sheet is now back to where it started before the price changes. Leverage is back down to the target level of 10.

Assets	Liabilities
Securities, 100	Equity, 10
	Debt, 90

In constrast to the textbook demand and supply responses to price changes, we see that investors with Value-at-Risk constraints exhibit perverse demand and supply responses where higher prices lead to purchases and lower prices lead to sales. To see how the magnitudes relate to the leverage targeted by the investor, note from (2.11) and (2.17) that the proportional change in equity can be written as

$$\frac{e_{t+1} - e_t}{e_t} = \tilde{r}_{t+1} \frac{p_t y_t}{e_t} = \tilde{r}_{t+1} \cdot L \tag{2.18}$$

while the proportional change in total assets as a consequence of the price change (but before the portfolio adjustment) is

$$\frac{p_{t+1} y_t - p_t y_t}{p_t y_t} = \tilde{r}_{t+1} \tag{2.19}$$

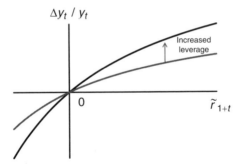

Figure 2.4: Upward-sloping demand response to $\tilde{r}_{t+1}$

Comparing (2.18) and (2.19), we see that for a leveraged investor, equity rises L times faster than total assets. The price response of the investor can be obtained by tracking the new quantity y_{t+1}. Since the investor maintains constant leverage L, we have

$$\frac{p_t y_t}{e_t} = \frac{p_{t+1} y_{t+1}}{e_{t+1}} = L \tag{2.20}$$

Hence

$$\frac{y_{t+1}}{y_t} = \frac{e_{t+1}/e_t}{p_{t+1}/p_t} = \frac{1 + \tilde{r}_{t+1} \cdot L}{1 + \tilde{r}_{t+1}} \tag{2.21}$$

The proportional increase in the holding of the risky security can be expressed as a function of the return on the risky asset $\tilde{r}_{t+1}$ and the degree of leverage L.

$$\frac{y_{t+1} - y_t}{y_t} = \frac{\tilde{r}_{t+1}}{1 + \tilde{r}_{t+1}} \cdot (L - 1) \tag{2.22}$$

The price response is upward-sloping in the return $\tilde{r}_{t+1}$, and is illustrated in Figure 2.4. The higher is the target leverage L maintained by the investor, the steeper is the demand response to price changes.

2.3 NOTES ON FURTHER READING

The widespread use of Value-at-Risk as a front-line risk management tool is reflected in the large selection of textbooks and manuals for its use. Textbook references include Crouhy, Galai, and Mark (2001), Pearson (2002), Holton (2003), Dowd (2005), McNeil, Frey, and Embrechts (2005) and Jorion (2006). These texts also discuss some other properties of Value-at-Risk that we have not dealt with in the text, such as the fact that VaR does not satisfy sub-additivity—that diversification may actually raise Value-at-Risk. The lesson, of course, is not that diversification is bad, but rather that VaR is not well-suited as a measure of extreme loss—a point that we have already addressed. Embrechts, McNeil, and Straumann (2002) show how correlation is a misleading summary measure of dependence away from the standard case of jointly normally distributed random variables, and instead urges the use of more sophisticated tools. Adrian and Brunnermeier's (2009) notion of CoVaR is one recent implementation of dependence for extreme outcomes. The April 2009 issue of the IMF's *Global Financial Stability Report* (IMF 2009) reports on measurements of extreme dependence during the financial crisis.

More far-reaching criticism of VaR as a risk management tool rests on the feedback effect that it generates. Danielsson, Shin, and Zigrand (2004) show simulated paths with and without VaR constraints, and argue that widespread use of Value-at-Risk amplifies the boom-bust cycle. Danielsson et al. (2001) is a report submitted to the Basel Committee in response to call for comments on the initial Basel II proposals, with the key conclusion being "The proposed regulations fail to consider the fact that risk is endogenous. Value-at-Risk can destabilise and induce crashes when they would not otherwise occur" (Danielsson et al. 2001, executive summary).

3

Boom and Bust Driven by Value-at-Risk

Does widespread adoption of Value-at-Risk as a risk management tool enhance financial stability or undermine it? Financial regulation based on Value-at-Risk, such as the Basel II rules for bank capital, is founded on the assumption that making each bank safe makes the system safe.

Of course, it is a truism that ensuring the soundness of each individual institution ensures the soundness of the system as a whole. But for this proposition to be a good prescription for policy, actions that enhance the soundness of a particular institution should promote overall stability. However, the proposition is vulnerable to the fallacy of composition. It is possible, indeed often likely, that attempts by individual institutions to respond to the waxing and waning of measured risks can amplify the boom-bust cycle. The "boom" part of the boom-bust cycle is especially important as we will see below.

We began this book with the quote from the anonymous risk manager who insisted that the value-added of a good risk management system is that one can take more risks. In this spirit, financial institutions have been encouraged to load up on exposures when measured risks are low, only to shed them as fast as they can when risks begin to materialize. Unfortunately, the recoiling from risk by one institution generates greater materialized risk for others. Put differently, there are externalities in the financial system where actions by one institution have spill-over effects on others.

But even more important than the realization that such externalities exist is the task of identifying the *mechanism* through which they operate. Traditionally, financial contagion has been viewed through the lens of cascading defaults, where if A has borrowed from B and B has borrowed from C, then the default of A impacts B, which then impacts C, and so on. This line of reasoning usually leads to analyses of interbank claims and financial networks, which are shocked by some hypothetical default by one or more constituents of the network. We could dub this the "domino" model of financial contagion, and the domino model has been a staple of much research on financial stability.

However, the near-universal conclusion from these studies have been that the potential for systemic crisis is small.[1] In the models, it is only with implausibly large shocks that the simulations generate any meaningful contagion. The global financial crisis has exposed the weakness of the domino model, although the

---

[1] For a comprehensive discussion of the performance of domino models of contagion used at central banks, see the recent work of Elsinger et al. (2006a, 2006b, 2006c).

appeal of the domino model still exerts a resilient hold, as witnessed by the large volume of research based on the domino model that is still produced by central banks and policy organizations.

One objective of this book is to show that a more potent channel through which externalities in financial markets exercise their influence is through the pricing of risk, and the resulting portfolio decisions of market participants. Actual defaults need not even figure in the mechanism, and the effects operate even in a setting where the financial institutions have not borrowed and lent to each other. The rest of this chapter is devoted to backing up these claims. The general equilibrium example that follows is therefore deliberately stark. It has two features that deserve emphasis.

First, there is no default in the model. The debt that appears in the model is risk-free. However, as we will see, the amplification of the financial cycle is very potent. John Geanakoplos (forthcoming) has highlighted how risk-free debt may still give rise to powerful spillover effects through fluctuations in leverage and the pricing of risk. Adrian and Shin (forthcoming) exhibit empirical evidence that bears on the fluctuations in the pricing of risk from the balance sheets of financial intermediaries.

The fact that our example has no default is useful in illustrating how booms and busts result from actions in anticipation of defaults, rather than the defaults themselves. Rather like a Greek tragedy, it is the actions taken by actors who want to avoid a bad outcome that precipitate disaster. It also draws our attention to where it belongs—the boom phase of the boom-bust cycle. In this respect, the analysis below is in line with Andrew Crockett's (2000) comment that risk *increases in booms and materializes in busts*.

Second, in our general equilibrium example, there is no lending and borrowing between financial institutions. So, any effect we see in the model cannot be attributed to the domino model of systemic risk. This is not to say that interlocking claims do not matter. Far from it. We will see in a later chapter that financial networks and interlocking claims and obligations do amplify the boom-bust cycle.

However, the key is the pricing of risk, and how balance sheet management based on Value-at-Risk amplifies the fluctuations in the price of risk. In order to demonstrate this claim, we work with a deliberately stark model where there are no interlocking claims and obligations between financial institutions, and where there is no default. Instead, the spillover effects operate through market prices, in particular the price of risk. We will see that even such a simple setting generates large amplifications.

3.1 GENERAL EQUILIBRIUM WITH VALUE-AT-RISK

Our example is set in a one-period asset market. Today is date 0. A risky security is traded today in anticipation of its realized payoff in the next period (date 1). Since trade takes place only once, we can drop the time subscripts, simplifying the notation. The payoff of the risky security is known at date 1.

When viewed from date 0, the risky security's payoff is a random variable $\tilde{w}$, with expected value $q > 0$. The uncertainty surrounding the risky security's payoff takes a particularly simple form. The random variable $\tilde{w}$ is uniformly distributed over the interval:

$$[q - z, q + z]$$

where $z > 0$ is a known constant. The mean and variance of $\tilde{w}$ is given by

$$E(\tilde{w}) = q$$

$$\sigma^2 = \frac{z^2}{3}$$

There is also a risk-free security, cash, that pays an interest rate of zero. Let p denote the price of the risky security. For an investor with equity e who holds y units of the risky security, the payoff of the portfolio is the random variable:

$$W \equiv \tilde{w}y + (e - py) \tag{3.1}$$

Let us now introduce two groups of investors—passive investors and active investors. The passive investors can be thought of as non-leveraged investors such as pension funds and mutual funds, while the active investors can be interpreted as leveraged institutions such as banks and securities firms who manage their balance sheets actively. The risky securities can be interpreted as loans granted to ultimate borrowers, but where there is a risk that the borrowers will not fully repay the loan. Figure 3.1 depicts the relationships. Under this interpretation, the market value of the risky securities can be hought of as the marked-to-market value of the loans granted to the ultimate borrowers. The passive investors' holding of the risky security can then be interpreted as the credit that is granted *directly* by the household sector (through the holding of corporate bonds, for example), while the holding of the risky securities by the

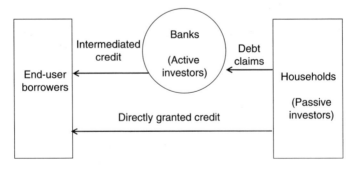

Figure 3.1: Intermediated and directly granted credit

active investors can be given the interpretation of *intermediated finance,* where the active investors are banks that borrow from households in order to lend to the ultimate borrowers.

We assume that the passive investors have mean-variance preferences over the payoff from the portfolio. They aim to maximize

$$U = E(W) - \frac{1}{2\tau}\sigma_W^2 \tag{3.2}$$

where $\tau > 0$ is a constant called the investor's "risk tolerance" and σ_W^2 is the variance of W. In terms of the decision variable y, the passive investor's objective function can be written as

$$U(y) = qy + (e - py) - \frac{1}{6\tau}y^2 z^2 \tag{3.3}$$

The optimal holding of the risky security satisfies the first-order condition:

$$q - p - \frac{1}{3\tau}z^2 y = 0 \tag{3.4}$$

The price must be below the expected payoff for the risk-averse investor to hold any of the risky security. The optimal risky security holding of the passive investor (denoted by y_P) is given by

$$y_P = \begin{cases} \dfrac{3\tau}{z^2}(q - p) & \text{if } q > p \\ 0 & \text{otherwise} \end{cases} \tag{3.5}$$

These linear demands can be summed to give the aggregate demand. If τ_i is the risk tolerance of the ith investor and $\tau = \sum_i \tau_i$, then (3.5) gives the aggregate demand of the passive investor sector as a whole.

Now turn to the portfolio decision of the active (leveraged) investors. These active investors are risk-neutral but face a Value-at-Risk (VaR) constraint, as is commonly the case for banks and other leveraged institutions. The general VaR constraint is that the capital cushion be large enough that the default probability is kept below some benchmark level. Consider the special case where that benchmark level is zero. Then, the VaR constraint boils down to the condition that leveraged investors issue only risk-free debt.

Denote by VaR the Value-at-Risk of the leveraged investor. The constraint is that the investor's capital (equity) e be large enough to cover this Value-at-Risk. The optimization problem for an active investor is:

$$\max_y E(W) \quad \text{subject to VaR} \leq e \tag{3.6}$$

If the price is too high (i.e. when $p > q$) the investor holds no risky securities. When $p < q$, then $E(W)$ is strictly increasing in y, and so the Value-at-Risk constraint binds. The optimal holding of the risky security can be obtained by solving VaR $= e$. To solve this equation, write out the balance sheet of the leveraged investor as

Assets	Liabilities
Securitics, py	equity, e
	debt, $py - e$

The Value-at-Risk constraint stipulates that the debt issued by the investor be risk-free. For each unit of the security, the minimum payoff is $q - z$. In order for the investor's debt to be risk-free, y should satisfy $py - e \le (q - z)y$, or

$$py - (q - z)y \le e \tag{3.7}$$

The left-hand side of (3.7) is the Value-at-Risk (the worst possible loss) relative to today's market value of assets, which must be met by equity e. Since the constraint binds, the optimal holding of the risky securities for the leveraged investor is

$$y = \frac{e}{z - (q - p)} \tag{3.8}$$

and the balance sheet is

Assets	Liabilities	
Securitics, py	equity, e	(3.9)
	debt, $py - e$	

Since (3.8) is linear in e, the aggregate demand of the leveraged sector has the same form as (3.8) when e is the *aggregate capital* of the leveraged sector as a whole.

Denoting by y_A the holding of the risky ecurities by the active investors and by y_P the holding by the passive investors, the market-clearing condition is

$$y_A + y_P = S \tag{3.10}$$

where S is the total endowment of the risky securities. Figure 3.2 illustrates the equilibrium for a fixed value of aggregate capital e. For the passive investors, their demand is linear, with the intercept at q. The demand of the leveraged sector can be read off from (3.8). The solution is fully determined as a function of e. In a dynamic model, e can be treated as the state variable (see Danielsson et al. 2009).

Now consider a possible scenario involving an improvement in the fundamentals of the risky security where the expected payoff of the risky securities rises from from q to q'. In our banking interpretation of the model, an improvement in the expected

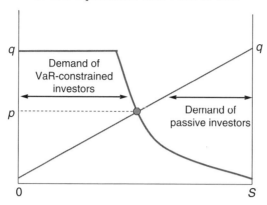

Figure 3.2: Market clearing price

payoff could result from an improvement in the macroeconomic outlook, lowering the probability that the borrowers would default on their loans. Figure 3.3 illustrates the scenario. The improvement in the fundamentals of the risky security pushes up the demand curves for both the passive and active investors, as illustrated in Figure 3.3. However, there is an amplified response from the leveraged institutions as a result of marked-to-market gains on their balance sheets.

From (3.9), denote by e' the new equity level of the leveraged investors that incorporates the capital gain when the price rises to p'. The initial amount of debt was $(q - z)y$. Since the new asset value is $p'y$, the new equity level e' is

$$e' = p'y - (q - z)y$$
$$= (z + p' - q)y \tag{3.11}$$

Figure 3.4 sets out the steps in the balance sheet expansion. The initial balance sheet is on the left, where the total asset value is py. The middle balance sheet shows the effect of an improvement in fundamentals that comes from an increase in q, but before any adjustment in the risky security holding. There is an increase in the value of the securities without any change in the debt value, since the debt was already risk-free to begin with. So the increase in asset value flows through entirely to an increase in equity. Equation (3.11) expresses the new value of equity e' in the middle balance sheet in Figure 3.4.

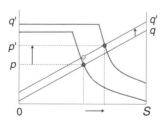

Figure 3.3: Amplified response to improvement in fundamentals q

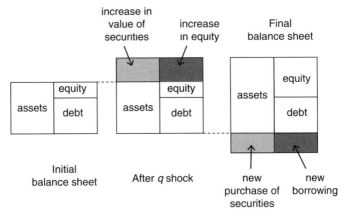

Figure 3.4: Balance sheet expansion from q shock

The increase in equity relaxes the Value-at-Risk constraint, and the leveraged sector can increase its holding of risky securities. The new holding y' is larger, and is enough to make the VaR constraint bind at the higher equity level, with a higher fundamental value q'. That is,

$$e' = p'y' - (q - z)y'$$
$$= (z + p' - q')y' \tag{3.12}$$

After the q shock, the investor's balance sheet has strengthened, in that capital has increased without any change in debt value. There has been an erosion of leverage, leading to spare capacity on the balance sheet in the sense that equity is now larger than is necessary to meet the Value-at-Risk.

In order to utilize the slack in balance-sheet capacity, the investor takes on additional debt to purchase additional risky securities. The demand response is upward-sloping. The new holding of securities is now y', and the total asset value is $p'y'$. Equation (3.12) expresses the new value of equity e' in terms of the new higher holding y' in the right-hand side balance sheet in Figure 3.4. From (3.11) and (3.12), we can write the new holding y' of the risky security as

$$y' = y\left(1 + \frac{q' - q}{z + p' - q'}\right) \tag{3.13}$$

From the demand of passive investors (3.5) and market clearing,

$$p' - q' = \frac{z^2}{3\tau}(y' - S)$$

Substituting into (3.13),

$$y' = y\left(1 + \frac{q' - q}{z + \frac{z^2}{3\tau}(y' - S)}\right) \tag{3.14}$$

This defines a quadratic equation in y'. The solution is where the right-hand side of (3.14) cuts the 45 degree line. The leveraged sector amplifies booms and busts if $y' - y$ has the same sign as $q' - q$. Then any shift in fundamentals gets amplified by the portfolio decisions of the leveraged sector. The condition for amplification is that the denominator in the second term of (3.14) is positive. But this condition is guaranteed from (3.13) and the fact that $p' > q' - z$ (i.e. that the price of the risky security is higher than its worst possible realized payoff).

Note also that the size of the amplification is increasing in leverage, seen from the fact that $y' - y$ is large when z is small. Recall that z is the fundamental risk. When z is small, the associated Value-at-Risk is also small, allowing the leveraged sector to maintain high leverage. The higher is the leverage, the greater is the marked-to-market capital gains and losses. Amplification is large when the leveraged sector itself is large relative to the total economy. Finally, note that the amplification is more likely when the passive sector's risk tolerance τ is high.

The price gap, $q - p$, is the difference between the expected payoff from the risky security and its price. It is one measure of the price of risk in the economy. The market-clearing condition and the demand of the passive sector (3.5) give an empirical counterpart to the price gap given by the size of the leveraged sector. Recall that y_A is the holding of the risky security by the leveraged sector. We have

$$q - p = \frac{z^2}{3\tau}(S - y_A) \tag{3.15}$$

which gives our first empirical hypothesis.

Empirical Hypothesis. Risk premiums are low when the size of the leveraged sector is large relative to the non-leveraged sector.

We will explore alternative notions of risk premiums in the next section. The amplifying mechanism works exactly in reverse on the way down. A negative shock to the fundamentals of the risky security drives down its price, which erodes the marked-to-market capital of the leveraged sector. The erosion of capital induces the sector to shed assets so as to reduce leverage down to a level that is consistent with the VaR constraint. The risk premium increases when the leveraged sector suffers losses, since $q - p$ increases.

3.2 PRICING OF RISK AND CREDIT SUPPLY

We now explore the fluctuations in risk pricing in our model more systematically. For now, let us treat S (the total endowment of the risky security) as being exogenous. Once we solve for the model fully, we can make S endogenous and address the issue of credit supply with shifts in economic fundamentals.

Begin with the market-clearing condition for the risky security, $y_A + y_P = S$. Substituting in the expressions for the demands of the active and passive sectors, we can write the market-clearing condition as

$$\frac{e}{z - (q - p)} + \frac{3\tau}{z^2}(q - p) = S \tag{3.16}$$

We also impose a restriction on the parameters from the requirement that the active investors have a strictly positive total holding of the risky security, or equivalently that the passive sector's holding is strictly smaller than the total endowment S. From (3.5) this restriction can be written as

$$\frac{3\tau}{z^2}(q - p) < S \tag{3.17}$$

Our discussion so far of the amplification of shocks resulting from the leveraged investors' balance-sheet management suggests that a reasonable hypothesis is that the risk premium for holding the risky security is falling as the fundamental payoff of the risky security improves. This is indeed the case. We have:

Proposition 1 The expected return on the risky security is strictly decreasing in q.

The expected return to the risky security is $(q/p) - 1$. It is more convenient to work with a monotonic transformation of the expected return given by

$$\pi \equiv 1 - \frac{p}{q} \tag{3.18}$$

We see that π lies between zero and one. When $\pi = 0$, the price of the risky security is equal to its expected payoff, so that there is no risk premium for holding the risky security over cash. As π increases, the greater is the expected return to holding the risky security. Using the π notation, the market-clearing condition (3.16) can be written as follows.

$$F \equiv e + \frac{3\tau}{z^2}q\pi(z - q\pi) - S(z - q\pi) = 0 \tag{3.19}$$

We need to show that π is decreasing in q. From the implicit function theorem,

$$\frac{d\pi}{dq} = -\frac{\partial F/\partial q}{\partial F/\partial \pi} \tag{3.20}$$

and

$$\frac{\partial F}{\partial q} = \pi\left(\frac{3\tau}{z}\left(1 - \frac{2\pi q}{z}\right) + S\right)$$

Dividing this expression by $3\tau\pi/z^2 > 0$, we see that $\partial F/\partial q$ has the same sign as

$$(z - \pi q) + \left(\frac{z^2}{3\tau}S - \pi q\right)$$
$$= (z - (q - p)) + \left(\frac{z^2}{3\tau}S - (q - p)\right)$$

(3.21)

The left-hand term in (3.21) is positive since price p is above the minimum payoff $q - z$. The right-hand term is positive from our parameter restriction (3.17) that ensures that the risky security holding by the leveraged sector is strictly positive. Hence, $\partial F/\partial q > 0$. Similarly, it can be shown that $\partial F/\partial\pi > 0$. Therefore, $d\pi/dq < 0$. This concludes the proof of Proposition 1.

The expected return on the risky security is falling as the fundamentals improve. We could rephrase this finding as saying that the risk premium in the economy is declining during booms. The decline in risk premiums is a familiar feature in boom times. Although the somewhat mechanical proof we have given for Proposition 1 is not so illuminating concerning the economic mechanism, the heuristic argument in the previous section involving the three balance sheets in Figure 3.4 captures the spirit of the argument more directly.

When fundamentals improve, the leveraged investors (the banks) experience mark-to-market gains on their balance sheets, leading to higher equity capital. The higher mark-to-market capital generates additional balance-sheet capacity for the banks that must be put to use. In our model, the excess balance-sheet capacity is put to use by increasing lending (purchasing more risky securities) with money borrowed from the passive investors.

Shadow Value of Bank Capital

Another window on the risk premium in the economy is through the Lagrange multiplier associated with the constrained optimization problem of the banks, which is to maximize the expected payoff from the portfolio $E(W)$ subject to the Value-at-Risk constraint. The Lagrange multiplier is the rate of increase of the objective function with respect to a relaxation of the constraint, and hence can be interpreted as the shadow value of bank capital. Denoting by λ the Lagrange multiplier, we have

$$\lambda = \frac{dE(W)}{de}$$
$$= \frac{dE(W)}{dy}\frac{dy}{de}$$
$$= (q - p)\cdot\frac{1}{z - (q - p)}$$

(3.22)

where we have obtained the expression for $dE(W)/dy$ from (3.1) and dy/de is obtained from (3.8), which gives the optimal portfolio decision of the leveraged investor. We see from (3.22) that as the price gap $q - p$ becomes compressed, the Lagrange multiplier λ declines. The implication is that the marginal increase of a dollar's worth of new capital for the leveraged investor is generating less expected payoff. As the price gap $q - p$ goes to zero, so does the Lagrange multiplier, implying that the return to a dollar's worth of capital goes to zero.

Furthermore, we have from (3.15) that the price gap $q - p$ is decreasing as the size of the leveraged sector increases relative to the whole economy. The shadow value of bank capital can be written as:

$$\lambda = (q - p) \cdot \frac{1}{z - (q - p)}$$
$$= \frac{z(S - y_A)}{3\tau + z(y_A - S)} \tag{3.23}$$

We have the following proposition.

Proposition 2 The shadow value of bank capital is decreasing in the size of the leveraged sector.

The *leverage* of the active investor is defined as the ratio of total assets to equity. Leverage is given by

$$\frac{py}{e} = \frac{p}{e} \times \frac{e}{z - (q - p)}$$
$$= \frac{p}{z - (q - p)} \tag{3.24}$$

As q increases, the numerator $p(q)$ increases without bound. Since the price gap is bounded below by zero, overall leverage eventually increases in q. Thus, leverage is high when total assets are large. In the terminology of Adrian and Shin (forthcoming), the leveraged investors exhibit *procyclical leverage*.

Proposition 3 For values of q above some threshold $\bar{q}$, leverage is procyclical.

In the run-up to the global financial crisis of 2007 to 2009, the financial system was said to be "awash with liquidity", in the sense that credit was easy to obtain. Adrian and Shin (2007) show that liquidity in this sense is closely related to the growth of financial intermediary balance sheets. When taken in conjunction with the findings of Adrian and Shin (forthcoming), Propositions 1 and 2 shed some light on the notion of liquidity. When asset prices rise, financial intermediaries' balance sheets generally become stronger, and—without adjusting asset holdings—their leverage becomes eroded. The financial intermediaries then hold surplus capital, and they will attempt to find ways in which they can employ their surplus capital. By analogy with manufacturing firms, we may see the financial system as having "surplus capacity". For such surplus capacity to be utilized, the intermediaries must expand their balance sheets. On the liability side, they take on more debt. On the asset side, they search for potential borrowers. When the set of potential borrowers is fixed, the greater willingness to lend leads to an erosion in the risk premium from lending, and spreads become compressed.

Feedback

A tell-tale characterstic of investors driven by the Value-at-Risk constraint is that their demands chase the most recent price changes. As long as the expected return is positive, the optimal policy is for the investor to buy the risky security up to the maximum permitted by his Value-at-Risk. In this sense, it makes sense to talk of an investor's "risk budget". In the market for the risky security with both active and passive traders, the market-clearing price is determined where the demands of both groups of traders sum to the total endowment of the risky security. In such a setting, an increase in the price of the risky security sets off an amplifying spiral of price increases and further purchases. The positive shock increases the marked-to-market capital of the VaR-constrained traders, relaxing the risk constraint and allowing the investor to buy more of the risky security. This pushes the demand up as a consequence. However, as more of the risky security ends up in the hands of the VaR-constrained investors, the market-clearing price is driven up further, which sets off another round of increases in the marked-to-market capital of the investors, pushing out the demands still further.

In this way, the presence of investors who manage their leverage actively has the potential to amplify shocks as price increases and balance-sheet effects become intertwined. The Millennium Bridge analogy applies in this feedback process. Note the importance of marking to market, and the dual role of market prices. Purchases drive up prices, but price increases induce actions (further purchases) on the part of the investors. The mechanism works in reverse on the way down. A negative shock to the price of the risky security drives down its price, which erodes the marked-to-market capital of the leveraged investor. The erosion of capital is a cue for the investor to shed some of the assets so as to reduce leverage down to a level that is consistent with the VaR constraint. The two circular figures in Figure 3.5, taken from Adrian and Shin (forthcoming) and Shin (2005a),

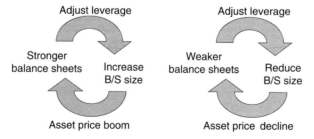

Figure 3.5: Feedback in booms and busts

depict the feedback from prices to actions to back to prices, both on the "way up" and on the "way down". Adrian and Shin (2008a, forthcoming) discuss the consequences of such balance-sheet dynamics for the financial system as a whole and for monetary policy.

Supply of Credit

Up to now, we have treated the total endowment of the risky securities S as fixed. However, as the risk spread on lending becomes compressed, the leveraged investors (the banks) will be tempted to search for new borrowers they can lend to. In terms of our model, if we allow S to be endogenously determined, we can expect credit supply to be increasing when the risk premium falls. Through this window, we could catch a glimpse of the way that *credit supply responds to overall economic conditions.*

To explore this idea further, we modify our model in the following way. Suppose there is a large pool of potential borrowers who wish to borrow to fund a project, from either the active investors (the banks) or the passive investors (the households). They will borrow from whomever is willing to lend.

Assume that the potential borrowers are identical, and each has identical projects to those which are already being financed by the banks and households. In other words, the potential projects that are waiting to be financed are perfect substitutes for the projects already being funded. Denote the risk premium associated with the pool of potential projects by the constant π_0. If the market risk premium were ever to fall below π_0, the investors in the existing projects would be better off selling the existing projects to fund the projects that are sitting on the sidelines. Therefore, the market premium cannot fall below π_0, so that in any equilibrium with endogenous credit supply, we have

$$\pi \geq \pi_0 \tag{3.25}$$

Define the *supply of credit function* $S(q)$ as the function that maps q to total lending S. When $\pi(q) \geq \pi_0$, there is no effect by a small change in q on the supply of credit. Define q^* as the threshold value of q defined as $q^* = \pi^{-1}(\pi_0)$. When $q > q^*$, then the equilibrium stock of lending S is determined by the market-clearing condition (3.19), where $\pi = \pi_0$. Hence, S satisfies

$$F \equiv e + \frac{3\tau}{z^2} q\pi_0(z - q\pi_0) - S(z - q\pi_0) = 0$$

The slope of the supply of credit function is given by

$$\frac{dS}{dq} = -\frac{\partial F/\partial q}{\partial F/\partial S} \tag{3.26}$$

We know from (3.21) that the numerator of (3.26) is positive, while $\partial F/\partial S = -(z - q\pi_0) = q - p - z < 0$. Therefore $dS/dq > 0$, so that credit supply is increasing in q. We can summarize the result as follows.

Proposition 4 The supply of credit S is strictly increasing in q when $q > q^*$.

The assumption that the pool of potential borrowers have projects that are perfect substitutes for existing projects being funded is a strong assumption, and unlikely to hold in practise. Instead, it would be reasonable to suppose that the project quality varies within the pool of potential borrowers, and that good projects are funded first. For instance, the pool of borrowers would consist of households that do not yet own a house, but would like to buy a house with a mortgage. Among the potential borrowers would be good borrowers with secure and verifiable income.

However, as the good borrowers obtain funding and leave the pool of potential borrowers, the remaining potential borrowers will be less good credits. If the banks' balance sheets show substantial slack, they will search for borrowers to lend to. As balance sheets continue to expand, more borrowers will receive funding. When all the good borrowers already have a mortgage, then the banks must lower their lending standards in order to generate the assets they can put on their balance sheets. In the subprime mortgage market in the United States in the years leading up to the financial crisis of 2007, we saw that when balance sheets are expanding fast enough, even borrowers that do not have the means to repay are granted credit—so intense is the urge to employ surplus capital. The seeds of the subsequent downturn in the credit cycle are thus sown.

3.3 LONG-SHORT STRATEGY HEDGE FUND

Some risk can be diversified away, but there are limits to diversification as long as there is aggregate risk. Some hedge funds claim to offer a *market-neutral* return in the sense that total return does not depend on whether the market as a whole goes up or down. How can such a statement be reconciled with the principle that diversification is limited by the extent of aggregate risk in the economy? We explore this issue in more detail here.

Let us address this question by putting ourselves in the shoes of a hedge fund manager. The hedge fund manager has raised $\$e$ million from investors (and possibly has put some of his/her own money into the fund). In this sense, the hedge fund starts with *capital* (or equivalently, *equity*) of $\$e$ million. The initial balance sheet of the hedge fund is extremely simple. It holds $\$e$ million of cash on the asset side, and all of this $\$e$ million is equity.

Assets	Liabilities
Cash ($\$em$)	Equity ($\$em$)

Suppose that the hedge fund manager has expertise in two securities in particular—call them security 1 and security 2. They could be shares, fixed income instruments, currencies, or other more complex traded securities. What's important for our discussion is that the hedge fund manager can use leverage, and both security 1 and security 2 can be sold short. That is, they can be borrowed from other investors who own them, and can be sold in the market for cash. Of course, the hedge fund manager has to return the security at the agreed date to the investor who has lent the security. The hedge fund can hold any combination of:

- Cash
- Security 1
- Security 2

The hedge fund can hold *negative* quantities of any of these three items. A negative holding of cash means that the hedge fund has borrowed the money, and the cash appears on the liabilities side of the balance sheet. A negative holding of a security means that the hedge fund has borrowed that security and so the market value of the borrowed security appears on the liabilities side of the balance sheet. Consider some examples in Figure 3.6, where the hedge fund starts with capital of $1 million, so that $e = 1$.

Example 1. Suppose our hedge fund borrows $2 million (recall that the hedge fund has $1 million of capital). With the total sum raised, the hedge fund buys security 1 and security 2 so that their market values are equal at $1.5 million each.

Example 2. Suppose our hedge fund borrows $1 million worth of security 2, sells it, and buys $2 million worth of security 1.

Example 3. Suppose our hedge fund borrows $1 million worth of security 1, borrows $1 million worth of security 2, sells all of both securities, and holds the proceeds in cash.

Notice that the size of the balance sheets in the three examples are not the same. Even though the hedge fund's equity is $1 million in all three examples, the

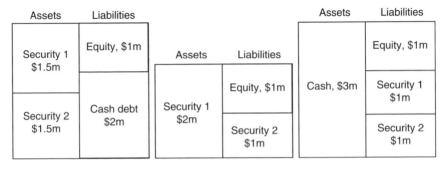

Figure 3.6: Three examples of hedge fund balance sheets

amount of assets controlled by the hedge fund differs depending on how much the hedge fund has taken on in liabilities. As before, the *leverage* of the hedge fund is defined as the ratio of total assets to equity.

$$\text{leverage} = \frac{\text{total assets}}{\text{equity}}$$

Let us put some more structure on the problem by considering what the optimal portfolio of the hedge fund is. We use the following notation.

- a_1 is the holding of security 1 (in $ millions)
- a_2 is the holding of security 2 (in $ millions)
- c is the holding of cash (in $ millions)

Any of these quantities could be negative numbers. For instance, if a_i is negative, this means that the hedge fund has sold short $|a_i|$ million dollars' worth of security i. If c is negative, this means that the hedge fund has borrowed $|c|$ million dollars. But no matter what the values of a_1, a_2, and c are, we know that the balance sheet must balance. This means that the holding of security 1 plus the holding of security 2 plus the holding of cash must sum to the total equity of the hedge fund, which is $1 million. In other words

$$a_1 + a_2 + c = e$$

Because of this balance-sheet identity we can work out the hedge fund's cash holding once we know its holdings of securities 1 and 2.

$$c = e - a_1 - a_2$$

So, in fact, when the hedge fund manager works out what the optimal portfolio of the fund is, it is enough to find the optimal values of a_1 and a_2. The cash holding is then fully determined by the balance-sheet identity.

Mean Variance Benchmark

Our main focus will be on a hedge fund that is subject to a Value-at-Risk constraint. But before we introduce that discussion, let us establish a benchmark case by supposing that the hedge fund aims to maximize the mean-variance objective function U, defined as:

$$U = E(r) - \frac{1}{2\tau} Var(r) \tag{3.27}$$

where r is the return from today to, say, this time next year on the hedge fund's initial investment of $1 million, $E(r)$ is the expected value of r, $Var(r)$ is the variance of r, τ is the hedge fund's *risk tolerance*, and is a positive constant.

Let us introduce some more notation to obtain the hedge fund's optimal portfolio. Suppose r_0 is the risk-free rate of return (return on cash), r_i is the return on security i, the expected return on security i is $\mu_i = E(r_i)$, $\sigma_i^2 = \text{Var}(r_i)$ is the variance of return on security i, $\sigma_{12} = \text{Cov}(r_1, r_2)$ is the covariance of return between securities 1 and 2. Then we can write the objective function U as:

$$U = E(r) - \frac{1}{2\tau}\text{Var}(r)$$

$$= cr_0 + a_1\mu_1 + a_2\mu_2 - \frac{1}{2\tau}\text{Var}(cr_0 + a_1r_1 + a_2r_2)$$

$$= (e - a_1 - a_2)r_0 + a_1\mu_1 + a_2\mu_2$$

$$- \frac{1}{2\tau}\left(a_1^2\sigma_1^2 + a_2^2\sigma_2^2 + 2a_1a_2\sigma_{12}\right)$$

$$= e \cdot r_0 + a_1(\mu_1 - r_0) + a_2(\mu_2 - r_0)$$

$$- \frac{1}{2\tau}\left(a_1^2\sigma_1^2 + a_2^2\sigma_2^2 + 2a_1a_2\sigma_{12}\right)$$

Example. Let the hedge fund's initial capital be $e = 1$. Suppose expected returns and other parameters are as follows. $\mu_1 = 0.1$, $\mu_2 = 0.05$, $r_0 = 0.02$, $\sigma_1^2 = \sigma_2^2 = 0.04$ (so that the standard deviation of return or 'volatility' σ is 20%), $\sigma_{12} = 0.037$ (so that the correlation of return is $\rho = 0.037/0.04 = 0.925$), the risk tolerance τ is $\tau = 0.25$. Given these parameters, we can plot the objective function U as a function of a_1 and a_2. In Figures 3.7 and 3.8, "asset i" refers to a_i.

It is apparent from Figure 3.7 that the maximum is reached when a_1 is positive but a_2 is negative. By looking at the contour diagram in Figure 3.8 from the top, we can get a better view of where the optimum is.

The contour diagrams verify that the objective function is a smooth concave function, and so we can use first-order conditions in deriving the optimal portfolio. The first-order conditions are:

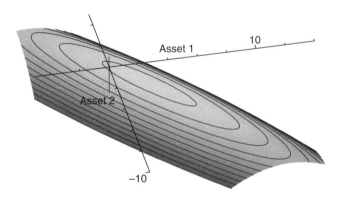

Figure 3.7: Utility surface for mean-variance preferences

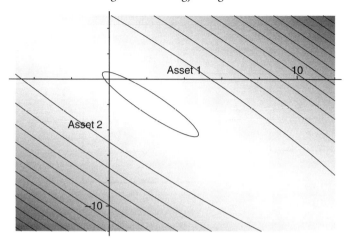

Figure 3.8: Utility contours for mean-variance preferences

$$\frac{dU}{da_1} = \overbrace{(\mu_1 - r_0)}^{\text{increase in mean}} - \frac{1}{\tau}\overbrace{\left(a_1\sigma_1^2 + a_2\sigma_{12}\right)}^{\text{increase in variance}} = 0$$

$$\frac{dU}{da_2} = (\mu_2 - r_0) - \frac{1}{\tau}\left(a_2\sigma_2^2 + a_1\sigma_{12}\right) = 0 \tag{3.28}$$

Equation (3.28) indicates that the choice of a_1 is dictated by the tradeoff between the increase in expected return against the increased variance of return. We can rearrange these two equations in matrix form, giving

$$\begin{bmatrix} \mu_1 - r_0 \\ \mu_2 - r_0 \end{bmatrix} = \frac{1}{\tau}\begin{bmatrix} \sigma_1^2 & \sigma_{12} \\ \sigma_{12} & \sigma_2^2 \end{bmatrix}\begin{bmatrix} a_1 \\ a_2 \end{bmatrix}$$

The optimal dollar holdings in the portfolio can then be calculated as:

$$\begin{bmatrix} a_1 \\ a_2 \end{bmatrix} = \tau\begin{bmatrix} \sigma_1^2 & \sigma_{12} \\ \sigma_{12} & \sigma_2^2 \end{bmatrix}^{-1}\begin{bmatrix} \mu_1 - r_0 \\ \mu_2 - r_0 \end{bmatrix} \tag{3.29}$$

For the numbers given in the numerical example above, we have

$$\begin{bmatrix} a_1 \\ a_2 \end{bmatrix} = 0.25\begin{bmatrix} 0.04 & 0.037 \\ 0.037 & 0.04 \end{bmatrix}^{-1}\begin{bmatrix} 0.08 \\ 0.03 \end{bmatrix}$$

$$= \begin{bmatrix} 2.2619 \\ -1.9047 \end{bmatrix}$$

The hedge fund's portfolio consists of \$2.26 million of security 1, − \$1.90 million of security 2 and a cash holding of $1 - a_1 - a_2 = 1 - 0.3572 = 0.6428$ million

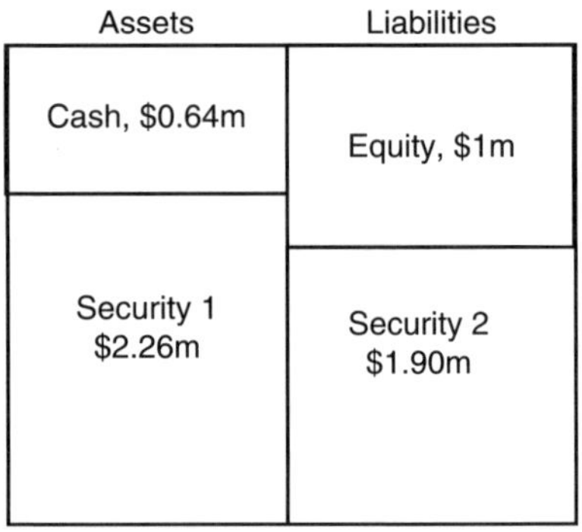

Assets	Liabilities
Cash, $0.64m	Equity, $1m
Security 1 $2.26m	Security 2 $1.90m

Figure 3.9: Balance sheet of hedge fund

dollars. The hedge fund holds 64% of its initial capital as cash, but has assets of $2.26 million of security 1. This position has been funded partly with its own cash (taking 357,200 dollars to buy security 1), but also by short-selling $1.9 million worth of security 2. The balance sheet of the hedge fund is given in Figure 3.9.

The *leverage* of the hedge fund is

$$\frac{\text{total assets}}{\text{equity}} \simeq \frac{2.26 + 0.64}{1}$$
$$= 2.9$$

The expected return on the portfolio is

$$r_0 + \begin{bmatrix} a_1 & a_2 \end{bmatrix} \begin{bmatrix} \mu_1 - r_0 \\ \mu_2 - r_0 \end{bmatrix} \simeq 0.144$$

The variance of the portfolio return is

$$\begin{bmatrix} a_1 & a_2 \end{bmatrix} \begin{bmatrix} \sigma_1^2 & \sigma_{12} \\ \sigma_{12} & \sigma_2^2 \end{bmatrix} \begin{bmatrix} a_1 \\ a_2 \end{bmatrix}$$
$$\simeq \begin{bmatrix} 2.262 & -1.905 \end{bmatrix} \begin{bmatrix} 0.04 & 0.037 \\ 0.037 & 0.04 \end{bmatrix} \begin{bmatrix} 2.262 \\ -1.905 \end{bmatrix}$$
$$\simeq 0.031$$

Volatility of return is $0.031 \simeq 0.176$. The expected return is higher than for either of the two risky assets, while the volatility is lower than both of them. Consider all the possible combinations of expected return and portfolio standard deviation of return from combinations of a_1 and a_2 that hold no cash. In other words, we consider all combinations a_1 and a_2 such that $a_1 + a_2 = 1$. The quadratic curve in Figure 3.10 plots the possible combinations of expected return and standard deviation of returns along this path.

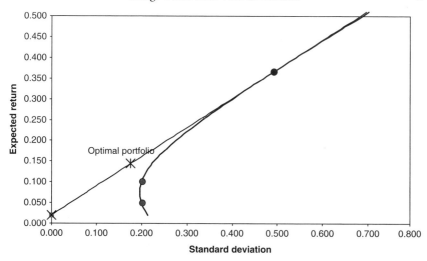

Figure 3.10: Mean-variance efficient portfolios

As well as the portfolios consisting of just security 1 and security 2, the hedge fund also has access to cash—both short and long positions. One point that is certainly accessible to the hedge fund is the portfolio consisting just of cash. This is the point marked on the vertical axis in Figure 3.10 where the combination of standard deviation and expected return is (0, 0.02). Also, by taking a combination of cash and a portfolio consisting of the two risky securities, the investor can achieve any point on a straight line that links (0, 0.02) with some point on the mean-variance surface. The optimal portfolio is marked with a cross in Figure 3.10. The combination of expected return and standard deviation dominates that of either of the securities taken individually.

3.4 HEDGE FUND WITH VaR CONSTRAINT

Let us now consider the optimal portfolio choice for a hedge fund that maximizes expected returns subject to a Value-at-Risk (VaR) constraint. The notation is kept the same as before. The balance-sheet identity is:

$$a_1 + a_2 + c = e$$

The hedge fund's optimization problem can be written as

$$\max_{a_1,a_2} E(r) \quad \text{subject to VaR} \leq e \tag{3.30}$$

where $E(r)$ is the expected return on the hedge fund's portfolio. We have already seen the expression $F(r)$ above in connection with the mean variance optimization case. The Value-at-Risk is some multiple of the standard devation of portfolio return, σ_r such that for some positive constant α, we have $\text{VaR} = \alpha\sigma_r$. The constraint faced by the hedge fund is that it has a large enough equity cushion e so as to meet its Value-at-Risk. That is

$$\text{VaR} \leq e$$

or equivalently, that $\alpha\sigma_r \leq e$. It will prove to be convenient to transform the constraint by squaring both sides and dividing by α^2 to give

$$\sigma_r^2 \leq \left(\frac{e}{\alpha}\right)^2 \tag{3.31}$$

Then, write the Lagrangian as

$$\begin{aligned}
\mathcal{L} &= E(r) - \lambda\left(\sigma_r^2 - \left(\frac{e}{\alpha}\right)^2\right) \\
&= E(r) - \lambda\sigma_r^2 + \lambda\left(\frac{e}{\alpha}\right)^2
\end{aligned} \tag{3.32}$$

Notice that the Lagrangian $\mathcal{L}$ has the same expression as the mean-variance utility function given by (3.27) above, except for the constant term $\lambda\left(\frac{e}{\alpha}\right)^2$ and the fact that λ is taking the place of $1/2\tau$. When taking first-order conditions with respect to a_1 and a_2, the constant term $\lambda\left(\frac{e}{\alpha}\right)^2$ will drop out, so that the first-order conditions turn out to be identical to the ones for the mean-variance portfolio case given by equations (3.28), except that we have the constant λ rather than the constant $1/2\tau$. The optimal portfolio is

$$\begin{bmatrix} a_1 \\ a_2 \end{bmatrix} = \frac{1}{2\lambda}\begin{bmatrix} \Sigma^{-1} \end{bmatrix}\begin{bmatrix} \mu_1 \\ \mu_2 \end{bmatrix} \tag{3.33}$$

where Σ is the covariance matrix of returns. The variance of return on the portfolio is given by the quadratic form:

$$\sigma_r^2 = a'\Sigma a \tag{3.34}$$

where a' is the transpose of a. From (3.33) we have

$$\begin{aligned}
\sigma_r^2 &= a'\Sigma a \\
&= \frac{1}{4\lambda^2}\mu'\Sigma^{-1}\mu
\end{aligned} \tag{3.35}$$

Finally, from the VaR constraint, we have $\sigma_r^2 = \left(\frac{e}{\alpha}\right)^2$. Thus,

$$\frac{1}{4\lambda^2}\mu'\Sigma^{-1}\mu = \left(\frac{e}{\alpha}\right)^2 \tag{3.36}$$

The Lagrange multiplier of the transformed constraint is

$$\lambda = \frac{\alpha}{2e} \sqrt{\mu' \Sigma^{-1} \mu} \qquad (3.37)$$

Substituting into the first-order condition (3.33) allows us to solve for the optimal portfolio.

$$\begin{bmatrix} a_1 \\ a_2 \end{bmatrix} = \frac{e}{\alpha} \cdot \frac{1}{\sqrt{\mu' \Sigma^{-1} \mu}} \left[\Sigma^{-1} \right] \begin{bmatrix} \mu_1 \\ \mu_2 \end{bmatrix} \qquad (3.38)$$

Note that the portfolio holdings of the two risky assets are proportional to the hedge fund's capital e. When the equity of the hedge fund doubles, so do the dollar values of the risky assets. In this sense, the portfolio holdings of the risky assets satify a "constant returns to scale" property. We saw this feature also in Section 3.3 when the choice was between the (single) risky asset and cash.

The implications are important. When the hedge fund suffers losses that deplete its equity, it will act more conservatively, and reduce its holding of the risky assets. Conversely, when favorable market outcomes increases the hedge fund's equity capital, it will hold a greater dollar value of risky securities.

The formal similarity between the solution of the mean-variance optimal portfolio and that of the Value-at-Risk constrained trader is revealing in another respect. We see that the VaR-constrained trader is acting like a mean-variance trader, except that it is as if the trader's risk tolerance τ is changing over time, in response to events as they unfold. Comparing (3.38) with the analogous optimal portfolio expression for the mean-variance optimal portfolio given by equation (3.29), we see that the portfolio of the hedge fund with a VaR constraint and equity level e acts like a mean-variance preference investor whose risk tolerance τ is given by

$$\tau = \frac{e}{\alpha} \cdot \frac{1}{\sqrt{\mu' \Sigma^{-1} \mu}} \qquad (3.39)$$

A hedge fund that is well-capitalized has a risk appetite that is higher than one that is not as well capitalized. For economists, preferences and beliefs would normally be considered as being independent of one another. However, it would be important to distinguish "risk appetite", which motivates traders' actions, from "risk aversion", which is a preference parameter hard-wired into agents' characteristics. A trader's risk appetite may change even if his preferences are unchanged. The reason is that risk taking may be curtailed by the constraints that traders operate under, such as those based on Value-at-Risk (VaR).

In the set-up here, the hedge fund is risk-neutral, but it operates under a Value-at-Risk (VaR) constraint. The Lagrange multiplier associated with the VaR constraint is the key quantity. It affects portfolio choice through shifts in risk appetite, but note that the Lagrange multiplier contains information about forecasts of future outcomes. Through the Lagrange multiplier, beliefs and risk appetite are thus linked.

To an outside observer, it would appear that market participants' preferences change with minute-by-minute changes in market outcomes. Crucially, shocks may be amplified through the feedback effects that operate from volatile outcomes to reduced capacity to bear risk. In this sense, the distinction between "risk appetite" and "risk aversion" is more than a semantic quibble. This distinction helps us understand how booms and crises play out in the financial system.

Example. Let $\sigma^2 = 1$, $\mu_1 = 0.1$, $\mu_2 = 0.05$, $\alpha = 2.33$.

For these parameters, the Lagrange multiplier of the transformed constraint is

$$\lambda = \frac{\alpha}{2e\sigma} \cdot \sqrt{\frac{\mu_1^2 + \mu_2^2 - 2\rho\mu_1\mu_2}{1 - \rho^2}}$$

From (3.33), we can solve for optimal portfolio:

$$\begin{bmatrix} a_1 \\ a_2 \end{bmatrix} = \frac{e}{\alpha\sigma((1 - \rho^2)(\mu_1^2 + \mu_2^2 - 2\rho\mu_1\mu_2))} \begin{bmatrix} \mu_1 - \rho\mu_2 \\ \mu_2 - \rho\mu_1 \end{bmatrix}$$

For the range where the correlation coefficient ρ satisfies $\rho \in \left[\frac{1}{2}, 1\right]$, leverage can be written as

$$L = 1 - \frac{a_2}{e}$$

$$= 1 + \frac{1}{\alpha\sigma} \cdot \frac{\rho\mu_1 - \mu_2}{(1 - \rho^2)(\mu_1^2 - 2\rho\mu_1\mu_2 + \mu_2^2)}$$

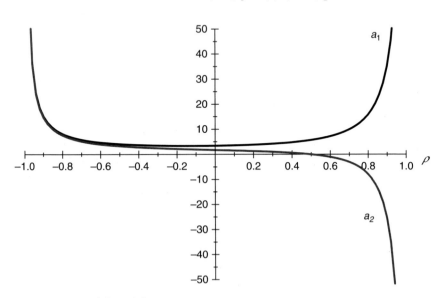

Figure 3.11: Portfolio weights

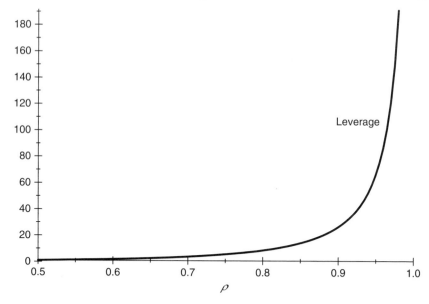

Figure 3.12: Leverage

We see that leverage is increasing in ρ and decreasing in σ. The portfolio weights are plotted in Figure 3.11, and the leverage of the hedge fund is plotted in Figure 3.12.

3.5 ENDOGENOUS RISK

The long-short hedging strategy rests on the stability of the statistical relationship in the returns across assets. When two securities have highly positively correlated returns, but there are small differences in the expected returns, the optimal portfolio has a long position in the security with the higher expected return and funds that position with a short position in the other risky security. Since it is often the illiquid security that has the higher expected return, this usually entails going long in the illiquid security and funding that position by selling short the liquid security.

We have seen that the empirical regularity in the correlation in returns plays a key role in such long-short strategies. In practice, the empirical relationships must be estimated from historical data, in particular, the covariance matrix Σ. By relying on such historical empirical regularities, the hedge fund manager is making the implicit assumption that future returns will conform to past experience. However, acting on such beliefs may undermine those very empirical regularities themselves. Just as the notion of endogenous risk applies to individual returns, it also applies to the vulnerability of historical correlations.

The experience of the hedge fund Long Term Capital Management (LTCM) is a good lesson in the endogeneity of correlations, and the pitfalls in relying on historical correlations as a guide to portfolio choice, especially when high levels of leverage are contemplated. The story of LTCM is well known from popular accounts such as Lowenstein (2000). The 1998 Interim Capital Markets Report of the International Monetary Fund (IMF 1998) is a good public source for the events at the time.

LTCM was known for its use of "convergence trades", many of which relied on the highly correlated returns that were common among fixed income securities. Holdings in risky fixed-income securities such as mortgage-backed securities, corporate bonds or swaps would be funded by selling short treasury securities. Indeed, the convergence trades could also be within the class of treasury securities, such as when the newly issued benchmark "on the run" treasuries would be sold short in order to fund the purchase of seasoned "off the run" treasuries, which would normally command a small additional yield to compensate for its illiquidity.

Another strategy was holding a long position in Italian government bonds funded by selling short German government bonds. Not only was there a yield difference between the two that favored the Italian government bonds, but the convergence trade was also a bet that the advent of the euro at the end of the 1990s would be preceded by the gradual convergence of the yield on German and Italian government bonds.

Although differences in the credit risk in the two government securities may persist, reflecting the respective creditworthiness of the two governments, the currency risk would be taken out of the picture, since both government bonds would be denominated in the same currency—euros. The repeated devaluation of the Italian lira which had undermined the value of Italian government bonds in the eyes of international investors, and which meant that Italian government bonds had to offer a higher risk premium over German government bonds, would no longer be in place after the adoption of the euro.

The early years of LTCM generated sustained high returns from such strategies, but the stability of the empirical regularity that underpinned the convergence trade was vulnerable to endogenous risk in the same way that the pedestrians on the Millennium Bridge were vulnerable to the self-reinforcing movements of the bridge. Suppose the convergence trade consists of being long in security 1 and being short in security 2. We can think of security 1 as being mortgage-backed securities and 2 as being treasuries, for instance. The feedback loop can be summarized in the following flow chart:

$$\text{Shock}\begin{cases} r_1 & \downarrow \\ r_2 & \uparrow \end{cases} \Rightarrow \rho \text{ down, } \mu_1 \text{ down, } \mu_2 \text{ up}$$

$$\Uparrow \qquad\qquad\qquad\qquad \Downarrow$$

$$\begin{matrix} r_1 & \downarrow \\ r_2 & \uparrow \end{matrix} \quad \Leftarrow \quad \text{Sell 1, Buy 2}$$

Consider an initial shock that delivers a setback to the convergence trade hedge fund, where security 1 experiences a price decline while security 2 experiences a price increase. For a convergence trade hedge fund that holds a long position in 1 and a short position in 2, this is a triple blow. This is because the hedge fund's portfolio choice rested on three empirical regularities—that the return on security 1 would be high, that the return on security 2 would be low, and that the correlation in returns between the two securities would be high—that μ_1 is high, μ_2 is low, and ρ is high. All three features are undermined by the realized returns where r_1 is low and r_2 is high simultaneously. For traders who forecast the future based on past outcomes, these outcomes have the effect of lowering the forecast return of security 1, raising the forecast return on security 2, and lowering the forecast correlation of the two returns. The optimal portfolio given by equation (3.33) will then reflect these changes in beliefs. The long-short convergence trade becomes less aggressively tilted toward security 1 and the leverage is likely to fall.

As well as these changes in beliefs, there is a more direct impact of the adverse shock. The capital of the hedge fund becomes depleted by the adverse shock. As we saw both in the single risky asset example in Section 3.3 and above in the expression for the optimal portfolio of the VaR-constrained hedge fund in equation (3.33), the dollar value of the holdings in the risky assets is proportional to the capital e of the hedge fund. When it suffers losses, its capital is depleted, pushing it to scale down its holdings of the risky assets—both positive and negative.

For all these reasons—the changes in beliefs, as well as the depletion of its capital—the upshot of the initial adverse shock in returns is that the hedge fund sells some units of security 1 and buys back some units in security 2. However, this is precisely the combination of trades that will put further downward pressure on the price of security 1 and upward pressure on the price of security 2. If a large swathe of the market began by holding similar positions, then the sale of security 1 and purchase of security 2 would affect the realized returns of the two securities, raising r_2 and lowering r_1. But this was precisely the combination of outcomes that set off the whole process. This is exactly like the wobble in the Millennium Bridge, where the initial gust of wind that moves the bridge gets amplified due to the responses of the pedestrians. The added dimension is that correlations are also subject to endogenous risk.

For a formal analysis of such endogenously varying correlations and feedback effects, the reader is referred to Danielsson, Shin, and Zigrand (2009). The starting point of the paper is to recognize the endogeneity of risk by treating it as the fixed point of the mapping that maps *perceived* risk to *actual* risk. In the dynamic asset pricing model that results, the stochastic volatility function is solved as a fixed point of the mapping that takes conjectured volatility functions to realized volatility functions. The equilibrium stochastic volatility is the "endogenous risk". In such a setting, even when the stochastic shocks that hit the underlying fundamentals of the risky assets are independent across the two securities, the resulting equilibrium dynamics exhibit time-varying and stochastic volatility, where higher volatilities coincide with increased correlations in returns.

Correlations emerge in equilibrium, even though the underlying shocks are constant, and independent across the risky assets, due to the type of feedback effects sketched above.

In a market where there is a uniformity of trading positions underpinned by a consensus over the superiority of particular trading strategies, any adverse shock has the potential of exerting a large and persistent impact. The breakdowns in correlations are a good example of endogenous risk—the risks that are generated and amplified within the system. They stand in contrast to exogenous risks that refer to shocks that originate from outside the system.

3.6 NOTES ON FURTHER READING

Lagrange multipliers associated with risk constraints have been examined in Gromb and Vayanos (2002), Danielsson, Shin, and Zigrand (2004, 2009), Oehmke (2008), Brunnermeier and Pedersen (2009) and Garleanu and Pedersen (2009). The role of Value-at-Risk in amplifying booms and busts is given a dynamic treatment in Danielsson, Shin, and Zigrand (2009) who solve for the equilibrium volatility and correlations as a fixed point of the mapping that takes perceived volatilities and correlations to realized volatilies and correlations.

The Bank for International Settlements has been consistent in warning of the damage done during financial booms. Andrew Crockett, its former Managing Director, William White, its former chief economist, and Claudio Borio, its head of research, have written a string of papers that have argued for the importance of "leaning against the wind" against such booms as a way to forestall the building up of vulnerabilities that build up during the boom. Two well-known papers are Borio and Lowe (2002) and Borio and White (2003). The latter paper was presented at the 2003 Jackson Hole Symposium, and the discussion and interventions from the floor following the presentation provide a fascinating snapshot of the state of thinking in mainstream central banking at the time.[2] Shin (2005a) examines a theoretical framework where loose monetary policy is an engine of housing market fluctuations through its interaction with bank balance sheets. Recently, Borio and Zhou (2008) have coined the term "risk-taking channel of monetary policy" to describe the way that monetary policy works through risk spreads and intermediary balance sheets in the way described in this book. The general equilibrium model in Section 3.1 is one possible formalization of the risk-taking channel of monetary policy. Many of the themes in this chapter have a long history, going back to the classic discussions of financial intermediation of Gurley and Shaw (1955) and the sign of muted risks as a prelude to crises in Minsky (1975). Brunnermeier and Sannikov (2009) is a macro model with a financial sector.

[2] <http://www.kc.frb.org/publicat/sympos/2003/sym03prg.htm>.

Long-short strategy hedge funds have been in the news more recently with the losses suffered by long-short equity hedge funds in the early weeks of the financial crisis, in August of 2007. The *Wall Street Journal's* article on September 7, 2007, is entitled "How Market Turmoil Waylaid the 'Quants'".[3] A rare glimpse into the detailed performance of the long-short funds is provided by Khandani and Lo (2007), who simulate the outcomes of a hypothetical long-short fund during early August of 2007.

[3] <http://online.wsj.com/article/SB118912592144720147.html>.

4

Dynamic Hedging

Some risk can be diversified away, and some of it can be hedged away through a matched position in a security that has a similar return process. In this chapter, I discuss a third way in which market participants attempt to deal with risk, namely *dynamic hedging*. Dynamic hedging refers to the practise of active adjustment of the portfolio in response to price changes in a manner that leaves the portfolio hedged against future shocks. We examine in particular the dynamic hedging of options—how they work and how they can be put into practise. Importantly, we will also see the limits of dynamic hedging, and what can go wrong. The 1987 stock market crash is an important lesson on the limits of dynamic hedging.

4.1 PORTFOLIO INSURANCE

In the 1980s, specialized fund managers put into practise the principles that underpin the Black and Scholes (1973) model for option pricing and set up funds that became known as portfolio insurers. Bookstaber (2007) gives a first-hand description from a practitioner on the scene at the time.

Portfolio insurance attempts to replicate the payoffs that arise from holding a put option by trading actively in the market. A put option gives the holder the right (but not the obligation) to sell a particular asset at a pre-agreed price (the *strike price*, or *exercise price*) at a particular date in the future (the *expiry date*). At the expiry date, the value of the put option is large when the price of the underlying asset is far below the exercise price, since the holder of the put can buy the underlying asset at the low prevailing market price, and then sell it at the higher exercise price, pocketing the difference. When the price of the underlying asset is *above* the exercise price, the holder of the option will not exercise the option, and the option will expire worthless. Figure 4.1 illustrates the payoff of a put option at expiry when the exercise price is X.

Before the expiry date, the option has a value that is above its value at expiry, since the price S of the underlying asset at expiry is uncertain. Even if the current price S is above the strike price X, there is a chance that S will drift below X before expiry. As long as this is a possibility, the option has a positive value. The farther in the future is the expiry date, the greater is the uncertainty, and the greater is the value of option for any given price of the underlying asset today as shown in Figure 4.2. The value of a

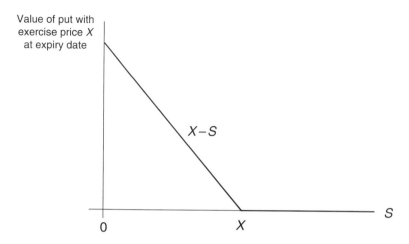

Figure 4.1: Payoff of put option at expiry date

put option is increasing when the price S falls. Also, *the rate* at which the option increases in value is itself increasing as S falls.

Replicating the payoff of a put option through dynamic hedging attempts to position one's portfolio in reaction to price changes in order to mimic the payoffs from a put option at expiry. There are two requirements. Since a put option pays out more when price is low, this means maintaining a short position in the underlying asset. Since the slope of the put option's value becomes steeper as the price falls, this means taking an even larger short position when the underlying asset falls in price. In other words, dynamic hedging dictates that when the price *falls*, you *sell* more of the asset. Replicating a put option through dynamic trading entails a "sell cheap, buy dear" strategy.

Why might it make sense to replicate a put option, rather than just buying a put option? Options that trade in organized exchanges are limited to certain well-established markets, and only for relatively short expiry dates. For very long-dated options, or for specific portfolios, dynamic replication may be the only avenue open to an investor if he/she wishes to attempt to hedge the value of an investment holding. You could approach one of the large banks or securities firms and ask it to sell an option to you. But you will need to pay for the privilege of buying the option. For instance, where a fund manager has sold long-term retail funds that guarantee the initial investment, the implicit put must be replicated in some way.

For the bank that sells you the option, it is incurring the liabilities generated by having sold the option. For this reason, even if the bank sells you an over-the-counter (OTC) option tailored to your needs, this does not mean that dynamic hedging becomes irrelevant. Once the bank sells the option to you, the bank is holding a risky liability, and will want to hedge this risk. The burden of replication is placed on the bank that has sold the option. So,

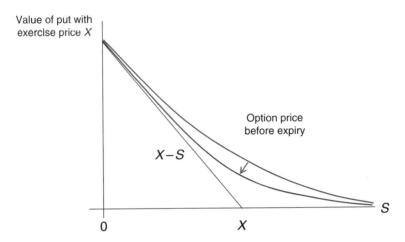

Figure 4.2: Put option price closer to expiry

as long as some party has to bear the risk of the liabilities generated by the option, dynamic hedging becomes relevant.

4.2 DELTA HEDGING

In its simplest form, dynamic hedging relies on the *delta* of the option. To fix ideas, let us focus on the task of replicating the payoff of a put option. The delta of a put option is the rate of change of the put option price with respect to the change in the price of the underlying asset. Thus, if P is the price of the put option and S is the price of the underlying asset, the delta Δ is given by $\Delta = dP/dS$. For a put option, its delta lies between -1 and 0. Black and Scholes, in their famous paper on option pricing, noted that the portfolio consisting of:

$$\begin{cases} \Delta & \text{underlying asset} \\ -1 & \text{put option} \end{cases}$$

is locally risk-free with respect to changes in S. This is because when the price changes slightly, the gain from the holding of the underlying asset (given by Δ) is matched by an exactly offsetting loss in the price of the put option $(-\Delta)$. This insight is used in the derivation of the Black-Scholes formula by arguing that the above portfolio must earn the same return as the risk-free asset.

The delta of a put option can be pictured in Figure 4.3. The delta is the slope of P with respect to S, and hence lies below the horizontal axis. The delta goes to -1 as the price of the underlying security S falls, and tends to 0 as the price of the underlying security increases. As the time of the expiry of the option approaches, the price of the option gets closer to the kinked curve, with the kink at the exercise

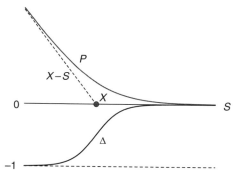

Figure 4.3: Delta of put option

price X. So, the delta behaves more like the step function that jumps from -1 to 0 at exercise price X. See Figure 4.4.

At expiry, there are two possible values of delta. If the option expires "in the money" so that $S < X$, then we are on the negatively sloped part of the curve in Figure 4.1 so that $\Delta = -1$. However, if the option expires "out of the money", we are on the flat part of the curve in Figure 4.1 so that $\Delta = 0$.

The payoff from the put option can be replicated by holding a suitable portfolio of the underlying asset and cash, and adjusting the position over time in response to realized outcomes. Suppose a trader starts with a cash balance of P, and suppose that P is also the market price of the put option that the trader wishes to replicate. With this wealth, the trader can either purchase the put option itself, or purchase the portfolio given by:

$$\begin{cases} \Delta & \text{underlying asset} \\ -S\Delta + P & \text{cash} \end{cases} \tag{4.1}$$

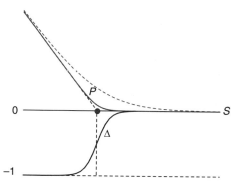

Figure 4.4: Delta of put option closer to expiry

The value of this portfolio is also P, since the Δ units of the underlying asset has price $-S\Delta$. Remember that Δ is negative since the trader wishes to replicate a put option. The portfolio given by (4.1) is financed by selling short $|\Delta|$ units of underlying asset at price S, and adding the proceeds to the cash balance.

Now, suppose price changes to S'. The value of the portfolio at the new price is

$$\overbrace{\Delta \cdot S'}^{\text{short asset}} + \overbrace{P - S\Delta}^{\text{cash}}$$
$$= P + \Delta(S' - S)$$
$$\simeq P'$$

where P' is the price of the put option given price S'. Figure 4.5 illustrates the change in the price of the portfolio following the price change, and how it relates to the shift in the price of the put option itself. The trader manages to approximate the wealth of a trader who starts out by holding the put option itself, in the sense that the trader's portfolio value moves along the tangency line at the old price S. Since the approximation is linear, the accuracy of the approximation is greater, the smaller is the price change.

After the price change, the trader can repeat his procedure at the new price S'. See Figure 4.6. At the new price S', the investor forms the new portfolio:

$$\begin{cases} \Delta' & \text{underlying asset} \\ -S'\Delta' + P' & \text{cash} \end{cases} \tag{4.2}$$

which is affordable (approximately), given his new wealth of P'.

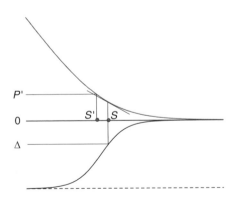

Figure 4.5: Delta prior to price change

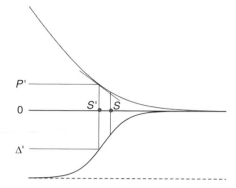

Figure 4.6: Delta following the price change

Suppose that the trader repeats this procedure of forming the new portfolio in response to price changes so that he maintains a position of Δ in the underlying security, and where the cash position adjusts as a result of the shift in the portfolio. When the price falls, the delta becomes more negative, meaning that the trader sells more of the underlying security, and thereby adds to the cash balance by the amount of the dollar value of securities sold short in that round. Conversely, if the price rises, then the delta becomes less negative, meaning that the trader has to buy back some of the security, thereby dipping into his cash balance to make the purchase. The cash balance will adjust in this way as a result of new sales and purchases

Proceeding in this way, let us suppose that the trader reaches the expiry date of the option. There are two cases we need to consider, depending on whether the option expires in the money or out of the money. If the option expires in the money (i.e. when the price S is below the exercise price X), we have $\Delta = -1$, so that the portfolio given by (4.2) is

$$\begin{cases} -1 & \text{underlying asset} \\ S + (X - S) & \text{cash} \end{cases}$$

In this case, the trader has a balance sheet in which he has cash of $S + (X - S)$ on the asset side, and 1 unit of the underlying security on the liabilities side. The difference between the two is the equity of the trader. Since the price of the underlying security is S, the value of equity is

$$\underbrace{S + (X - S)}_{\text{asset}} - \underbrace{S}_{\text{liability}} = X - S \tag{4.3}$$

Another way to think about this is to imagine the trader buying back the 1 unit of the security at expiry, at the price of S. With a cash balance of $S + (X - S)$, paying out S leaves the trader with $X - S$.

The second case is when the option expires out of the money. In this case, the price of the underlying security S lies above the exercise price X.

So, the portfolio (4.2) takes the particular simple form:

$$\begin{cases} 0 & \text{underlying asset} \\ 0 & \text{cash} \end{cases} \qquad (4.4)$$

In this case, the equity of the trader is zero. So, taking account of the two possible cases taken by the trader's portfolio at the expiration date, the final value of the trader's portfolio is the larger of $X - S$ and zero. In other words, the payoff at expiry of the trader who follows the strategy of keeping a delta position in the underlying security is given by

$$\max\{X - S, 0\}$$

But this payoff is exactly the payoff achieved by the alternative strategy for the trader in which he pays P to buy one unit of the put option, and holds it to expiry. In this way, the strategy of hedging by holding a delta position in the underlying security enables the trader to mimic the payoff of buying a put option and holding it.

Examples without Feedback

Let us first examine a numerical example in the standard case where there is no feedback. This is the case dealt with in textbooks, such as Hull (2009). Suppose the initial price of the underlying security is 100. A trader wishes to replicate the payoff of the put option with strike price 90 by rebalancing his portfolio at the end of each week. We suppose that the trader starts with a zero cash balance, but can borrow and lend at some risk-free rate r. The option expires in 20 weeks. Suppose also that the process governing the evolution of the security's price is such that the Black-Scholes option pricing formula is valid. We will examine some numerical examples of delta hedging.

According to the Black-Scholes formula for option pricing, the delta of a put option at time t is given by

$$N(d_1) - 1$$

where $N(.)$ is the cumulative distribution function of the standard normal, and d_1 is given by the following function

$$d_1 = \frac{\ln\left(\frac{S}{X}\right) + \left(r + \frac{\sigma^2}{2}\right)(T - t)}{\sigma\sqrt{T - t}} \qquad (4.5)$$

where X is the exercise price of the option, S is the price of the underlying asset, r is the risk-free interest rate, T is the expiry date of the option and σ is the standard deviation of return on the underlying security. For convenience, let us set the risk-free interest rate r to zero. The Black-Scholes formula for the price for the put at t is

$$P = Xe^{-r(T-t)}N(-d_2) + S(N(d_1) - 1)$$

where

$$d_2 = d_1 - \sigma\sqrt{T-t}$$

We first examine two cases where the delta hedging goes according to plan. The first case is when the put option expires out of the money. Table 4.1 reports the results.

Quantities such as the time to expiry T and volatility σ will be measured in units of years. In the case we want to examine, there are 20 weeks to expiry, so that the time to expiry at the initial date is 0.38 years, which we can see from the second column in the table. The third column is a set of random draws from a normal return density for weekly returns-that is consistent with a 25% yearly volatility σ. The returns each week are assumed to be independent. The yearly standard deviation is converted to a weekly standard deviation by dividing by the square root of 52, the number of weeks in a year. For the particular set of random draws in Table 4.1, the price path is given by the fourth column. We see that the

Table 4.1: No feedback, out of the money

Week	$T-t$	Random	Price	log(p/x)	d_1	Delta	Purchases	Cash flow	Cash stock
0	0.385		100.000	0.105	0.757	−0.224	−0.224	22.450	22.450
1	0.365	0.041	104.052	0.145	1.036	−0.150	0.074	−7.732	14.718
2	0.346	0.002	104.272	0.147	1.074	−0.141	0.009	−0.922	13.795
3	0.327	0.095	114.230	0.238	1.739	−0.041	0.100	−11.464	2.332
4	0.308	−0.004	113.729	0.234	1.757	−0.039	0.002	−0.172	2.160
5	0.288	0.016	115.534	0.250	1.927	−0.027	0.012	−1.444	0.716
6	0.269	−0.036	111.422	0.214	1.711	−0.044	−0.017	1.847	2.563
7	0.250	−0.067	103.950	0.144	1.215	−0.112	−0.069	7.128	9.690
8	0.231	0.016	105.664	0.160	1.396	−0.081	0.031	−3.252	6.438
9	0.212	0.032	109.001	0.192	1.723	−0.042	0.039	−4.244	2.194
10	0.192	0.027	111.945	0.218	2.045	−0.020	0.022	−2.461	−0.267
11	0.173	−0.026	109.068	0.192	1.900	−0.029	−0.008	0.907	0.640
12	0.154	−0.069	101.502	0.120	1.276	−0.101	−0.072	7.340	7.980
13	0.135	−0.019	99.549	0.101	1.145	−0.126	−0.025	2.488	10.468
14	0.115	0.041	103.618	0.141	1.702	−0.044	0.082	−8.459	2.009
15	0.096	−0.005	103.067	0.136	1.788	−0.037	0.007	−0.771	1.238
16	0.077	0.024	105.521	0.159	2.329	−0.010	0.027	−2.849	−1.612
17	0.058	−0.010	104.476	0.149	2.514	−0.006	0.004	−0.413	−2.024
18	0.038	0.009	105.458	0.159	3.257	−0.001	0.005	−0.570	−2.595
19	0.019	0.002	105.658	0.160	4.644	0.000	0.001	−0.059	−2.654
20	0.000	0.024	108.182	0.184		0.000	0.000	0.000	−2.654

returns draws are favorable to the security and the security ends up at the price of 108.18 at the end of the 20 weeks, meaning that the put option with strike of 90 ends up out of the money. The rest of the columns of the table show the details of the delta hedging.

At the outset, the price of the underlying security is 100. For the parameters assumed above, the Black-Scholes delta is -0.22, as we can see from the first entry in the column labelled "Delta". Accordingly the investor who follows the delta-hedging strategy sells 0.22 units of the underlying security, yielding a positive increment to the cash balance of 22.45, which is the product of the price of the security ($= 100$) and the number of units sold short ($= 0.22$). So, after the initial trade, the trader goes into the next period with a portfolio consisting of 22.45 worth of cash and a short position of 0.22 of the risky security. The investor maintains this portfolio until the end of the first week.

Over the first week, the random draw from the return density of the security indicates that the security had a positive return of 4.05%. We see this from the third and fourth columns of Table 4.1. The price of the security thus rises to 104.05. The delta thus goes up from -0.22 to -0.15. When faced with an increase in the delta, the investor must adjust his portfolio to meet the new delta. An increase in the delta means that the trader needs to cut back his short position by buying some of the underlying security. The trader buys the underlying security by the amount of the increase in the delta, namely

$$-0.15 - (-0.22) = 0.07$$

The change in the delta with respect to the price of the underlying asset is known as the option's "gamma". The trader thus buys 0.07 units of the risky security at the prevailing price, which is 104.05. The expenditure is therefore $0.07 \times 104.05 = 7.73$, and so the cash balance decreases by this amount. We see this from the negative second entry in the column labelled "Cash Flow". The final column now reflects the fact that the cash balance now falls to 14.72 due to the cash outflow. The investor is now positioned to meet the random return in the second week.

Proceeding in this way, the investor rebalances his portfolio at the end of each week, in response to the price change that has occurred during that week. We see from Table 4.1 that as time progresses, the delta of the put option goes to zero fairly quickly. This is because the random returns keep the security's price substantially above the exercise price, so that the option price is close to zero and insensitive to changes in the price of the underlying security. Since the delta itself does not change very much (i.e. the gamma is close to zero), we see that the portfolio rebalancing is not very active either. The purchases and sales quickly taper off to zero.

At the expiry of the option after 20 weeks, the trader holds a zero position in the underlying security, reflecting the zero delta. The cash balance is negative, and is given by -2.65. The investor has lost this much. However, the right comparison is with what the investor would have ended up with, if he had purchased the option instead, and held it to expiry. Since the option expires out of the money, the investor would have incurred losses by purchasing the put option also. So, the right comparison is with someone who bought the option at date 0. The Black-Scholes price at date 0 for the put option with strike price of 90 can be calculated to be 2.17. This is the amount that the investor would have lost had he purchased the put option instead, rather than attempting to replicate the payoff of the put option through delta hedging. There is a difference between 2.65 and 2.17, reflecting the approximate nature of a strategy of dynamic hedging that rebalances the portfolio only once a week.

We now turn to an example where the option ends up in the money, although there is still no feedback effect and the returns are exogenous. Table 4.2 is a table of outcomes of delta hedging for a different draw of random returns from the same density as in the previous example, but where the returns are unfavorable to the security value, so that the put option ends up in the money. The starting point is the same as in the previous example; the price is 100, and the trader begins with a short position in the underlying security of -0.22. However, the return in the first week is -2.6%, lowering the price to 97.38. The delta becomes more negative, at -0.2753, which is met by the trader selling additional units of the risky security, and adding 4.94 to the cash balance. At the end

Table 4.2: No feedback, in the money

Week	$T-t$	Random	Price	$\log(p/x)$	d_1	Delta	Purchases	Cash flow	Cash stock
0	0.385		100.000	0.105	0.757	−0.224	−0.224	22.450	22.450
1	0.365	−0.026	97.378	0.079	0.597	−0.275	−0.051	4.944	27.394
2	0.346	0.014	98.738	0.093	0.704	−0.241	0.034	−3.397	23.997
3	0.327	−0.046	94.213	0.046	0.392	−0.348	−0.107	10.065	34.062
4	0.308	0.015	95.617	0.061	0.506	−0.306	0.041	−3.944	30.118
5	0.288	0.006	96.144	0.066	0.559	−0.288	0.018	−1.764	28.353
6	0.269	0.021	98.138	0.087	0.732	−0.232	0.056	−5.502	22.851
7	0.250	−0.047	93.485	0.038	0.366	−0.357	−0.125	11.684	34.535
8	0.231	0.024	95.685	0.061	0.570	−0.284	0.073	−6.955	27.580
9	0.212	−0.037	92.180	0.024	0.266	−0.395	−0.111	10.227	37.807
10	0.192	−0.010	91.283	0.014	0.184	−0.427	−0.032	2.901	40.708
11	0.173	−0.048	86.910	−0.035	−0.284	−0.612	−0.185	16.054	56.762
12	0.154	−0.045	83.001	−0.081	−0.777	−0.781	−0.170	14.072	70.834
13	0.135	−0.037	79.944	−0.118	−1.246	−0.894	−0.112	8.977	79.811
14	0.115	−0.043	76.546	−0.162	−1.864	−0.969	−0.075	5.761	85.572
15	0.096	−0.020	75.005	−0.182	−2.312	−0.990	−0.021	1.557	87.129
16	0.077	0.044	78.313	−0.139	−1.971	−0.976	0.014	−1.093	86.036
17	0.058	−0.036	75.531	−0.175	−2.889	−0.998	−0.022	1.692	87.728
18	0.038	−0.047	71.989	−0.223	−4.530	−1.000	−0.002	0.139	87.867
19	0.019	0.011	72.788	−0.212	−6.105	−1.000	0.000	0.000	87.867
20	0.000	−0.035	70.236	−0.248		−1.000	0.000	0.000	87.867

of the first week, the trader has a cash balance of 27.39, as seen in the last column.

Proceeding in this way, the trader adjusts his portfolio at the end of each week in response to the weekly realized return. The random draws push the security price down, so that at the end of the 20 weeks, the security price ends up at 70.24. The option ends up in the money, and the delta goes to -1 rapidly in the last few weeks. The cash balance at the end of the 20 weeks is 87.87.

At the end of the 20 weeks, the trader has a portfolio consisting of a cash balance of 87.87 and a liability of 1 unit of the risky security. Since the price of the security is 70.24 at that date, the equity of the trader is given by

$$87.87 - 70.24 = 17.63$$

Having started off with a zero cash balance, 17.63 is the net gain from having replicated the put option. We can compare this outcome to the alternative that was open to the trader of buying 1 unit of the put option and then waiting for the expiry of the option at the end of 20 weeks. The Black-Scholes price of the option at date 0 with strike price 90 is 2.17. Meanwhile, the option ends up in the money by the difference between 90 and 70.24. Hence, the net gain to the trader is

$$90 - 70.24 - 2.17 = 17.59$$

which is very close to the 17.63 that is made by the trader who uses delta hedging to replicate the put option. In this particular numerical example, the outcome of the delta hedging is extremely close to the outcome given by buying and holding the put.

Examples with Feedback

Delta hedging rests on being able to sell the security when the price falls, and buying the security when its price rises. In other words, it is a strategy that chases price moves up or down. The strategy rests on there being someone who buys when you want to sell. However, when there is feedback from the actions of traders to the price moves seen on the market, then there is the potential for amplified responses, where price falls elicit more selling, which pushes price down, which then elicits further selling. When the conditions are ripe (on which more below), delta hedging can generate a price spiral where selling and market dynamics create a feedback loop.

To illustrate such a possibility, let us examine a slightly modified version of the examples examined previously, where the modification consists of incorporating a price feedback effect where sales and purchases impact on price changes in the market. The idea is that selling creates downward pressure on price and buying creates upward pressure on price.

Table 4.3: With feedback, out of the money

Week	$T-t$	Random	Theoretical Price	Actual Price	Delta	Purchases	Cash flow	Cash stock
0	0.385		100.000	100.000	− 0.224	− 0.224	22.450	22.450
1	0.365	0.041	104.052	104.052	− 0.150	0.074	− 7.732	14.718
2	0.346	0.002	104.272	112.004	− 0.059	0.091	− 10.179	4.538
3	0.327	0.095	114.230	132.880	− 0.003	0.057	− 7.538	− 3.000
4	0.308	− 0.004	113.729	139.835	− 0.001	0.002	− 0.279	− 3.278
5	0.288	0.016	115.534	142.333	0.000	0.000	− 0.047	− 3.326
6	0.269	− 0.036	111.422	137.315	0.000	0.000	0.027	− 3.299
7	0.250	− 0.067	103.950	128.079	− 0.002	− 0.002	0.193	− 3.106
8	0.231	0.016	105.664	129.998	− 0.001	0.001	− 0.137	− 3.243
9	0.212	0.032	109.001	134.241	0.000	0.001	− 0.093	− 3.336
10	0.192	0.027	111.945	137.960	0.000	0.000	− 0.023	− 3.359
11	0.173	− 0.026	109.068	134.437	0.000	0.000	0.001	− 3.358
12	0.154	− 0.069	101.502	125.111	0.000	0.000	0.035	− 3.323
13	0.135	− 0.019	99.549	122.668	0.000	0.000	− 0.002	− 3.325
14	0.115	0.041	103.618	127.684	0.000	0.000	− 0.038	− 3.363
15	0.096	− 0.005	103.067	127.042	0.000	0.000	− 0.002	− 3.364
16	0.077	0.024	105.521	130.069	0.000	0.000	0.000	− 3.365
17	0.058	− 0.010	104.476	128.781	0.000	0.000	0.000	− 3.365
18	0.038	0.009	105.458	129.991	0.000	0.000	0.000	− 3.365
19	0.019	0.002	105.658	130.239	0.000	0.000	0.000	− 3.365
20	0.000	0.024	108.182	133.349	0.000	0.000	0.000	− 3.365

For concreteness, let us consider the case where the realized return from date $t-1$ to t is given by

$$1 + r_t + y_t \qquad (4.6)$$

where r_t is the exogenous random return given in the third column of the tables examined above and y_t is the *purchase* of the security as given by the column in the tables labelled as "Purchases". This is the purchase dictated by delta hedging, where the portfolio is required to be rebalanced after the price change to reflect the new value of the optional delta. Since the trader maintains a position in the security of delta of the option, the "Purchases" column reflects the change in the delta from one date to the next.

The first example with feedback is given by Table 4.3, which is the analogue of the example shown earlier in Table 4.1. The third column gives the same set of "fundamental" returns in Table 4.3 as it does in the earlier case of Table 4.1. However, the difference is that the trading decisions affect the subsequent outcome. Selling at one date leads to downward pressure on prices at the subsequent date. There are now two columns for the price sequence. First there is a "Theoretical Price" column that reflects just the exogenous returns. This column is identical to the price series column in Table 4.1. However, with feedback, the actual price sequence reflects the purchases and sales, and is given under the heading "Actual Price".

At the end of week 1, there is a purchase of 0.0743. The actual price at the end of week 2 reflects both the "fundamental" return of $+0.2\%$, but also the upward pressure on price from the purchase in the previous period of 0.0743. The combined return is

$$0.002 + 0.0743 = 0.0763$$

so that the actual price at the end of week 1 is

$$104.05 \times 1.076 = 112$$

This compares with a theoretical price of only 104.27. The difference is due to the large purchases in the previous period following the positive return. At the actual price of 112, the delta now rises to -0.15, which implies a big increase compared to the initial situation. But this big leap in delta then directly feeds into further purchases of the security, since the trader aims to maintain a delta position in the risky security. The additional purchase of the security dictated by the change in delta is 0.09, as can be seen in the "Purchases" column of Table 4.3. After each purchase or sale, the subsequent price change reflects the trade, thereby amplifying the initial price change. For any given exogenous return, a purchase in the previous period makes it more likely that there is a higher return this period, necessitating further purchases. Conversely, a sale in the previous period makes it more likely that there is a *lower* return this period, necessitating further *sales*. The price paths in the two cases—with and without feedback—are plotted in Figure 4.7.

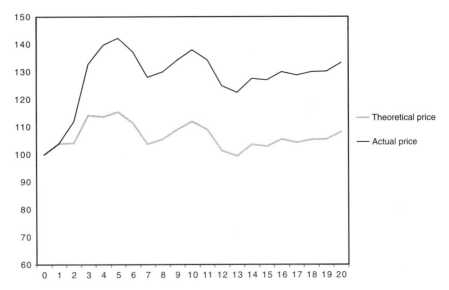

Figure 4.7: Price paths with and without feedback, out of the money case

The upshot is that the delta hedging does a much worse job of mimicking the outcome of buying and holding the option at the initial date. In the case depicted in Table 4.3, the option ends up out of the money. But compared to the Black-Scholes option price of 2.17, the loss made by the delta hedger is 3.36. The gap has widened considerably in this case with feedback than in the case examined in Table 4.1 without feedback. Alternatively, we can interpret the outcome as suggesting that the Black-Scholes option formula underprices the true value of the put option.

The final case we will examine is the most interesting one. This is the case where the option ends up in the money, but where, in addition, we have price feedback effects amplifying the price change. This is the case that is reminiscent of a market collapse driven by the amplifying sales of traders. Table 4.4 tracks the outcome over time. The "fundamental" returns given in Table 4.4 are identical to those in Table 4.2 for the case with no feedback. The starting point at date 0 is as before. The starting price of the security is 100, the delta is −0.22, so that the trader's portfolio at the end of date 0 consists of a short position of 0.22 units of the security and a cash balance of 22.45. At the end of week 1, the fundamental return is −2.26%, which drives down the price to 97.38, as before in Table 4.2.

However, this is when the downward spiral begins to gather momentum. The sale at the end of date 1 feeds into the return for week 2. The "fundamental"

Table 4.4: With feedback, in the money

Week	T−t	Random	Theoretical price	Actual price	Delta	Purchases	Cash flow	Cash stock
0	0.385		100.000	100.000	−0.224	−0.224	22.450	22.450
1	0.365	−0.026	97.378	97.378	−0.275	−0.051	4.944	27.394
2	0.346	0.014	98.738	93.793	−0.362	−0.086	8.095	35.490
3	0.327	−0.046	94.213	81.400	−0.736	−0.374	30.480	65.969
4	0.308	0.015	95.617	52.133	−1.000	−0.264	13.759	79.728
5	0.288	0.006	96.144	38.662	−1.000	0.000	0.002	79.730
6	0.269	0.021	98.138	39.461	−1.000	0.000	0.000	79.730
7	0.250	−0.047	93.485	37.591	−1.000	0.000	0.000	79.730
8	0.231	0.024	95.685	38.475	−1.000	0.000	0.000	79.730
9	0.212	−0.037	92.180	37.066	−1.000	0.000	0.000	79.730
10	0.192	−0.010	91.283	36.705	−1.000	0.000	0.000	79.730
11	0.173	−0.048	86.910	34.946	−1.000	0.000	0.000	79.730
12	0.154	−0.045	83.001	33.375	−1.000	0.000	0.000	79.730
13	0.135	−0.037	79.944	32.145	−1.000	0.000	0.000	79.730
14	0.115	−0.043	76.546	30.779	−1.000	0.000	0.000	79.730
15	0.096	−0.020	75.005	30.160	−1.000	0.000	0.000	79.730
16	0.077	0.044	78.313	31.490	−1.000	0.000	0.000	79.730
17	0.058	−0.036	75.531	30.371	−1.000	0.000	0.000	79.730
18	0.038	−0.047	71.989	28.947	−1.000	0.000	0.000	79.730
19	0.019	0.011	72.788	29.268	−1.000	0.000	0.000	79.730
20	0.000	−0.035	70.236	28.242	−1.000	0.000	0.000	79.730

return in week 2 is positive, namely 1.4%. However, this positive fundamental return is swamped by the downward pressure on prices exerted by the sale of 0.0508 units of the security at the end of week 1. The realized return that combines the fundamental shock and the downward pressure on price from sales is given by

$$0.014 - 0.0508 = -0.0368$$

so that the actual price at the end of week 2 is given by

$$97.38 \times (1 - 0.0368) = 93.79$$

This compares with the theoretical price of 98.74 that takes account only of the exogenous return. The potency of the feedback effect then get a grip on the price process. With each massive sale in one period, the return in the subsequent period is depressed, which generates more sales, and so on.

The upshot of the feedback is clear from the price path in Table 4.4. The price falls very rapidly from the starting price of 100. By the end of week 4, the price has crashed to 52.13, compared to the theoretical price of 95.62. The column tracking the delta of the option reflects the rapid price decline. By the end of week 4, the delta has in effect reached its lower bound of -1. Once the delta reaches -1, the price of the security remains deep in the money, and so the delta remains at -1 until the expiry of the option. Since there is no further change in the delta, there is no trading of the security either. Figure 4.8 plots the price paths with and without feedback for the case where the option ends up in the money.

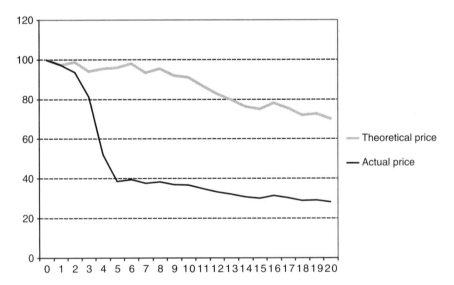

Figure 4.8: Price paths with and without feedback, in the money case

At expiry, the security's actual price has crashed to 28.24. The cash balance of the delta-hedging trader stands at 79.73. Since the trader has a liability of 1 unit of the security, the equity of the trader is

$$79.73 - 28.24 = 51.49$$

Had the trader bought the put option at date 0 at the Black-Scholes price of 2.17, the net position at the time of expiry would have been

$$90 - 28.24 - 2.17 = 59.59$$

which is substantially larger than the outcome of the delta hedging. Again, this is evidence that when there is feedback, the Black-Scholes formula is underpricing the put option.

4.3 STOCK MARKET CRASH OF 1987

As we have seen, the dynamic hedging strategy that replicates a put option has the property that it dictates selling of the underlying asset when its price *falls*, and dictates buying the underlying asset when its price *rises*. It is a "sell cheap, buy dear" strategy.

When the trader is small relative to the market as a whole, or when the active traders in the market hold diverse positions, one would expect little or no feedback of the traders' decisions on the market dynamics itself. However, when a large segment of the market is engaged in such trading strategies, the market dynamics may be affected by the trading strategy itself, and hence lead to potentially destabilizing price paths.

The stock market crash of 1987 is a classic example of the potentially destabilising feedback effect on market dynamics of concerted selling pressure arising from dynamic hedging. Figure 4.9 shows the S&P 500 index in the latter part of 1987, including the crucial period in October 1987 during the dramatic collapse of the major US stock indices. On Monday, October 19, the major stock indices fell by more than 20%.

After the 1987 crash, a Presidential commission of inquiry was set up, chaired by Nicholas Brady (who was to become Treasury Secretary in 1988), to investigate the causes of the crash. The Brady Commission's report, published in January 1988 (Brady 1988) attributed the magnitude and swiftness of the price decline in the 1987 stock market crash to portfolio insurance and dynamic hedging techniques. Bookstaber (2007) gives a first-hand account of the events at the time, from the perspective of a practitioner. Best estimates in 1987 suggested that around $100 billion in funds were following formal portfolio insurance programs, representing around 3% of the pre-crash market value. However, the Brady Commission noted that this was almost certainly an underestimate of

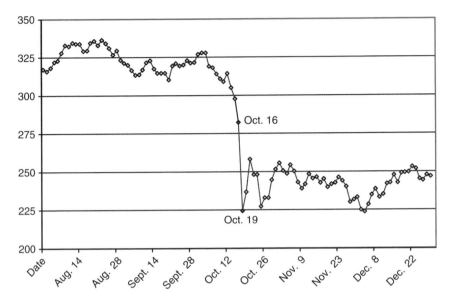

Figure 4.9: S&P 500 Index, 1987

total selling pressure arising from other funds that were also following similar strategies, albeit informally.

The Brady Commission report noted that whereas some portfolio insurers rebalanced several times a day, many more followed the strategy of rebalancing their portfolios once a day—at the open, based on the prior day's close. The favored hedging instrument were the futures contracts in the underlying stock market indices, rather than the constituent stocks themselves. The futures contract for the S&P index was traded (as it is today) at the Chicago Mercantile Exchange (CME). If any gap opened up between the futures contract price and the underlying constituent stocks of the S&P index, then index arbitrageurs would step in and trade profitably until the gap closed again. The sparse trading ensured that transaction costs would be low, but this was achieved at the cost of the accuracy of the approximation, especially if the price moved in one direction only over several days.

The key issue was the price pressure that was generated by the endogenous risk of selling generating falls in price, that generated further selling. The selling pressure arising from the dynamic hedging rule of the traders had the potential to influence the price of the underlying asset itself, thereby introducing further rounds of selling.

The picture of the wobbly Millennium Bridge is very much of relevance in this case too. The feedback process operates as in Figure 4.10. When wide segments of the market are following delta hedging, a downward shock to the price generates sales, which pushes price down. But a decline in price entails a fall in the delta of

Figure 4.10: Feedback due to delta hedging

the option that is being dynamically replicated. When the delta falls, the imperative for the traders is to sell more. We see the double-edged nature of prices in this process. Not only is the price affected by the actions of the traders, the price is also an imperative to actions—the price changes force certain actions on traders. Price declines induce them to sell more.

During the days leading up to the crash of October 19, the US stock market had experienced sharp falls. In the period from Wednesday October 14 to Friday October 16, the market declined around 10%, as we can see from Figure 4.9. The sales dictated by dynamic hedging models were estimated by the Brady Commission to be around $12 billion. This much had to be sold either in the cash market or in the futures market. However, the actual sales up to Friday were estimated to have been only around $4 billion. This was due mainly to the fact that much of the price declines on Friday happened in the last hour of so of trading, so that many of the portfolio insurers had been unable to position their portfolios according to their desired hedged positions reflecting the lower price.

As a result, there was pent-up selling pressure over the weekend. Experienced market observers who were familiar with the nature of portfolio insurance activity knew that by the time of the open on Monday morning, there would be large quantities of shares on sale, reflecting the substantial amount of pent-up selling pressure.

The market opened on Monday, October 19 with a large gap in the price, and the price continued to fall during the day. But no one quite imagined how large the price falls would be. Both the S&P and Dow Jones fell over 20% on October 19. At times, the imbalance between purchases and sales meant that much of the underlying market for stocks did not function. Instead, traders attempted to use the index futures market to hedge their exposures. The S&P index futures sold at large discounts to the cash market on Monday 19 and Tuesday 20 for this reason.

The important lesson to emerge from the 1987 stock market crash is that uncertainty governing stock returns is better described as being *endogenous* rather than *exogenous*. The returns are generated partly by increased selling pressure from traders, which then interacts with price falls. As the market adage has it, "you should never try to catch a falling knife", meaning that it would be foolhardy to stand in the way of a market rout, and it is best to let the market fall and pick up assets cheaply once the market has found its bottom. A variation of this adage counsels that "you should never try to catch a falling piano". Delta hedging rests on the ability to sell when the price falls—that is, on there being someone who buys when you want to sell. However, in a one-sided market where the selling pressure is high, and the potential buyers stand on the sidelines, the basic premise on which delta hedging rests is no longer valid. When risk is endogenous, the basic premise of delta hedging needs to be reconsidered and qualified.

5

Asset-Liability Management

Pension funds and university endowments seem to be at the opposite pole from the world of hedge funds and high finance. But the double-edged nature of market prices can be glimpsed in the operation of such seemingly sedate institutions also. Market prices serve as a signal of the underlying fundamentals that underpin the balance sheets of such institutions. For this reason, balance sheet values are often revealing about the underlying solvency of a pension fund or the strength of a university endowment in meeting its future obligations.

However, precisely because the balance sheet is so informative about the underlying fundamental health of such institutions, balance sheet information is used as an input in how the institution manages its affairs—in particular, how it manages its balance sheet going forward. The two-way flow between balance sheet information and actions comes from the dual nature of balance sheet information.

Let us consider the example of a pension fund. The pension fund holds various assets—both financial assets and real assets—in order to meet the obligations to its policy holders. The stylized balance sheet of a pension fund could be depicted as follows.

Assets	Liabilities
Securitics	Annuities
Property	Pensions

In this example, the pension fund has pension liabilities to a group of retired workers in that it has promised a stream of payments to them. In addition, the pension fund has sold annuities—claims on a stream of income that lasts for the lifetime of the beneficiary. Such liabilities have long-term, bond-like cash-flow streams. It is as if the pension fund has issued bonds and must make payments over time.

On the asset side of the pension fund's balance sheet are various assets that back up the promises. The larger is the value of the asset pool, the more secure are the promises that the pension fund has made. But both sides of the balance sheet are quite sensitive to interest rate movements, since the key items on the balance sheet involve long-term cash flows. When judging the ability of the pension fund to fulfil its promise—that is, in judging the solvency of the pension fund—one way would be to use the prevailing market prices to convert the balance sheet items to their current market price. Even if an item is not traded in the market, it would be feasible to convert the cash flows into some hypothetical market price by discounting the cash flows at some given market discount rate. Thus, marking to market is applicable to such long-term claims and obligations, just as it is applicable to the more exotic balance sheets of hedge funds and securities firms.

In some countries, pension funds are required by their regulators to mark their liabilities to market. In the UK, the accounting rule FRS 17 (Financial Reporting Standard 17) requires pension funds to mark their liabilities to market using the discount rates implicit in the prices of high grade corporate bonds. The European counterpart is the International Accounting Standard 19 (IAS 19), issued by the International Accounting Standards Board (IASB).

However, the debate on the desirability of fair value accounting applies with equal controversy in the case of pension funds and other similar institutions with long-term liabilities. The proponents of marking to market have emphasized many of its merits. The market value of an asset reflects the amount at which that asset could be bought or sold in a current transaction between willing parties. Similarly, the market value of a liability reflects the amount at which that liability could be incurred or settled in a current transaction between willing parties. A measurement system that reflects the market values of assets and liabilities would, it is argued, provide a more accurate indicator of the true economic exposures faced by a firm, and hence lead to better insights into the risk profile of the firm currently in place so that investors could exercise better market discipline and corrective action on the firm's decisions. See Borio and Tsatsaronis (2004) for a wide-ranging discussion of accounting and financial stability.

The accounting scandals of recent years have further strengthened the hands of the proponents of fair value accounting. By shining a bright light into the dark corners of a firm's accounts, fair value accounting precludes the dubious practices of managers in hiding the consequences of their actions from the eyes of investors. Good corporate governance and fair value accounting are seen as two sides of the same coin.

The US Savings and Loans (S&Ls) crisis is a case in point. The crisis stemmed in part from the fact that the (variable) interest rates on the S&Ls' deposit liabilities rose above the (fixed) rates earned on their mortgage assets. Traditional historical cost accounting masked the problem by allowing it only to show up gradually through negative annual net interest income. The insolvency of many S&Ls became clear eventually, but a fair value approach would arguably have highlighted the problem much earlier, and resolved it at lower fiscal cost. See Michael (2004) for further elaboration of this point.

However, the arguments are far from being one-sided. As we have emphasized so far, market prices play a dual role. Not only are they a reflection of the underlying fundamentals and actions, but they are also an imperative to action. In this way, market prices also influence the market outcome through their influence on the actions of market participants.

One example we have emphasized up till now is the effect of Value-at-Risk (VaR) constraints in amplifying price shocks. However, the feedback from prices to actions also works through more subtle channels. The managers of a publicly traded financial firm are accountable to their shareholders. The various mechanisms put in place to ensure good governance, accountability and transparency will place subtle (and sometimes not so subtle) constraints on actions. Thus, the management of a bank whose return on equity is lagging behind its peer group will feel pressure to remedy this by leveraging up its balance sheet, changing the composition of its portfolio, or cutting costs. Hedge funds, or hedge fund-like institutions which have promised a minimum absolute return on equity will feel such pressures even more acutely. Accounting numbers provide a powerful spur to managers in their actions. They serve a certification role, and hence provide justification for actions.

If decisions are made not only because you believe that the underlying fundamentals are right, but because the prices give you the external validation to take such decisions, then there is the potential for a loop whereby prices affect actions, and actions affect prices. Once the loop is established, price changes may be amplified by endogenous responses within the financial system. Mark-to-market accounting gives added potency to market prices by endowing them with the external validation role for actions.

The arguments of the proponents of fair value accounting would be overwhelming in the context of completely frictionless markets where market prices fully reflect the fundamental values of all assets and liabilities. The benchmark results from economics—the efficiency properties of competitive equilibria—could then be invoked, and no further argument would be necessary. However, when there are imperfections in the market, the superiority of a mark-to-market regime is no longer so immediate. The relevant analogy here is with the 'theory of the second best' from welfare economics. When there is more than one imperfection in a competitive economy, removing just one of these imperfections need not be welfare improving. It is possible that the removal of one of the imperfections magnifies the negative effects of the other imperfections to the detriment of overall welfare. Thus, simply moving to a mark-to-market regime without addressing the other imperfections in the financial system need not guarantee a welfare improvement.

The main issue is the problem generated by the kind of feedback loop that is typified by the Millennium Bridge. The feedback loop is generated by the actions of managers of institutions that attempt to manage risks through dynamic hedging—that is, by adjusting their balance sheets in response to price changes. Just as with delta hedging, or with Value-at-Risk-based risk management, attempts by individual institutions to hedge can generate aggregate fluctuations that are unintended and sub-optimal.

5.1 REVIEW OF BASIC CONCEPTS

In order to develop the point more systematically, it is useful to review some very basic notions of present values and duration. The reader is referred to textbooks such as Brealey, Myers, and Allen (2008) for further details.

Start with a stream of payments over time, where the payments are identical and equally spaced. Today is date 0, and suppose the payments start from date 1. When the payments have no terminal date and the payments are all equal so that $C_1 = C_2 = \cdots = C$, the stream of payments is known as a *perpetuity*. The present value of a perpetuity is the infinite sum

$$PV = \frac{C}{1+r} + \frac{C}{(1+r)^2} + \frac{C}{(1+r)^3} + \cdots \tag{5.1}$$

where r is the discount rate.

Multiplying (5.1) by $1 + r$ gives

$$(1+r)PV = C + \frac{C}{1+r} + \frac{C}{(1+r)^2} + \cdots \tag{5.2}$$

Subtracting (5.1) from (5.2), we have $rPV = C$. So the present value of a perpetuity is given by

$$PV = \frac{C}{r}$$

A *growing perpetuity* is a perpetuity where the payment grows at a constant rate g per period. The convention is to treat today as date 0, and assume that the first payment of C is made at date 1, the second payment of $C(1+g)$ is made at date 2, third payment of $C(1+g)^2$ at date 3, and so on. The present value of a growing perpetuity is

$$PV = \frac{C}{1+r} + \frac{C(1+g)}{(1+r)^2} + \frac{C(1+g)^2}{(1+r)^3} + \cdots \tag{5.3}$$

Multiplying through by $(1+r)/(1+g)$ gives

$$\frac{1+r}{1+g}PV = \frac{C}{1+g} + \frac{C}{(1+r)} + \frac{C(1+g)}{(1+r)^2} + \cdots \tag{5.4}$$

Subtracting (5.3) from (5.4),

$$\left(\frac{1+r}{1+g} - 1\right)PV = \frac{C}{1+g}$$

Multiplying through by $1 + g$,

$$(r - g)PV = C$$

$$PV = \frac{C}{r - g}$$

The present value is well-defined (i.e. finite) only when $r > g$.

If the stream of payments starts from date 1, is constant at C, and ends at a known date T, then the payment stream is referred to as an *annuity*. The present value of an annuity with terminal date T is

$$PV = \frac{C}{1+r} + \frac{C}{(1+r)^2} + \cdots + \frac{C}{(1+r)^T}$$

The present value can be expressed as the difference between the values of two perpetuities:

$$PV = \left(\frac{C}{1+r} + \frac{C}{(1+r)^2} + \cdots \right) - \left(\frac{C}{(1+r)^{T+1}} + \frac{C}{(1+r)^{T+2}} + \cdots \right)$$

$$= \frac{C}{r} - \frac{C}{(1+r)^T} \underbrace{\left(\frac{1}{1+r} + \frac{1}{(1+r)^2} + \cdots \right)}_{=1/r}$$

$$= \frac{C}{r} \left(1 - \frac{1}{(1+r)^T} \right)$$

We now introduce the important notion of the *duration* of a cash-flow. Consider the cash-flow stream $C_1, C_2, \cdots, C_T$. Let PV be the present value of this cash-flow stream discounted at the rate r. Then $PV = \sum_{t=1}^{T} C_t/(1-r)^t$. The *duration* of the cash flow is defined as

$$D = \frac{1}{PV} \sum_{t=1}^{T} \frac{t \cdot C_t}{(1+r)^t}$$

$$= \frac{1}{PV} \left(\frac{C_1}{1+r} + \frac{2C_2}{(1+r)^2} + \frac{3C_3}{(1+r)^3} + \cdots + \frac{TC_T}{(1+r)^T} \right)$$

We interpret the notion of duration in the following terms. Notice that

$$\frac{1}{PV} \frac{C_s}{(1+r)^s} = \frac{C_s/(1+r)^s}{\sum_{t=1}^{T} C_t/(1+r)^t} \qquad (5.5)$$

Hence, $(1/PV)(C_s/(1+r)^s)$ is the proportion of the present value of the cash-flow stream that is attributable to the cash flow at date s. The duration of the cash flow is the *weighted average of the dates*, where the weights are given by these proportions. In other words,

$$D = w_1 \cdot 1 + w_2 \cdot 2 + \cdots + w_T \cdot T$$

where

$$w_s = \frac{C_s/(1+r)^s}{\sum_{t=1}^{T} C_t/(1+r)^t}$$

The duration of the cash-flow stream is a measure of how far in the future the cash flow arrives. The longer the duration, the more long term is the cash flow. As well as a summary measure of how long term the cash flow is, the notion of duration carries importance as a first-order approximation of the proportional change in the present value arising from a change in its discount rate. To see this, begin with the present value formula for a finitely lived cash flow:

$$PV = \sum_{t=1}^{T} \frac{C_t}{(1+r)^t}$$

The sensitivity of the present value to changes in the discount rate r can be found by differentiating the present value expression by r.

$$\frac{d}{dr} PV = \sum_{t=1}^{T} \frac{(-t) \cdot C_t}{(1+r)^{t+1}} = -\frac{1}{1+r} \sum_{t=1}^{T} \frac{t \cdot C_t}{(1+r)^t} \qquad (5.6)$$

The proportional change in the present value to shifts in the discount rate can then be obtained by dividing (5.6) by the present value itself. We have,

$$\frac{d(PV)/dr}{PV} = -\frac{1}{1+r} \frac{1}{PV} \sum_{t=1}^{T} \frac{t \cdot C_t}{(1+r)^t}$$

$$= -\frac{D}{1+r}$$

For small r, we have the approximation:

$$\frac{d(PV)/dr}{PV} \simeq -D \qquad (5.7)$$

Because of its usefulness, the expression

$$\frac{D}{1+r}$$

is used in its own right, and is sometimes called the *modified duration* measure.

Another important concept in present value analysis is that of the internal rate of return of a cash flow. The *internal rate of return* (IRR) of a cash-flow stream is defined as the discount rate that makes the present value of the cash-flow stream equal to zero. In other words, for a cash-flow stream given by

$$C_0, C_1, C_2, \cdots, C_T$$

the internal rate of return is the discount rate r that solves

$$C_0 + \frac{C_1}{1+r} + \frac{C_2}{(1+r)^2} + \cdots + \frac{C_T}{(1+r)^T} = 0$$

The internal rate of return is closely related to the notion of the *yield* on a bond. The yield on a bond is the discount rate that sets the price of the bond equal to the discounted value of the coupon payments and principal. If C_0 is the negative cash flow entailed by buying the bond ($C_0 = -P$), and C_t is the coupon at date t, then the internal rate of return is the yield on this bond.

$$P = \frac{C_1}{1+r} + \frac{C_2}{(1+r)^2} + \cdots + \frac{C_T}{(1+r)^T}$$

Let us consider an example. This example comes from Irving Fisher's book, *The Theory of Interest*, first published in 1930 (Fisher 1930). The numbers have been adapted, but otherwise the example is faithful to Fisher's original story.

Suppose there is a plot of land that is on sale today for 100. There are three possible uses of the land: for farming, forestry or mining. Farming generates a steady cash flow of 25, and the cash flow starts immediately. Forestry does not generate any cash for 11 years, while the trees mature. Thereafter, it generates a cash flow of 60 in perpetuity. Mining generates a high cash flow of 50 for the next five years, but then the land is useless and generates no cash. The cash flow from the three projects are shown in Table 5.1.

The cash flow from farming is a perpetuity. The net present value of farming at discount rate r is

$$-100 + \frac{25}{r}$$

The cash flow from forestry is also a perpetuity, but the cash flows are delayed. At year 11, the present value of the cash flow would be $60/r$. In today's value, this amount is discounted by $1/(1+r)^{11}$. Hence, the net present value of forestry when viewed from today is

Table 5.1: Cash flow from three projects

Year	Farming	Forestry	Mining
0	−100	−100	−100
1	25	0	50
2	25	0	50
3	25	0	50
4	25	0	50
5	25	0	50
6	25	0	0
⋮	25	0	0
10	25	0	0
11	25	0	0
12	25	60	0
thereafter	25	60	0

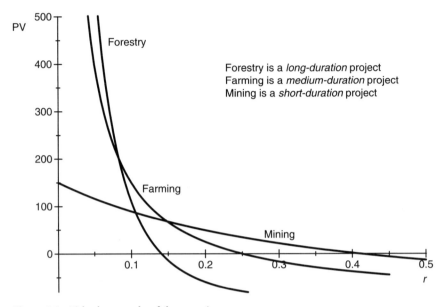

Figure 5.1: Fisher's example of three projects

$$-100 + \frac{60}{r} \cdot \frac{1}{(1+r)^{11}}$$

The cash flow from mining is an annuity, with a five year term and per period cash flow of 50. The net present value of mining is given by

$$-100 + \frac{50}{r} \left(1 - \frac{1}{(1+r)^5} \right)$$

The net present value of the three projects can be plotted as in Figure 5.1. We can calculate the internal rate of return on the three projects as follows.

The internal rate of return (IRR) for a project is the discount rate r that makes the net present value equal to zero. For farming, the IRR is the discount rate r that solves

$$-100 + \frac{25}{r} = 0$$

This gives $IRR_{FARM} = 25\%$. For forestry, the IRR is the discount rate r that solves

$$-100 + \frac{60}{r} \cdot \frac{1}{(1+r)^{11}} = 0$$

This gives $IRR_{FOREST} = 14.1\%$. For mining, the IRR is the discount rate r that solves

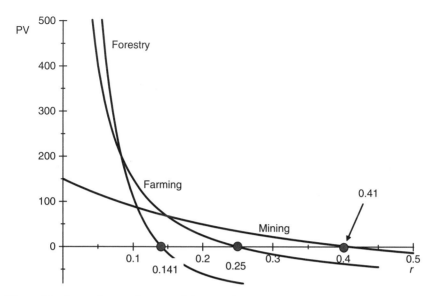

Figure 5.2: Internal rates of return of three projects

$$-100 + \frac{50}{r}\left(1 - \frac{1}{(1+r)^5}\right) = 0$$

This gives $\text{IRR}_{\text{MINE}} = 41\%$. Mining has the highest IRR, followed by farming, with forestry last. Figure 5.2 illustrates the ranking of the three projects by their internal rates of return.

It is clear that choosing the project with the highest internal rate of return would not be the right policy. The best project in terms of maximizing the net present value of the project depends on what the prevailing discount rate r is. Figure 5.3 shows the respective intervals over which one or other project is optimal. Forestry is best for low values of r, and in particular when $r < 8.3\%$. This is because low values of r give high weight to payoffs that arrive far in the future. Forestry is a project that provides such long-term payoffs. We could say that patient investors favor long-range projects such as forestry. More accurately, we should say that long-range projects such as forestry is favored when the market prices evaluate projects according to preferences of patient investors.

In contrast, note that mining does best for high values of r, in particular when $r > 14.9\%$. High discount rates are associated with impatient investors. For such impatient investors, mining offers the best project since the cash flow is immediate and large. As an investor, you dig up the land, extract the resources, and then leave. The long-term cash flow is zero, but for a short-term investor, the long run is irrelevant. Farming is the intermediate case. Farming does best for intermediate discount rates when r lies between 8.3% and 14.9%.

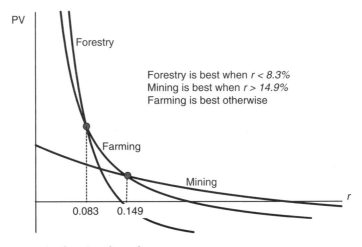

Figure 5.3: Optimal project depends on *r*

This example shows that maximizing the internal rate of return is not the same as maximizing the net present value per dollar invested. All three projects involve an investment of 100. Their net present values depend on the discount rate *r*. At low discount rates, long-duration projects such as forestry do best. At high discount rates, short-duration projects like mining do best. At intermediate discount rates, intermediate-duration projects like farming do best.

Fisher's example has a modern resonance, too. When we translate Fisher's example to a modern stock market context, then technology stocks are rather like forestry. They could have high cash flow in the distant future. Utility stocks are like farming. They have steady cash flow. Finally, tobacco stocks are like mining. Tobacco stocks have high yield, and so high cash flow. But as tobacco use dwindles, the cash flow will dwindle/cease at some time in the future.

5.2 EXAMPLE OF A PENSION FUND

Let us consider the example of a pension fund that marks to market its liability stream, and attempts to ensure its solvency by making sure that it holds the right types of assets that fluctuate in value in the same way (and to the same extent) as the fluctuations in its liabilities. We will see that when liabilities are marked to market and pension funds attempt to meet a solvency condition by matching the duration of its assets to the duration of its liabilities, the response for some long-maturity fixed income securities can become perverse. Rather than the demand response being downward-sloping, the demand response can slope *upward*. That is, as price rises, the demand for the asset rises. Consider an example.

A pension fund is responsible for running a final salary pension plan. It has liabilities that grow at the rate g due, say, to the growing wages of each successive cohort of retirees who joined the pension plan. The liabilities of the pension fund is a growing perpetuity with cash flows

$$C, \quad (1+g)C, \quad (1+g)^2 C, \cdots$$

If there were an asset that pays out exactly such a cash flow, then the pension fund could buy the right quantity of the asset, thereby matching the cash-flow obligations exactly. Such assets are very rare in practise. As such, the pension fund has to make do with assets that are similar, but not perfect replicas of the liability stream.

Suppose there is a close cousin, given by a perpetuity that pays a constant coupon of 1 each period. Let us further suppose that this perpetuity is riskless, meaning that the payment of 1 each period is guaranteed. We can think of this perpetuity as a govenment bond that pays a coupon in perpetuity. UK government *consols* are one such example.

This perpetuity is traded in the market, and has a market price p. The yield on the perpetuity is the discount rate r such that

$$p = \frac{1}{r}$$

The pension fund has made promises to its beneficiaries that it must keep. Because the keeping of pension promises has important public policy and consumer protection implications, pension funds are subject to regulation so that they have enough financial resources to back up those promises.

As we have mentioned in passing, in the UK, the accounting rule FRS 17 (Financial Report Standard 17) requires pension funds to mark to market its liabilities by discounting the liability stream at a discount rate that applies to a highly rated corporate bond. The analogous accounting standard of the International Accounting Standards Board (IASB) is IAS 19 (International Accounting Standard 19), which similarly requires a pension fund to mark to market its liabilities at the discount rate given by the current market price of a high grade (AA-rated) corporate bond.[1]

For the pension fund in our example, it has a growing perpetuity as its liability. If there were an asset that matches the cash flow exactly, the regulatory authorities could require the pension fund to mark to market its liabilities at the market discount rate. However, in the absence of such an asset, the regulators would be in search of an alternative.

Let us suppose that the pension fund is required by regulation to mark to market its pension liability by discounting the cash-flow promises at the discount

---

[1] The Accounting Standards Board of the Financial Reporting Council gives details of FRS 17; see <http://www.frc.org.uk/images/uploaded/documents.FRS17_revisedz.pdf>. For details of IAS 19, see <http://eur-lex.europa.eu/LexUriServ/site/en/oj/2003/1_261/1_26120031013en00540183,pdf>.

rate associated with the traded perpetuity—that is, the perpetuity with price p and discount rate r. Since the constant perpetuity is the closest substitute for the pension fund's liability stream, such a regulation could be justified as using market prices that are closest to the specific case at hand.

Since the pension fund is required to mark to market its liabilities at the same discount rate as the constant perpetuity, one natural way to hedge risks would be for the pension fund to hold the constant perpetuities as assets. If the modified duration of the assets were kept equal to the modified duration of the liabilities, then fluctuations in the discount rate would have equal effects on both assets and liabilities, meaning that the equity of the pension would be kept constant. Constant equity would guarantee the solvency of the pension fund in the marked-to-market sense.

To implement such a strategy, the pension fund would first need to know the modified duration of both the constant perpetuity and its pension liabilities. Recall that p is the price of the perpetuity that pays 1 each period.

The modified duration of this perpetuity is

$$-\frac{dp/dr}{p} = \frac{1/r^2}{1/r}$$
$$= 1/r \qquad\qquad (5.8)$$
$$= p$$

So, the modified duration of the perpetuity is just its price.

Now let us turn to the liabilities side of the balance sheet. Denote by L the market value of the pension fund's liability. By hypothesis, the pension fund is required by regulation to discount the cash flows of its liability at the rate r—the discount rate associated with the constant perpetuity. Hence, the market value of the pension liability is given by

$$L = \frac{C}{r-g} \qquad\qquad (5.9)$$

The modified duration of the liability is then

$$-\frac{dL/dr}{L} = \frac{C/(r-g)^2}{C/(r-g)}$$
$$= \frac{1}{r-g} \qquad\qquad (5.10)$$

So, in order to match modified duration of its assets and liabilities, the pension fund must hold y units of the constant perpetuity, where y satisfies

$$py \cdot \frac{1}{r} = L \cdot \frac{1}{r-g} \qquad\qquad (5.11)$$

The left-hand side of (5.11) gives the rate of change of the asset side of the pension fund's balance sheet to small changes in the discount rate r. It is the product of the modified duration of assets and the market value of total assets. The right-hand side of (5.11) is the rate of change of the liabilities side of the pension fund's balance sheet to small changes in the discount rate r, given by the product of the modified duration of its liabilities and the market value of its liabilities. By satisfying condition (5.11), the pension fund can immunize itself from fluctuations in its equity that results from shifts in the discount rate r. Solving for the holding y, we have

$$
\begin{aligned}
y &= C\left(\frac{r}{r-g}\right)^2 \\
&= C\left(\frac{1/p}{1/p-g}\right)^2 \\
&= C\left(\frac{1}{1-gp}\right)^2
\end{aligned}
\tag{5.12}
$$

Figure 5.4 plots y as a function of p when $g = 3\%$ and $C = 100$.

We can see from the demand function (5.12) and Figure 5.4 that the demand y for the perpetuity is increasing in its price p. This is because the duration of the pension fund's liability is rising much faster than the duration of assets when r falls (when p rises). As the yield falls, more of the constant perpetuity is demanded so as to keep pace with the growing duration of the liabilities L. Plantin, Sapra, and Shin (2005) examine the potential for macroeconomic

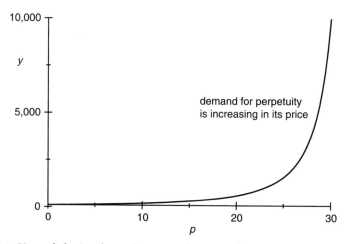

Figure 5.4: Upward-sloping demand response for perpetuity

feedback through the housing and capital markets that results from widespread adoption of mark-to-market rules for pension funds.

There is, of course, a limit to how low the discount rate can go before the pension fund finds itself insolvent. As the discount rate continues to fall, the number of units y of constant perpetuity that is needed to match duration increases. With the fall in r, there is an increase in the size of the balance sheet that is needed to match the duration of liabilities. But for a pension fund with a finite pool of assets, there is a resource limit to how far it can purchase the number of units of the constant perpetuity that it needs. As r falls, the pension fund will eventually find itself insolvent. The early years of decade beginning in 2000 presented something of a "perfect storm" for pension funds in this respect. Many of them had started the decade by holding a large proportion of their assets in stocks. But the stock market began to decline from 2000, leading to falls in the value of their assets. At the same time, long-term interest rates began to fall, meaning that the value of its liabilities were increasing. The pension funds' equity cushion was caught in between, squeezed from both directions. On a marked-to-market basis many pension funds found themselves insolvent.

The upward-sloping demand response for the constant perpetuity in our example is reminiscent of some long-standing anomalies in the long-dated government bond market in several countries. Before the financial crisis of 2007 and 2008, long-dated government bonds were very much in demand from pension funds and other institutions seeking the long duration that they offered. They were cost-effective sources of modified duration that would be put to work in meeting the duration of long-term liabilities. The yield curve for UK government bonds ("gilts") remained inverted, with yields on long-dated bonds being much lower than the yields on short-dated bonds. The inversion has subsequently been reversed as short-term interest rates have been cut to close to zero by central banks around the world. Figure 5.5 gives a snapshot of the UK government bond yield curve for April 27, 2007, showing the inverted yield curve.

5.3 EXAMPLE OF IVY COLLEGE

Let us examine another example of duration matching, but in the context of a private college that funds its activities with its own endowment. Ivy College (our hypothetical example) is a private college that charges no tuition fees, and must fund its activities purely from its endowment. It has pledged to spend x million dollars at date 1, and to increase its expenditure at the constant rate $1 + \pi$ over time, so that its expenditure from date 1 is given by the growing perpetuity:

$$x, \quad x(1 + \pi), \quad x(1 + \pi)^2, \cdots \tag{5.13}$$

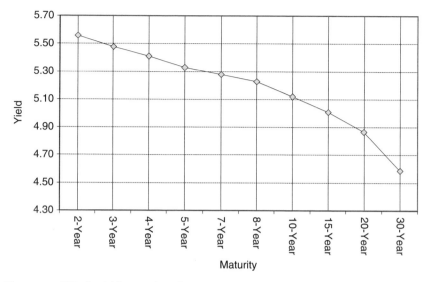

Figure 5.5: UK gilt yield curve (April 27, 2007)

Suppose that $\pi = 0.03$, reflecting the growing wage bill for faculty and staff and the increase in the cost of upkeep of facilities. The future expenditure stream of Ivy College could be regarded as a type of liability in that the college sees itself as an on-going entity pursuing its goal of educating students and pursuing scholarship. The expenditure that is needed to employ the faculty and staff, the costs of the facilities of the college, and the scholarships that are granted to the students can all be regarded as elements of the college's overall "liability". Of course, such liabilities are not as rigid as the liabilities that arise from legally binding promises, as when a company issues corporate bonds that promise a coupon and principal. Indeed, when push comes to shove, Ivy College may be able to distinguish some activities that it regards as being its core activities and scale down some of its other activities.

However, the management of Ivy's endowment would share many of the same features as the pension fund's balance sheet management, since one of Ivy's objectives would be to make reasonably sure that it can conduct its core activities with some sense of security. So, in what follows, let us regard the expenditure stream (5.13) in the same way as the pension fund's obligation to pay its retired beneficiaries. The present value of this expenditure stream is regarded by Ivy College as its liability on the balance sheet.

To make the problem more stark, suppose that there are no perpetual securities available to meet the liabilites. Instead, the longest dated bond is a three-period riskless bond whose cash payoffs are given by

date	payoff ($)
1	5
2	5
3	105

The bond pays a constant coupon of 5, and at the end of date 3 pays back the principal amount 100. Suppose that the yield curve is flat at 5%. Today is date 0. Ivy College wishes to buy just enough of the three-period bond and hold the rest of its endowment in cash in order to match the modified duration of its assets with the modified duration of its liabilities. How many units of the three-period bond must Ivy hold today in order to achieve its aim of matching the modified duration of its assets with the modified duration of its liabilities? How large must Ivy's endowment be in order to achieve its aim?

The present value L of Ivy's expenditures is obtained from the formula for the present value of a growing perpetuity.

$$L = \frac{x}{r - \pi} \tag{5.14}$$

The modified duration of L is

$$-\frac{dL/dr}{L} = \frac{x/(r - \pi)^2}{x/(r - \pi)}$$

$$= \frac{1}{r - \pi}$$

For $r = 0.05$ and $\pi = 0.03$, the modified duration is 50. Meanwhile, the price of the price of the three-period bond with a flat yield curve at 5% is given by

$$\frac{5}{1.05} + \frac{5}{(1.05)^2} + \frac{105}{(1.05)^3} = 100$$

When the coupon rate is equal to the yield, the bond trades at par. The modified duration of the three-period bond is given by

$$\frac{5}{1.05} \cdot \frac{1}{100} \left(1 \times \frac{5}{1.05} + 2 \times \frac{5}{(1.05)^2} + 3 \times \frac{105}{(1.05)^3} \right) \tag{5.15}$$

$$= 2.7232$$

The ratio of the modified duration of liabilities to the modified duration of the three-period bond is $50/2.7232 = 18.361$. Hence, for each dollar's worth of liabilities, Ivy must hold 18.361 dollars' worth of the three-period bond. Total liabilities are

$$L = \frac{x}{0.02} = 50x \text{ million dollars}$$

Hence, Ivy must hold $18.361 \times 50x = 918.05x$ million dollars' worth of the three-period bond. Since the price of the three-period bond is 100, Ivy must hold 9.1805 million units of the three-period bond.

Another way to obtain the solution is by setting up the problem as one where the change in Ivy's net worth to a parallel shift dr in the yield curve leads to no change in Ivy College's net worth, V. Write the change in Ivy's net worth due to a small change in the yield r as

$$dV = pyD_3 dr - LD_L dr$$

where p is the price of the three-period bond, y is the number of units of the bond. In order to have $dV = 0$, we have

$$pyD_3 = LD_L$$

hence

$$y = \frac{LD_L}{pD_3} = \frac{50x \times 50}{100 \times 2.7232}$$

in units of 1 million. Hence, $y = 9.18x$ million. Ivy needs an endowment of at least $918.05x$ million dollars.

The size of the endowment needed by Ivy College in order to immunize itself perfectly against fluctutations in the value of its liabilities is very large. The fact that it has to match durations using a relatively short-term three-period bond explains why it needs such a large endowment, since the short-term bond delivers very little "bang for the buck" in terms of duration per dollar. However, the lesson is quite general. The liabilities of a pension fund or a university endowment that is linked to future wages is likely to be a longer duration cash-flow stream than the cash flows that are available from the fixed income instruments available in the financial markets.

In general, when interest rates are low, the present value of a pension fund's liability stream becomes large. Unless the assets of the pension fund grow at a pace that is at least as large as the growth in liabilities, the pension fund will show a deficit and will have liabilities that are larger than the assets that are held to cover them.

5.4 PRICES AS SIGNALS FOR INVESTMENT

We conclude this chapter with an example of the role of market prices as an imperative to action, but this time where the action being dictated by prices comes from a real investment decision.

Beginning in early 2000, many European governments conducted formal auctions to sell the exclusive rights to particular frequencies of the radio spectrum to operate so-called "third generation" (3G) mobile phones (cell phones). Paul Klemperer (2002) describes the design and performance of the auctions.

Technically, the third generation of mobile phones was a leap ahead of existing technology in terms of its capacity, enabling download speeds that were similar to broadband internet connections. In the boardrooms of telecommuncations companies in Europe, all manner of exciting prospects were discussed. The auctions just happened to coincide with the peak in the technology bubble in the stock market of the late 1990s. Some of the ideas that were floated by the internet entrepreneurs seem rather far-fetched today. But they did not seem so far-fetched in the breathless atmosphere at the time. For the advocates of the "new economy", the argument was that the market was pricing technology assets at very high prices precisely because the future payoffs of the new technologies were very high, and the discount rates being applied to such long-term payoffs were very low. As in the Irving Fisher example of the three possible uses of land between farming, forestry and mining, the market prices of technology firms were high, it was argued, because the market was applying a very low discount rate to the very long-term cash flows associated with the technology firms. Market prices were the arbiter. The market had decreed that such firms had high value. Who would second-guess the market?

The same argument was influential in the boardrooms of the major telecoms companies. For the incumbent firms, getting a license was seen not only as a matter of seizing a profitable opportunity, but as a matter of survival. For an incumbent firm, not winning a license would have relegated it to the second tier of telecom companies. With hindsight, 3G licenses were not the critical next generation technology after all. Newer technologies now are considered as a credible and in some cases superior alternative. It is now clear (again with the benefit of hindsight) that many companies overpaid for their licenses. Many of the highest payers experienced severe financial distress subsequently.

Let us first examine what happended at the time. The series of auctions kicked off in the UK, right at the peak of the Nasdaq bubble. Over the next two years, eight other European countries conducted auctions for the 3G licenses. Some countries (like France) chose not to conduct a formal auction, but instead relied on "beauty contests", where bidding companies were asked to write proposals for why they should be the recipient of a license. Figure 5.6 plots the revenues raised in the auctions in each country, where the revenue is measured in euros per capita (i.e. total sum raised divided by the country's population). The data are from Klemperer (2002). The line series is the Nasdaq stock index.

We draw on the formula for growing perpetuities once more. Suppose the Nasdaq index represents the present value of cash flows that grow at the rate g. The price of a growing perpetuity with initial cash flow of 1 is

$$p = \frac{1}{r - g} \tag{5.16}$$

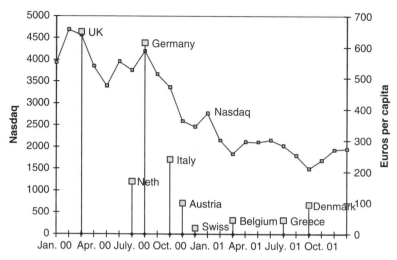

Figure 5.6: Auction revenue per capita (in euros)

Let us treat p as the value of the Nasdaq index. If we knew the growth rate g, we could infer what discount rate the market was applying to the Nasdaq index as a whole. Suppose that the 3G licenses will yield a faster growing stream of cash flows net of set-up costs. Say that the cash flows are growing at the rate γ, where

$$\gamma > g \qquad (5.17)$$

Then the net present value of a 3G license (denoted by q) will be

$$\begin{aligned} q &= \frac{1}{r - \gamma} \\ &= \frac{1}{\left(g + \frac{1}{p}\right) - \gamma} \qquad (5.18) \\ &= \frac{1}{\frac{1}{p} - (\gamma - g)} \end{aligned}$$

Then, q is increasing in p, but in a non-linear way. Figure 5.7 is a plot of q as a function of p when $\gamma - g = 0.01$. If the telecom executives (and their consultants from investment banks running their spreadsheets) looked to market prices to ascertain the true value of the licenses, then they would be willing to pay more as the value of the Nasdaq rose. In fact, the willingness to pay would be increasing in a non-linear way.

Indeed, there is some evidence that market prices can explain the per capita revenue raised in the auctions. Figure 5.8 is a scatter chart plotting the relationship between the revenue raised per capita and the squared value of the Nasdaq

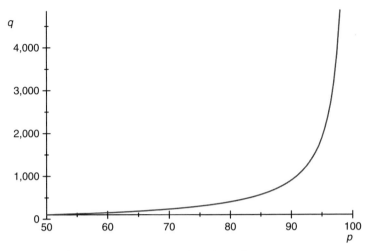

Figure 5.7: Value of 3G license as function of Nasdaq index

at the beginning of the month in which the auction was conducted. The scatter
chart suggests that the square of the Nasdaq does a reasonably good job of
explaining the revenue generated in the auctions. The R^2 from the ordinary
least squares regression is 82%. Wong (2008) shows that other "fundamental"
variables such as subscriber growth and population density have no additional

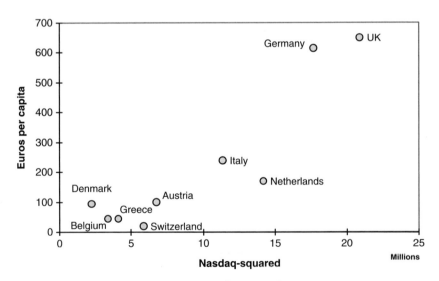

Figure 5.8: Scatter chart revenue against Nasdaq-squared

explanatory power in explaining the auction outcome once the Nasdaq index is taken into account.

The lesson from the example above calls into question the maxim often found in corporate finance textbooks that, when uncertain of the discount rate, one should look to market prices. Bidders would have looked to market prices to give them guidance on what they should do. If they had decided that they would bid, and the only remaining uncertainty was what price to pay, then the market price would act as a guide to action. In the case of the 3G mobile auction, those bidders that heeded the imperative did not fare well, with several of the telecoms firms experiencing financial distress in the subsequently bust.

A useful check for such problems would have been the so-called "payback rule" in capital budgeting (see Brealey et al. 2008). On this rule, the project should be taken on if the project generates enough cash flow within a fixed horizon to pay off the cost of investment. It is a rule that favors short-term projects, such as the mining project in the Irving Fisher example, at the expense of long-term projects such as the forestry project. The payback rule is inconsistent with the textbook net present value (NPV) rule. However, the lesson from the 3G auction case is that the payback rule may be a useful check on the NPV rule under extreme circumstances. The NPV rule beats other rules, but it is useful to have something else as a check on the calculations. If mechanical applications of a rule give nonsensical answers, then perhaps we are better off exercising some caution. The payback rule favors short-termism. In some cases (as in a stock market bubble), a little dose of short-termism may not be all bad.

6

Financial System

What is the financial system for? Asking this question and taking an opportunity to step back and address the question from a distance helps us to focus on the bigger picture. One answer to this bald question is that the purpose of the financial system is to channel the funds of savers in the economy to those who need the funds to finance real economic activity.

At one extreme, there is the textbook "Robinson Crusoe" or "yeoman farmer" economy, where there is no role for financing decisions. Everyone is identical, and firms and households are the same entity. The typical balance sheet reflects this. The asset side of the balance sheet consists of the real project (farming, say), and the projects are wholly owned by the farmer. The liabilities side is therefore 100% equity.

Assets	Liabilities
Projects	Equity

However, if it becomes possible for the claims on the projects to be transferred to others, and the legal and accounting systems are in place to enforce contractual provisions, then one of the functions of the financial system is to organize the transfer of such claims. In such a world, the *firm* would be financed by *households*, with the potential separation of ownership and management of the projects. Figure 6.1 illustrates. The balance sheets would reflect the new relationships. The firms hold projects as assets, and issue claims on those assets, where the claims can differ by seniority of the claims. For instance, the firm could issue debt and equity claims, with the debt promising a fixed payment and with a senior claim on the firm, and the equity holders being the residual claimholders, and the owners of the firm. These liabilities of the firms would then be the *assets* of these households who hold claims on the firms. The liabilities side of the households reflect the fact they do not owe money to anyone else. The whole of their liabilites are their own equity.

Firm's balance sheet		Household's balance sheet	
Assets	Liabilities	Assets	Liabilities
Projects	Debt (bonds)	Firms' bonds	Equity
	Equity	Firms' equity	

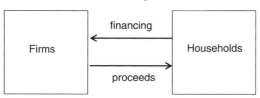

Figure 6.1: Simple financing relationship

As well as holding direct marketable claims on the firms, the households could provide funding indirectly to the firms through *financial intermediaries*. One example of a financial intermediary is a deposit-taking bank. The deposit-taking bank takes in deposits from the households, and lends the funds to the firms. Although the bank is a special type of firm, it is a firm nevertheless, and the bank also has its own shareholders. The balance sheet of a deposit-taking bank looks as follows.

Bank's balance sheet

Assets	Liabilities
Loans to firms	Deposits
Other assets	Equity

The balance sheets of the firms and households reflect these new claims and obligations.

Firm's balance sheet			Household's balance sheet	
Assets	Liabilities		Assets	Liabilities
	Debt (bonds)		Firms' bonds	
Projects	Bank debt		Deposits	Equity
	Equity		Equity of firms, banks	

The firms owe money to households directly through the marketable debt they have issued (e.g. bonds), but they also owe money to the banks because they borrowed from them. The households have three types of assets on their balance sheet. They own the bonds issued by the firms, they have deposit claims in the banks, and they also hold the equity of the firms and banks. The relationships can be depicted as in Figure 6.2.

Of course, financial intermediation does not occur just between firms and households. In the real world, the relationships are more complex. The banks not only intermediate between firms and households, they also intermediate between households themselves. When a young household wants to buy a house, it must borrow. The bank lends to the young households, and can fund such loans by taking

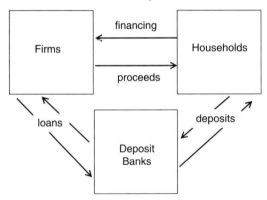

Figure 6.2: Intermediation through a bank

deposits from the old households. As an illustration, let us abstract from firms for a while, and just concentrate on the interaction between the households and the banks. The assets are the houses that people live in. There are young households who have an income stream from working, but who must borrow in order to buy a house. For young households, they hold assets in the form of property (their house). But they have mortgage liabilities to the bank. If their house is worth more than their mortgage, they have positive equity. As per the terminology we have used throughout these lectures, "net worth" is synonymous with "equity".

The banks hold as assets the loans made to young households (mortgage loans), and fund these loans with the deposits of old households, and whatever was the initial capital (equity) that the bank's owners put up in establishing the bank. The old households own property, have deposits in the banks, and are also the owners of the banks (see Figure 6.3).

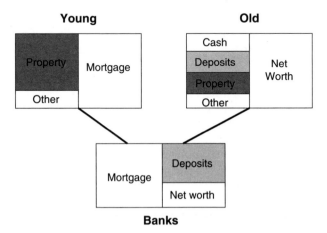

Figure 6.3: Financial intermediation between households

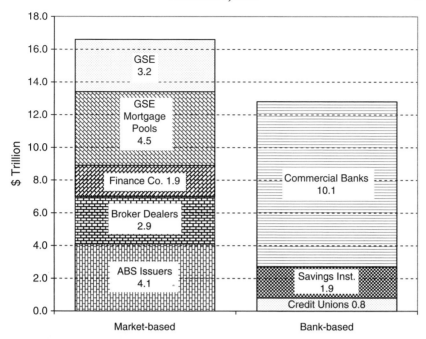

Figure 6.4: Total assets of US financial intermediaries (2007 Q2)

As well as banks, other financial intermediaries associated with securitization have played an increasingly important role in the development of the financial system, especially in the United States. Traditionally, banks were the dominant suppliers of credit, but their role has increasingly been supplanted by market-based institutions – especially those involved in the securitization process.

Securitization refers to the practise of parceling and selling loans and other debt claims to other financial institutions, who then hold those purchased claims and then issue liabilities backed by such claims. The best-known example of securitization is the process by which household residential mortgages are sold to "mortgage pools"—passive firms whose sole role is to hold the mortgage assets and then issue liabilities backed by them.[1] Mortgage pools are less conspicuous as compared to banks, but they play a vital role in financial intermediation, especially in the United States. Figure 6.4, taken from Adrian and Shin (2009), compares total assets held by banks with the assets of securitization pools or at institutions that fund themselves mainly by issuing securities.

By the end of June 2007 (on the eve of the global financial crisis), the assets of this latter group, "market-based assets", were substantially larger than bank assets. In Figure 6.4, "GSE" refers to government-sponsored enterprises such as

---

[1] See Gorton and Souleles (2006) for a description of the institutions that underpin the securitization process in the United States

Fannie Mae and Freddie Mac which have played the linchpin role in the US securitization process. Until the global financial crisis, the GSEs were private institutions with private shareholders, but which operated with implicit backing from the US government. In the crisis of 2008, the implicit backing came into play, and the GSEs are now (at the time of writing) effectively under public ownership. The GSEs issued securities under their own name, and also guaranteed the mortgage-backed securities of the GSE mortgage pools. We see from Figure 6.4 that the size of the total lending that passed through either the GSE or one of its mortgage pools amounted to $7.7 trillion, which compares to $10.1 trillion for the whole of the commercial banking sector in the United States.

Note also the size of the sector called the "ABS issuers", which refers to passive companies much like the mortgage pools, but which hold other loans as assets, such as credit card receivables, car loans and student loans. Crucially, the ABS issuers also held mortgages, but these mortgages were not guaranteed by GSEs such as Fannie Mae and Freddie Mac. They were so-called "private label" mortgage securitizations. Many of the subprime mortgage securities were intermediated through these entities. Their size on the eve of the financial crisis was $4.1 trillion, amounting to over 40% of the total commercial banking sector assets.

Taking account of the various ways in which credit is allocated in the financial system, we can depict the flows as in Figure 6.5. Leaving aside the allocation of equity funding, Figure 6.5 depicts the various ways in which credit is allocated by the financial system, from ultimate lenders to ultimate borrowers. The ultimate lenders are households, either directly or indirectly through institutions such as pension funds, mutual funds and life insurance

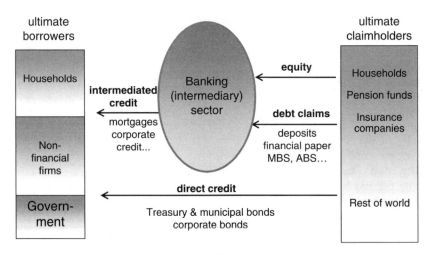

Figure 6.5: Stylized financial system for credit

Figure 6.6: Short intermediation chain

companies. Some credit will be directly provided from the lender to the borrower. Treasury bonds, municipal bonds, and corporate bonds are good examples of such direct credit, where the lender holds a direct claim on the borrower. However, the sizeable borrowing of the household sector—either mortgages or consumer debt—is almost always intermediated through the banking system, broadly defined. At the end of 2008, US household sector mortgage liabilities amounted to around $10.6 trillion, and consumer debt accounted for another $2.5 trillion.

An important feature to note from the picture of the modern financial system is that financial intermediaries play the role both of lenders and of borrowers. They borrow in order to lend. Not only do they borrow from ultimate creditors—the household savers—but they also borrow and lend to each other. For instance, if a commercial bank holds mortgage-backed securities issued by Fannie Mae, then one financial intermediary (the bank) holds the liabilities issued by another financial intermediary (Fannie Mae). In this way, chains of financial intermediaries can form whereby the ultimate flow of credit from savers can pass through many balance sheets before finally reaching the borrower.

Indeed, a characteristic feature of financial intermediation based on the US-style securitization system is the long chains of financial intermediaries involved in channeling funds from ultimate creditors to ultimate borrowers. The difference can be illustrated in Figures 6.6 and 6.7. Figure 6.6 depicts a traditional deposit-taking bank that collects deposits and holds mortgage assets against household borrowers. Until around 1990, the bulk of home mortgage assets in the United States were held by savings institutions and commercial banks (see Adrian and Shin 2008c).

In recent years, however, government-sponsored enterprise (GSE) mortgage pools have become the dominant holders of home mortgages. The chain of

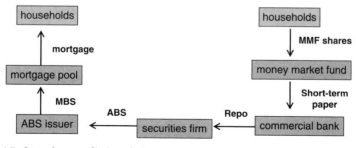

Figure 6.7: Long intermediation chain

financial intermediation has become correspondingly much longer and more heavily dependent on overall capital market conditions. Figure 6.7 illustrates one possible chain of lending relationships whereby credit flows from ultimate creditors (household savers) to ultimate debtors (households who obtain a mortgage to buy a house).

In this illustration, the mortgage asset is held in a mortgage pool—a passive firm whose sole role is to hold mortgage assets and issue liabilities (MBSs—mortgage-backed securities) against those assets. The mortgage-backed securities might then be owned by an asset-backed security (ABS) issuer who pools and tranches the MBSs into another layer of claims, such as collateralized debt obligations (CDOs). Then, a securities firm (a Wall Street investment bank, say) might hold CDOs on their own books for their yield, but finances such assets by collateralized borrowing through repurchase agreements (repos) with a larger commercial bank. In turn, the commercial bank would fund its lending to the securities firm by issuing short-term liabilities, such as financial commercial paper. Money market mutual funds would be natural buyers of such short-term paper, and ultimately the money market fund would complete the circle, since household savers would own shares in these funds.

Of course, the illustration in Figure 6.7 is a simple example of potentially much more complex and intertwined relationships. For instance, the same security could be used several times in repo lending as the lender turns round and pledges the same security as collateral to another lender (the practise known as "re-hypothecation"). In that case, the chain would be much longer and more involved. Nor does the illustration take account of off-balance sheet vehicles such as structured investment vehicles (SIVs) or ABCP conduits that the commercial bank might set up in order to finance the direct holding of CDOs and other asset-backed securities.

What is noticeable from the institutions involved in Figure 6.7 is that they were precisely the institutions that were at the sharp end of the financial crisis of 2007 and 2008. Subprime mortgages cropped up in this chain, and the failure of Bear Stearns and Lehman Brothers was owing to problems in the smooth function of this chain. This realization begs the question of what advantages can be gained by such long intermediation chains. We return to this important question later.

The short illustrative discussion above shows that we need to have an accounting framework to discuss the interweaving of claims and obligations in the financial system. We turn to this as the first step in our formal modeling of the financial system.

6.1 ACCOUNTING FRAMEWORK

A stylized financial system for the intermediation of credit follows Figure 6.5. There are *n* leveraged intermediaries that we call "banks" for convenience, but in principle, they could encompass intermediaries such as broker dealers, mortgage pools, and government-sponsored enterprises such as Fannie Mae and Freddie Mac involved in the securitization process. The banks are indexed by $i \in \{1, \cdots, n\}$.

In addition, there is a non-leveraged sector which we label $n+1$. The non-leveraged sector brings together household claimholders who have direct equity and debt claims against the banks, as well as non-leveraged institutions such as mutual funds and pension funds that hold claims on the banks on behalf of the household beneficiaries. In turn, the banks have claims against end-users of credit such as non-financial firms and households who have mortgage loans or consumer loans granted by the banks. Denote by $\bar{y}_i$ the face value of claims held by bank i against such end-user borrowers. "Face value" refers to the promised amount. We will later see that the market value of such promises may fall short of the promised amount due to the possibility of default. The bar notation is used to indicate face values. The non-leveraged sector $n+1$ could lend directly to the end-user borrowers without passing through the banking sector. We see this from the picture of the stylized credit system in Figure 6.5. We denote by $\bar{y}_{n+1}$ the face value of debt claims held directly by the non-leveraged sector.

As well as end-user loans, we also introduce claims between banks. The liability of one party in the system will be the asset of another party. Denote by $\bar{x}_i$ the face value of the total obligations of bank i, and by π_{ij} the share of bank i's obligations that are held by bank j. Then, the balance sheet identity of bank i in terms of face values is:

$$\bar{y}_i + \sum_{j=1}^{n} \bar{x}_j \pi_{ji} = \bar{x}_i + \bar{e}_i \tag{6.1}$$

The left-hand side of (6.1) is the total assets of bank i in notional values, consisting of the loans made to end-users $\bar{y}_i$, and the claims held against the other leveraged entities (the "banks") in the financial system, $\sum_{j=1}^{n} \bar{x}_j \pi_{ji}$. The right-hand side of (6.1) gives the total liabilities of bank i in notional values, and consists of the total promised repayment $\bar{x}_i$ by bank i plus the notional equity $\bar{e}_i$ that equates the two sides of the balance sheet. The interlocking claims and obligations can be depicted in terms of the following table, where $\bar{x}_{ij}$ denotes the notional value of bank i's obligations to bank j.

	bank 1	bank 2	$\cdots$	bank n	outside	debt
bank 1	0	$\bar{x}_{12}$	$\cdots$	$\bar{x}_{1n}$	$\bar{x}_{1,n+1}$	$\bar{x}_1$
bank 2	$\bar{x}_{21}$	0		$\bar{x}_{2n}$	$\bar{x}_{2,n+1}$	$\bar{x}_2$
$\vdots$	$\vdots$	$\vdots$	$\ddots$	$\vdots$	$\vdots$	$\vdots$
bank n	$\bar{x}_{n1}$	$\bar{x}_{n2}$	$\cdots$	0	$\bar{x}_{n,n+1}$	$\bar{x}_n$
end-user loans	$\bar{y}_1$	$\bar{y}_2$	$\cdots$	$\bar{y}_n$		
total assets	$\bar{a}_1$	$\bar{a}_2$		$\bar{a}_n$		

Summing the ith row of the matrix gives the total liabilities of bank i, since it sums the obligations of bank i to other banks and to the outside claimholders (sector $n+1$). The sum of the entries in the ith column of the matrix gives the total notional assets of bank *i*, since it sums the claims that bank *i* has on all other banks in the system, plus the loans it has made to end-users. The total notional assets of bank *i* are denoted as $\bar{a}_i$.

6.2 REALIZED ALLOCATIONS

Let there be two dates 0 and 1. Loans are made at date 0 and are repaid at date 1. Recall that $\bar{y}_i$ is the total face value of loans made by bank *i* to the end-user borrowers in the economy. We now allow the possibility that some the face value of debt. Hence, realized values of bank debt at state ω satisfy

$$x_1(\omega) = \min(a_1(x(\omega)), \bar{x}_1)$$
$$x_2(\omega) = \min(a_2(x(\omega)), \bar{x}_2)$$
$$\vdots$$ (6.2)
$$x_n(\omega) = \min(a_n(x(\omega)), \bar{x}_n)$$

where $x(\omega) = (x_1(\omega), x_2(\omega), \cdots, x_n(\omega))$ is the profile of the realized values of debt at state ω, and $a_i(x(\omega))$ indicates the realized value of assets of bank *i* at state ω, where the notation makes clear that this asset value in turn depends on the profile of realized value of the claims held against the other banks in the financial system.

The system of equations (6.2) defines a mapping from the vector of realized values $(x_1(\omega), x_2(\omega), \cdots, x_n(\omega))$ to the actual payments that the banks can make, given those realized values. Denote this mapping by $F(.)$, which is a function that maps one *n*-vector of realized values of debt on to the *n*-vector of realized values of debt when the debts are settled. Then (6.2) can be written more succinctly as

$$x = F(x, \bar{x})$$ (6.3)

Since the realized value of debt depends on the realized value of debt, the problem calls for solving a fixed point problem in coming up with a consistent set of realized values. In other words, in getting at a consistent set of allocations at the final date (date 1), we need to ensure that the allocation is a fixed point of the mapping $F(.)$. Eisenberg and Noe (2001) have shown that under unobjectionable conditions on the nature of the problem, we can ensure that there is a unique fixed point of the mapping (6.3), so that there is no ambiguity in talking about *the* realized values of debt at the final date.

Nature of the Problem

To gain some intuition into the result of Eisenberg and Noe (2001), it is useful to address the issue from the point of view of someone attempting to solve the problem through an iterative process. Start from a "conservative" viewpoint, where the claims against other banks are given zero value, to reflect a conservative stance on the possibility that the claims might turn out to be worthless. Bank i's assets would then be calculated by putting the most pessimistic value on the claims against other banks.

However, even if bank i were to write off all the claims against the other banks, it would still have the realized value of the loans made to the final end-user borrowers, given by y_i. Provided that $y_i > 0$, the realized value of bank i's debt will be strictly positive, since it will be able to pay out a positive amount by paying out y_i. Thus, even on the most pessimistic scenario, the profile of bank debt values may not be zero, implying that the initial, very conservative assumption can be moderated somewhat. The initial estimate x^1 for debt values based on the conservative assumption is

$$x^1 = F(0, \bar{x}) \geq 0 \qquad (6.4)$$

Note the superscript notation on x^1 indicating that it is a value that appears in a sequence, rather than the debt of bank 1 (for which we have used the subscript notation). The vector x^1 is the realized values of the debt when valuing the claims on the other banks in the most conservative way.

Then, we can repeat the reasoning, starting from x^1. Since x^1 is the most conservative estimate of the realized values of the debt that is consistent with the nature of the problem, we can come to a revised estimate of the realized values of debt by substituting in x^1 in place of the zero vector 0 in (6.4). We then arrive at a revised conservative estimate of debt values x^2 given by

$$x^2 = F(x^1, \bar{x}) \geq x^1 \qquad (6.5)$$

We can iterate the reasoning further. Since x^2 is the most conservative estimate of debt values consistent with the nature of the problem, we can arrive at a further adjustment x^3, and so on. In this way, we have the non-decreasing sequence $x^1, x^2, x^3, \cdots$ defined by

$$x^{t+1} = F(x^t, \bar{x}) \geq x^t \qquad (6.6)$$

Now, if the inequality in (6.4) holds as an equality, that would be the end of the matter. However, if the realized values $\{y_i(\omega)\}$ of the loans made to end-users are not all zero, the banks' promises will have some assets to back them up. In this case, we would have

$$0 \lneq x^1 \qquad (6.7)$$

where the notation $0 \lneq x^1$ indicates that $0 \neq x^1$ and $0 \leq x^1$. Furthermore, since F is a non-decreasing function of x, applying F to both sides of (6.7) preserves the inequality. If $x^1 = x^2$, then we have found a fixed point. Otherwise, we have

$0 \lneqq x^1 \lneqq x^2$. By iteration, we either have a fixed point xk for finite k, or we have the inequalities

$$0 \lneqq x^1 \lneqq x^2 \lneqq x^3 \lneqq \cdots \tag{6.8}$$

Since each component x_i of the vector x lies in the closed and bounded interval $[0, \bar{x}_i]$, the sequence in (6.8) converges from below to some limit. Since F is a continuous function, such a limit would be a fixed point of the mapping F, and so we will have found one set of consistent debt values at the final date.

Unique Value of Realized Debt

The argument above shows that we can find at least one set of debt values based on a conservative valuation principle that is consistent with the nature of the problem, but it does not guarantee that there is not yet another consistent set of debt values. However, Eisenberg and Noe (2001) have shown that under very mild regularity conditions, there is a unique consistent profile of realized debt values, and hence a fixed point of the mapping F.

Here, we follow a slight variation in the argument, using a stronger regularity condition in order to simplify the argument. The argument here (as well as that in Eisenberg and Noe 2001) makes use of tools from lattice theory, as popularized in economics by Topkis (1978) and Milgrom and Roberts (1990, 1994). Afonso and Shin (2008) apply the techniques to flows in the payment system.

For completeness of the discussion, we give a proof of uniqueness. We begin by covering some preliminary ground from lattice theory. Readers who are willing to take the uniqueness of realized debt values on faith should skip this sub-section, and go to Section 6.3.

A *complete lattice* is a partially ordered set $(X, \leq)$ with the property that every non-empty subset $S \subseteq X$ has both a greatest lower bound inf (S) and a least upper bound sup (S) that belong to the set X. In our context, we can define a complete lattice with the set X given by

$$X \equiv [0, \bar{x}_1] \times [0, \bar{x}_2] \times \cdots \times [0, \bar{x}_n]$$

and the ordering $\leq$ is given by the usual component-wise order so that $x \leq x'$ when $x_i \leq x_i'$ for all components i. Tarski (1955) showed that monotonic functions on complete lattices have a highest and lowest fixed point.

Proposition 5 (Tarski's Fixed Point Theorem) Let $(X, \leq)$ be a complete lattice and F be a non-decreasing function on X. Then there are x_* and x^* such that $F(x_*) = x_*$, $F(x^*) = x^*$, and for any fixed point x, we have $x_* \leq x \leq x^*$.

For the sake of self-contained discussion, as well as for later adaptation for use in argument, we retrace the proof of Tarski's fixed point theorem here. Define the set S as

$$S = \{x | x \leq F(x)\} \tag{6.9}$$

and define x^* as $x^* \equiv \sup S$. For any $x \in S$, $x \leq x^*$, since by definition x^* is the least upper bound of S. By definition of the set S, if $x \in S$ then $x \leq F(x)$. Also, from the fact that $x \leq x^*$ and the fact that F is non-decreasing, we have $F(x) \leq F(x^*)$. We thus have $x \leq F(x) \leq F(x^*)$. Since we picked x arbitrarily from the set S, this means that $F(x^*)$ is also an upper bound for S. But recall that x^* was defined as the *least* upper bound of S. Thus

$$x^* \leq F(x^*) \tag{6.10}$$

Applying F to both sides of (6.10), we have $F(x^*) \leq F(F(x^*))$. But this implies that $F(x^*) \in S$, so that $F(x^*)$ is bounded by x^*. That is, $F(x^*) \leq x^*$. Taken together with (6.10), this means that $F(x^*) = x^*$. Any other fixed point of F must belong to S, and so x^* is the largest fixed point. The smallest fixed point x_* is defined as $\inf\{x | x \geq F(x)\}$, and the argument is exactly analogous.

The application of Tarski's fixed point theorem gives us the conclusion that in our debt pricing problem, there is always a smallest and largest consistent set of realized debt values. If we impose some additional structure on the problem, we can show that there is a unique fixed point. We impose the following condition.

Assumption. For all banks i we have $\pi_{i,n+1} > 0$.

The condition is that the final claimholder sector is owed some money by all the banks in the system. This condition is stronger than is necessary to obtain uniqueness. Eisenberg and Noe (2001) rely on the mild condition that the string of claims and obligations are such that they tie together all banks in the system directly or indirectly to someone with positive equity. Such a condition seems entirely unobjectionable in a modern financial system with interlocking claims and obligations. The stronger regularity condition allows for a simpler argument. The uniqueness result can be stated as follows.

Proposition 6 There is a unique profile of debt prices x that solves $x = F(x, \bar{x})$.

The argument for Proposition 6 is as follows. From Tarski's fixed point theorem (Proposition 5), there are solutions x and x' such that $x_i \leq x'_i$ for all i. Suppose, contrary to the proposition, that there is more than one solution. Then, for some j, we have

$$x'_j > x_j \tag{6.11}$$

From our regularity assumption, the final claimholder sector $n+1$ (which is unleveraged) holds some fraction of this debt. Denote by e'_{n+1} the equity of the

Financial System

non-leveraged sector $n+1$ under x', and denote by e_{n+1} the equity of the non-leveraged sector under x. For the unleveraged investor, the realized value of equity is just the realized value of assets. The realized value of assets consists of the value of directly provided credit, y_{n+1}, that does not pass through the banking system, and the realized value of claims on all the banks. Thus,

$$
\begin{aligned}
e'_{n+1} &= y_{n+1} + \sum_j \pi_{j,\,n+1} x'_k \\
&> y_{n+1} + \sum_j \pi_{j,\,n+1} x_k \\
&= e_{n+1}
\end{aligned}
\tag{6.12}
$$

In other words, the unleveraged sector's equity under x' is strictly larger than its equity value under x.

Meanwhile, from the fact that $x \le x'$, the asset value of bank i under x' is at least as large as its asset value under x. This is true for all banks in the financial system. Since the value of a bank's equity cannot fall when the value of its assets rises, the equity value of bank i under x' is at least as large as that under x. That is, for all banks i, $e'_i > e_i$. From (6.12) and the fact that $e'_i > e_i$ for all i, we have the strict inequality:

$$
\sum_{i=1}^{n+1} e'_i > \sum_{i=1}^{n+1} e_i
\tag{6.13}
$$

But we can also calculate aggregate equity for the whole financial system (including the non-leveraged sector) by adding up the balance sheets across banks and the non-leveraged sector.

$$
\begin{aligned}
\sum_{i=1}^{n+1} e_i &= \sum_{i=1}^{n+1} a_i - \sum_{i=1}^{n+1}\sum_{j=1}^{n+1} x_{ij} \\
&= \sum_{i=1}^{n+1} \left(y_i + \sum_{j=1}^{n+1} x_{ji} \right) - \sum_{i=1}^{n+1}\sum_{j=1}^{n+1} x_{ij} \\
&= \sum_{i=1}^{n+1} y_i \\
&= \sum_{i=1}^{n+1} \left(y_i + \sum_{j=1}^{n+1} x'_{ji} \right) - \sum_{i=1}^{n+1}\sum_{j=1}^{n+1} x'_{ij} \\
&= \sum_{i=1}^{n+1} e'_i
\end{aligned}
\tag{6.14}
$$

where (6.14) follows from the fact that

$$\sum_{i=1}^{n+1}\sum_{j=1}^{n+1} x_{ij} = \sum_{i=1}^{n+1}\sum_{j=1}^{n+1} x_{ji}$$

In other words, we have

$$\sum_{i=1}^{n+1} e_i = \sum_{i=1}^{n+1} e_i' \tag{6.15}$$

But then we have a contradiction, since (6.15) is incompatible with (6.13). Thus, we conclude that $x' = x$, and so Proposition 6 holds.

The intuition behind Proposition 6 comes out clearly from the argument above. The argument rests on the principle that the equity value of the *whole financial system* depends only on the assets that are not the obligation of any other investor. By (6.14), the equity value of the whole financial system is the value of claims on end-user borrowers.

This is natural, since when all claims and obligations are summed across banks, the total value of claims against others must match exactly the total value of obligations to others. Thus, as long as the value of the fundamentals is unchanged, the equity value of the whole system is conserved. By Tarski's fixed point theorem, if there is more than one solution, then one must be strictly larger than the other in at least one component. However, this turns out to imply that the total equity values can be strictly ordered, which is a contradiction.

The argument can be re-expressed as follows. If there is more than one fixed point, there are fixed points x and x' such that $x \le x'$ and $x_i < x_i'$ for some i. From our regularity condition that the non-leveraged sector holds a piece of every bank's debt, the asset value of the non-leveraged sector is strictly higher at x' than at x. The equity value of all banks are (weakly) higher at x' than at x. Hence, the equity value of the whole financial system is strictly higher at x' than at x. But the equity value of the system is the total value of realized repayments, $\sum_{i=1}^{n+1} y_i$, which must be invariant across any fixed point of $F(.)$. Hence, we have a contradiction if we suppose that there is more than one fixed point of $F(.)$. This proves the uniqueness of the fixed point of F.

6.3 MARKET VALUE OF DEBT

In our framework, there are two dates, date 0 and date 1, where loans are made at date 0 and repaid at date 1. Up to now, we have focused on date 1, when the realized values of the loans to end-user borrowers are known, and the issue is how to allocate the value in the system among all the claimholders.

We now shift our focus to date 0, when the loans are made. At date 0, the constituents do not yet know which state of the world ω will be realized.

However, they will have some idea of the likelihood of one state or another. When the probabilities of the states are known, the expected value of claims and obligations can then be calculated. We will now turn to these expected values. They can be given the interpretation of market values of claims when the prices are determined by a risk-neutral marginal investor. Before we go into details, we need to spend some time on a change of notation that will simplify the dicussion.

Notation. From here on, we will use the following notation.

$\hat{x}_i$ is the realized value of i's debt at date 1
$\bar{x}_i$ is the face value of i's debt
x_i is the market value of i's debt at date 0, defined as the expected value of $\hat{x}_i$.

The notation for the face value of debt remains the same at $\bar{x}_i$, but we are changing our notation of the realized value of debt to $\hat{x}_i$. The hat "^" notation will be used from now on to denote realized values at date 1. This is in order to reserve x_i (without hats or bars) to denote the market value of bank i's debt at date 0. Similarly, y_i is the market value of the loans to end-users made by bank i.

Financial System Accounting Identities

Using our new notation, we state some accounting identities for the financial system as a whole. The accounting identities listed below will be in terms of market values, but the same identities hold for face values, and for realized values at date 1. But since our applications of the framework will make reference to market values most of the time, it is most useful to state the accounting identities in terms of market values.

Begin with the total assets of bank i expressed in market values. Total assets can be written as

$$a_i = y_i + \sum_j x_j \pi_{ji} \qquad (6.16)$$

where y_i is the market value of the loans made by bank i to the end-user borrowers, and x_j is the market value of the debt of bank j. The balance sheet identity for bank i in market values is

$$y_i + \sum_j x_j \pi_{ji} = e_i + x_i \qquad (6.17)$$

The left-hand side is the market value of assets and the right-hand side is the market value of the liabilities side of the balance sheet, where e_i denotes the market value of equity of bank i. The matrix of claims and obligations between banks can then be written in market values, as below. The *i*th row of the matrix can be summed to give the market value of debt of bank *i*, while the *i*th column of the matrix can be summed to give the market value of the total assets of bank *i*.

	bank 1	bank 2	$\cdots$	bank n	outside	debt
bank 1	0	x_{12}	$\cdots$	x_{1n}	$x_{1,\,n+1}$	x_1
bank 2	x_{21}	0		x_{2n}	$x_{2,\,n+1}$	x_2
$\vdots$	$\vdots$	$\vdots$	$\ddots$	$\vdots$	$\vdots$	
bank n	x_{n1}	x_{n2}	$\cdots$	0	$x_{n,\,n+1}$	x_n
end–user loans	y_1	y_2	$\cdots$	y_n		
total assets	a_1	a_2		a_n		

From the balance sheet identity (6.17), we can express the vector of debt values across the banks as follows, where Π is the $n \times n$ matrix where the (i, j)th entry is π_{ij}.

$$[x_1, \cdots, x_n] = [x_1, \cdots, x_n][\ \Pi\ ] + [y_1, \cdots, y_n] - [e_1, \cdots, e_n] \tag{6.18}$$

or more succinctly as

$$x = x\Pi + y - e \tag{6.19}$$

Equation (6.19) shows the recursive nature of debt in a financial system. Each bank's debt value is increasing in the debt value of other banks. The reason is that when debt values are generally high, the value of claims against other banks is also high, meaning that asset values are high. Therefore, the promises that are written against high asset values are valued more highly. Solving for y,

$$y = e + x(I - \Pi)$$

Define the leverage of bank *i* as the ratio of the value of its assets to the value of its equity. Denote leverage by λ_i. In terms of market values, leverage is defined as

$$\lambda_i \equiv \frac{a_i}{e_i} \tag{6.20}$$

Since $x_i/e_i - \lambda_i - 1$, we have $x = e(\Lambda - I)$, where Λ is the diagonal matrix whose *i*th diagonal entry is λ_i. Thus

$$y = e + e(\Lambda - I)(I - \Pi) \tag{6.21}$$

Thus, the profile of total lending by the n banks to the end-user borrowers depends on the interaction of three features of the banking system—the distribution of equity e in the banking system, the profile of leverage Λ and the structure of the financial system given by Π. Total lending to end-users is increasing in equity and in leverage, as one would expect. More subtle is the role of the financial system, as given by the matrix Π. Define the vector z as

$$z \equiv (I - \Pi)u \tag{6.22}$$

where u is the unit column vector given by

$$u \equiv \begin{bmatrix} 1 \\ \vdots \\ 1 \end{bmatrix}$$

so that $z_i = 1 - \sum_{j=1}^{n} \pi_{ij}$. In other words, z_i is the proportion of bank i's debt held by the outside claimholders—the sector $n+1$. Then, total lending to end-user borrowers $\sum_i y_i$ can be obtained by post-multiplying equation (6.21) by u so that

$$\sum_{i=1}^{n} y_i = \sum_{i=1}^{n} e_i + \sum_{i=1}^{n} e_i z_i (\lambda_i - 1) \tag{6.23}$$

Equation (6.23) is the balance sheet identity for the financial sector as a whole, where all the claims and obligations between banks have been netted out. The left-hand side is the total lending to the end-user borrowers. The first term on the right-hand side of (6.23) is the total equity of the banking system, and the second term is the total funding to the banking sector provided by the outside claimholders (note that the second term can be written as $\sum_{i=1}^{n} x_i z_i$). Thus, from equation (6.23), we see the importance of the structure of the financial system for the supply of credit. Ultimately, credit supply to end-users must come from either the equity of the banking system, or the funding provided by non-banks. Greenlaw et al. (2008) use this framework to calibrate the aggregate consequences of banking sector lending contraction that results from the combination of capital losses and deleveraging from subprime losses.

The aggregate balance sheet identity of the financial intermediary sector given by (6.23) can be explained more intuitively as follows. Take the balance sheet of an individual bank, given by Figure 6.8. The bank has assets against ultimate

Assets	Liabilities
Loans to firms, households	Liabilities to non-banks (e.g. deposits)
Claims on other banks	Liabilities to other banks
	Equity

Individual bank

Figure 6.8: Balance sheet of individual bank

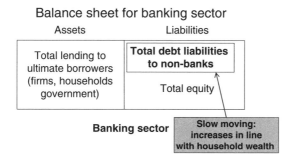

Figure 6.9: Aggregate balance sheet of banking sector

borrowers (loans to firms and households), but it also has assets that are claims against other banks. On the liabilities side, the bank has obligations to outside creditors (such as retail depositors), but it also has obligations to other banks.

Now, consider the aggregate balance sheet of the banking sector as a whole, where the assets are summed across individual banks and the liabilities are also summed across the banks. Every liability that a bank has to another bank is an asset when viewed from the point of view of the lending bank. One asset cancels out another equal and opposite liability. In aggregate, all the claims and obligations across banks cancel out. Thus, in aggregate, the assets of the banking sector as a whole against other sectors of the economy consist of lending to non-bank borrowers. This lending must be met by two sources—the total equity of the banking system, and the liabilities that banks have to lenders *outside* the banking system. Figure 6.9 illustrates.

Equation (6.23) is a statement of the aggregate balance sheet identity. What is useful is the fact that equation (6.23) tells us how the leverage of the financial intermediary sector as a whole depends on the leverage of the individual institutions.

Banking Sector Leverage

A given degree of leverage for the banking system as a whole is consistent with a wide range of leverage levels for the individual banks. This is true in terms of both the face value of claims, as well as market values. First consider face values. A financial system in face values can be represented as the array $(\bar{e}, \bar{y}, \bar{x}, \Pi)$ that satisfies the balance sheet identity:

$$\bar{x} = \bar{x}\Pi + \bar{y} - \bar{e} \qquad (6.24)$$

Then, for positive constant ϕ, we can construct a financial system where the aggregate equity, lending, and leverage are all unchanged, but where the debt to equity ratio of all individual banks is ϕ times as large. Here is how. Consider the financial system ($\bar{e}'$, $\bar{y}'$, $\bar{x}'$, Π') where $\bar{e}' = \bar{e}$, $\bar{x}' = \phi\bar{x}$, and Π' is any matrix of interbank claims whose ith row sums to $1 - z_i/\phi$. Finally, $\bar{y}'$ is defined as

$$\bar{y}' = \bar{e}' + \bar{x}'(I - \Pi') \tag{6.25}$$

Then, aggregate lending is given by

$$\sum_{i=1}^{n} \bar{y}_i' = \bar{e}'u + \bar{x}'(I - \Pi')u$$
$$= \sum_{i=1}^{n} \bar{e}_i' + \sum_{i=1}^{n} \bar{x}_i' \frac{z_i}{\phi}$$
$$= \sum_{i=1}^{n} \bar{e}_i + \sum_{i=1}^{n} \bar{x}_i z_i$$
$$= \sum_{i=1}^{n} \bar{y}_i$$

Hence, aggregate notional leverage of the banking sector in both financial systems is $\sum_{i=1}^{n} \bar{y}_i / \sum_{i=1}^{n} \bar{e}_i$. However, by construction, the debt to equity ratio of all individual banks is ϕ times larger in the second financial system. The only restriction on the constant ϕ comes from the feature that the ith row of Π' sums to $1 - z_i/\phi$. So, ϕ should not be so small that $1 - z_i/\phi < 0$ for some i. This puts a lower bound on ϕ. But there is no upper bound. We can construct a financial system where aggregate notional leverage is unchanged, but where individual bank notional leverage can be as high as we want. The intuition is that banks can lend and borrow from each other in large amounts so that their leverage can be raised, without altering the aggregate relationship between the banking sector and its ultimate creditors.

The construction presented above can also be made for the balance sheet quantities expressed in market values, but with one difference. It is still true that two financial systems can have the same aggregate market leverage and where the individual market leverage for the banks differs by a positive factor ϕ. However, for market leverage, the constant factor ϕ cannot be chosen to be arbitrarily large. This is because the market value of debt x_i cannot be larger than the market value of assets a_i, and the market value of assets is underpinned by the value of fundamental assets $\{y_k\}$. Thus, there is an upper bound in choosing the constant factor ϕ. Subject to this condition, the construction follows an exactly analogous process.

The leverage of the aggregate banking sector itself is related to the leverage of individual banks in the following way. If we denote by L the leverage of the banking sector as a whole, we can write it as

$$L = \frac{\sum_{i=1}^{n} y_i}{\sum_{i=1}^{n} e_i}$$
$$= 1 + \frac{\sum_{i=1}^{n} e_i z_i (\lambda_i - 1)}{\sum_{i=1}^{n} e_i} \tag{6.26}$$

where (6.26) follows from (6.23). Thus, other things being equal, the leverage of the banking sector as a whole is increasing in the amount of funding obtained from outside claimholders, as given by the quantities $\{z_i\}$. We summarize this feature by means of the following proposition.

Proposition 7 For any given profile of leverage for individual banks, the leverage of the banking sector as a whole is increasing in the proportion of funding obtained from creditors outside the banking sector.

So far, we have examined accounting identities for the financial system as a whole. We now examine how the accounting identities can be given meaning by combining them with the actions of the constituents of the financial system. We will put to use the insights gained from accounting relationships to see how the overall flow of credit to end-user borrowers depends on the behavior of financial intermediaries and the structure of the financial system, and how the two interact.

7

Lending Booms

In our framework, loans are granted at date 0 and are repaid at date 1 when the state of the world ω is realized. At date 0 when the loans are granted, the market values reflect the probability density over the states of the world ω to be realized at date 1. The density over the states of the world can be defined once we adopt a model of credit risk on the realized credit losses from the loans granted to end-users.

7.1 CREDIT RISK MODEL

We will use the model of credit risk due to Vasicek (2002)—the so-called Vasicek one-factor model—which has served as a benchmark textbook model of credit risk, and which has found wide applicability in setting regulatory capital ratios. The Vasicek one-factor model has been adopted as the backbone of the Basel II capital regulations. It has also been used by economists to study the role of capital regulation in financial stability, as in Alizalde and Repullo (2006), and Repullo and Suarez (2008).

Under the Vasicek one-factor model, the end-user borrower j of bank i repays the loan in full when the realization of random variable Z_{ij} is non-negative, where Z_{ij} is defined as

$$Z_{ij} = -\Phi^{-1}(p_i) + \sqrt{\rho}Y + \sqrt{1 - \rho}X_{ij} \tag{7.1}$$

In this definition, $\Phi(.)$ is the cumulative distribution function (c.d.f.) of the standard normal, Y and $\{X_{ij}\}$ are mutually independent standard normal random variables, and ρ and p_i are constants. Y is interpreted as the common risk factor that affects all banks and X_{ij} as the idiosyncratic risk factor that affects the particular loan j made by bank i. The probability of default of any borrower j of bank i is p_i since

$$\Pr(Z_{ij} < 0) = \Pr\left(\sqrt{\rho}Y + \sqrt{1 - \rho}X_{ij} < \Phi^{-1}(p_i)\right)$$
$$= \Phi\left(\Phi^{-1}(p_i)\right) = p_i$$

Conditional on the common factor Y, defaults are independent across borrowers, and the parameter ρ gives the ex ante correlation in defaults between any two loans made by bank i.

Suppose that bank i's portfolio includes N loans to end-user borrowers, each with face value $\bar{y}_i/N$. But letting N become large, the loan portfolio to end-users consists of many small loans whose defaults are independent, conditional on the realization of Y. By the law of large numbers, the repayment w_i on the loan book of face value $\bar{y}_i$ then becomes a deterministic function of Y. The repayment on the loans made by bank i is given by the product of the face value of loans to end-users, $\bar{y}_i$, and the probability that a particular loan by bank i is repaid, conditional on the realization of Y.

$$w_i(Y) \equiv \bar{y}_i \Pr(Z_{ij} \geq 0 | Y)$$
$$= \bar{y}_i \Pr\left(Y\sqrt{\rho} + X_{ij}\sqrt{1-\rho} \geq \Phi^{-1}(p_i)\right)$$
$$= \bar{y}_i \Phi\left(\frac{Y\sqrt{\rho} - \Phi^{-1}(p_i)}{\sqrt{1-\rho}}\right)$$

The c.d.f. over the repayment on bank i's loan book is thus

$$F_i(z) = \Pr(w_i(Y) \leq z)$$
$$= \Pr\left(Y \leq w_i^{-1}(z)\right)$$
$$= \Phi\left(\frac{\Phi^{-1}(p_i) + \sqrt{1-\rho}\,\Phi^{-1}\left(\frac{z}{\bar{y}_i}\right)}{\sqrt{\rho}}\right) \tag{7.2}$$

Note the following features of the credit risk model we have adopted. A change in p_i (the probability of default on a particular loan made by bank i) implies a first-degree stochastic dominance shift in the repayment density. A fall in p_i pushes down the c.d.f., implying a first-degree stochastic shift to the right in repayments. When p_i is fixed, the mean repayment remains unchanged. However, a change in the parameter ρ, keeping p_i fixed, implies a second-degree stochastic dominance shift in the repayment density. An increase in ρ is associated with a mean-preserving spread of the repayment density, making the loan book more risky.

The realized values of the loans to end-user borrowers fully determine the state of the world ω at date 1. We can then draw on the discussion from Section 6.2 in determining the realized values of the profile of bank liabilities $(\hat{x}_1(\omega), \cdots, \hat{x}_n(\omega))$ at state ω from the fixed point characterization of the value of interbank claims. The realized value of repayment on the loans to end-users will determine the realized value of the claims held between the banks, since the ability of one bank to fulfill its promise will depend on the resources it has to meet its obligations. Recall that we are now using the hat notation "^" to denote realized values at date 1. Thus, $\hat{y}_i$ is the realized repayment on bank i's loans to end-users, $\hat{x}_i$ is the realized repayment by bank i and so on. We maintain the assumption that all debt is of equal seniority, so that if $\hat{x}_i < \bar{x}_i$, then bank j receives share π_{ij} of $\hat{x}_i$. Creditors receive the full value of the assets of the bank if the realized value of the assets falls short of the face value. Realized values of debt satisfy

$$\hat{x}_1 = \min{(a_1(\hat{x}),\bar{x}_1)}$$
$$\hat{x}_2 = \min{(a_2(\hat{x}),\bar{x}_2)}$$
$$\vdots \tag{7.3}$$
$$\hat{x}_n = \min{(a_n(\hat{x}),\bar{x}_n)}$$

where $\hat{x} = (\hat{x}_1, \hat{x}_2, \cdots, \hat{x}_n)$ is the profile of realized values of debt. Since the realized values $\{\hat{y}_i\}$ are determinstic functions of Y, we can write the realized value of the assets of bank i as a deterministic function of the common factor Y. Hence, we write

$$\hat{a}_i(Y) = \hat{y}_i(Y) + \sum_j \pi_{ji}\hat{x}_j(\hat{y}(Y)) \tag{7.4}$$

The notation "$\hat{y}(Y)$" makes clear that the vector of realized repayments $\hat{y}$ on the end-user loans is a deterministic function of the common factor Y. In turn, the vector of realized values of bank j's debt $\hat{x}_j$ is a function of the vector of realized repayments $\hat{y}$ from the fixed point argument we encountered in Section 6.2. It is intuitively plausible that the realized value of bank debt $\hat{x}_j$ is high when the realized value of Y is high, since a high realization of Y means that all banks receive more from their loans to end-users, thereby giving them larger resources with which to meet their obligations. We can formalize this intuition by appealing to the comparative statics of the fixed point obtained in Section 6.2 with respect to shifts in the common factor Y. The following comparative statics result is due to Milgrom and Roberts (1994, theorem 3).

Proposition 8   *Let $\hat{x}(Y)$ be the unique fixed point of the mapping (7.3) given the realized value Y of the common factor. Then $\hat{x}(Y)$ is increasing in Y. That is, when $Y' \geq Y$, we have $\hat{x}(Y') \geq \hat{x}(Y)$.*

Note that Y is a scalar variable, while $\hat{x}(Y)$ is the vector of all realized values of bank debt. The comparative statics result states that when Y increases, the value of bank debt for all banks go up. The proof follows from the definition of the set S given by (6.9) in Section 6.2, where we proved the uniqueness of the fixed point problem. Using the notation there, and noting the dependence of F on the realized Y, let us denote

$$S(Y) \equiv \{x|x \leq F(x, Y)\} \tag{7.5}$$

As Y becomes larger, the condition for inclusion becomes more accommodative. Formally, if $Y' \geq Y$, then $S(Y') \supseteq S(Y)$. Since $x(Y') = \sup S(Y')$ and $x(Y) = \sup S(Y)$, we have $x(Y') \geq x(Y)$. This proves the result.

7.2 VALUE-AT-RISK AND LENDING

We now turn to the decision rule followed by the banks. From this, we can address comparative statics questions on how lending to end-users depends on the underlying parameters that drive credit risk. For this purpose, we now return to our theme of banks employing the notion of Value-at-Risk to manage their balance sheets. We will assume that banks behave according to the prescriptions that flow from the notion of Value-at-Risk and investigate the consequences of such actions. In particular, assume that bank i aims to set market equity e_i equal to its value at risk V_i, so that

$$e_i = V_i \tag{7.6}$$

In this context, let us examine the consequences of more favorable macroeconomic conditions as reflected in the decline of default probabilities $\{p_i\}$ in the Vasicek one-factor model. For simplicity, let $p_i = p$ for all i, and we suppose that p has fallen. This is the analogue of the exercise we examined in Chapter 3 where we followed the consequences of an improvement in the fundamentals of the single risky asset when the risky asset is widely held by leveraged institutions that follow the Value-at-Risk rule in managing their balance sheets. We will see a similar scenario emerging in our richer framework outlined here.

Recall that the c.d.f. for realized repayments $\hat{y}_i$ on bank i's loans to end-users is given by

$$\Phi\left(\frac{\Phi^{-1}(p) + \sqrt{1-\rho}\,\Phi^{-1}\left(\frac{z}{\hat{y}_i}\right)}{\sqrt{\rho}}\right) \tag{7.7}$$

Notice that when the default probability p_i for bank i declines, there is a rightward shift in the density over the realized loan values $\bar{y}_i$ in the sense of first-degree stochastic dominance. Moreover, we now appeal to Proposition 8. Since the value of interbank claims are increasing in the aggregate factor Y, a fall in p entails a first-degree stochastic dominance shift in the density over realized values of interbank assets $\sum_{j=1}^{n} \pi_{ji}\hat{x}_j$ held by bank i. Hence, there is a first-degree stochastic dominance shift in the density over bank i's total asset value $\hat{a}_i$. Figure 7.1 illustrates the shift. The market value of assets following the fall in p is given by a'_i, and the market equity is given by e'_i. We have $e'_i > e_i$, since the ex post value of equity at the terminal date is increasing in the realized values $\hat{y}_i$, and there is a first-degree stochastic dominance shift in $\hat{y}_i$. At the same time, there is a decline in the Value-at-Risk of bank i. This is because the c.d.f. over asset values shifts lower following the fall in p. Therefore, the $(1-c)$-quantile of the realized asset value shifts upward. The Value-at-Risk is smaller than before, and is given by V'_i. Thus, following the decline in p, we have

$$e'_i > e_i > V'_i \tag{7.8}$$

so that $e'_i > V'_i$.

Following the fall in the default probability p, bank i has surplus equity in the sense that its equity is now larger than the amount required to meet its Value-at-Risk. The surplus equity could, in principle, be paid out as a dividend to

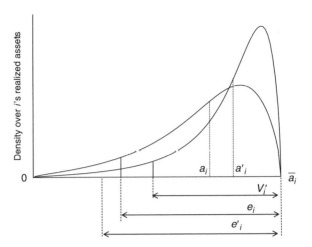

Figure 7.1: Value-at-Risk and leverage

shareholders, or by buying back equity by issuing more debt. However, in practise, the evidence points to banks "remedying" surplus equity by raising the size of total balance sheets instead, rather than paying out the surplus equity. For the empirical evidence, the reader is referred to Adrian and Shin (forthcoming). Consistent with this evidence, let us assume that if bank i has surplus equity, it expands its balance sheet by increasing the notional value of debt $\bar{x}_i$ and using the proceeds to take on more assets.

Assumption 1.   When $e_i' > V_i'$ after the decline in p, bank i increases the face value of its debt $\bar{x}_i$.

As banks raise new debt, they will acquire assets with the proceeds. The interbank claims matrix Π will therefore change. Since our focus here is on the effect on aggregate lending, the exact way in which the interbank claims matrix changes is not of direct interest. Suppose the new interbank claims matrix is given by Π^* after the adjustment of face values, and the profile of market value of debt is given by x^* after the adjustment of face values. The comparative statics result on the fixed point of increasing functions on lattices given by Proposition 8 above can be adapted easily to show that when the face value of bank i's debt increases, the market value of debt is increasing for all banks.[1] Hence, given Assumption 1, we have

$$x_i^* \geq x_i \text{ for all } i \tag{7.9}$$

Let us make one further assumption. As banks increase their borrowing in response to the appearance of surplus equity, they will search for new sources

----

[1] See also Eisenberg and Noe (2001) for details.

of funding. If financial innovation through securitization is available, the banks may tap new sources of funding by borrowing from the outside creditor sector— sector $n + 1$ in our notation. We therefore make the following assumption.

Assumption 2. When banks increase notional debt in response to a fall in p, the proportion of funding raised from the outside creditor sector is non-decreasing.

This assumption places a restriction on the new interbank claims matrix Π^* so that the sum of the ith row of Π^* is no larger than the sum of the ith row of the initial interbank matrix Π. In other words,

$$(I - \Pi^*)u \geq (I - \Pi)u \qquad (7.10)$$

We will see later that Assumption 2 is much stronger than is necessary for the result that follows. So, it should be seen as a strong sufficient condition for the results to be reported below rather than an essential feature of the argument. We will return to this issue later.

Proposition 9   When p falls, the value of aggregate lending to end-users increases, both in notional values and in market values.

Proposition 9 is about the *supply of credit*. When the fundamentals of the economy improve in terms of a decline in the fundamental risks of the loans to end-user borrowers, there is an increase in the supply of credit from the banking sector. The intuition for this result is very much in tune with the analogous mechanism for the expansion of the balance sheets of leveraged institutions in Chapter 3. Indeed, Proposition 9 is the analogue of Proposition 4 in Chapter 3. The mechanism can be illustrated as in Figure 7.2, which sets out the steps in the balance sheet expansion.

The initial balance sheet is on the left. The middle balance sheet shows the effect of an improvement in fundamentals that comes from a fall in default probability p.

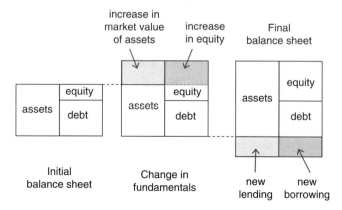

Figure 7.2: Increase in supply of credit from fall in p

There is an increase in market value of equity e, even as the Value-at-Risk declines (not shown in Figure 7.2). There is excess capacity on the bank's balance sheet following these changes. The "excess" balance sheet capacity is utilized by taking on more debt in order to expand the size of the balance sheet, and lend more. Part of the increased lending will flow to end-user borrowers in the form of increased y.

The argument for Proposition 9 starts with the balance sheet identities before and after the change in face values of debt. The balance sheet identities in face values are

$$\bar{y} - \bar{e} + \bar{x}(I - \Pi)$$
$$\bar{y}^* = \bar{e}^* + \bar{x}^*(I - \Pi^*)$$

(7.11)

where * indicates variables after the change. The face value of equity remains unchanged ($\bar{e}^* = \bar{e}$), so that the change in aggregate notional lending is given by

$$(\bar{y}^* - \bar{y})u = (\bar{x}^* - \bar{x})(I - \Pi)u + \bar{x}^*(\Pi - \Pi^*)u$$

(7.12)

The first term on the right-hand side is positive from our assumption that banks react to surplus equity by expanding their balance sheets, while the second term on the right-hand side is positive from our assumption (7.10) that an increasing proportion of the funding comes from the outside sector. Thus, $(\bar{y}^* - \bar{y})u > 0$, so that total lending to end-user borrowers in terms of notional values increases.

The argument for the increase in the market value of loans to end-users following the decline in p is similar. The balance sheet identities in market values before and after the change are

$$y = e + x(I - \Pi)$$
$$y^* = e^* + x^*(I - \Pi^*)$$

(7.13)

The change in the market value of loans to end-users is

$$(y^* - y)u = (e^* - e)u + (x^* - x)(I - \Pi)u + x^*(\Pi - \Pi^*)u$$

(7.14)

Equation (7.14) differs from the analogous one for face values in that the banks' balance sheets now reflect the capital gain on their loan portolio as given by $(e^* - e)u$, where $e^* = e'$, and e' is the value given in (7.8). The increased equity is an additional funding source when loans are valued at market values. All three terms on the right-hand side of (7.14) are positive, and so $(y^* - y)u > 0$.

7.3 CREDIT BOOM

We can now sketch the scenario for a lending boom by using the results derived so far. The first ingredient is the relationship between the probability of default p on the loan book and the aggregate lending to end-user borrowers, who may be interpreted as being households who borrow in order to buy a house. Proposition 9 gives a declining function that maps p to total lending. Figure 7.3 depicts the negative relationship between total (notional) lending and p, where total lending appears on the horizontal axis. The arrows indicate that for each level of p, there is an associated level of total lending $\sum_i \bar{y}_i$. In our framework, it is the *supply* of credit that determines the total volume of lending in the economy. There are always household borrowers who stand ready to borrow in order to buy a house or to take out consumer loans in order to increase consumption. The question is how much credit is actually supplied to this group of potential borrowers.

To complete the picture we need macroeconomic feedback going from the volume of total lending to more buoyant macroeconomic conditions—say, through increased consumption of households who borrow more. When macroeconomic conditions are more buoyant, incomes and asset values rise, implying that the measured probability of default on loans to households actually falls. Feedback effects of this kind can be expected to lead to amplifications of shocks to the economy from the interplay between strengthening balance sheets and increased lending that we have seen in Chapter 3. Indeed, Adrian and Shin (2008c) exhibit evidence that expansions of intermediary balance sheets help explain future growth of GDP components such as housing investment and durable good consumption.

If increased loan supply feeds through to more buoyant aggregate conditions, it is possible to sketch a scenario for a lending boom. For the purpose of illustration, the feedback effect can be illustrated with the function g, which maps aggregate lending $\sum_i \bar{y}_i$ to the probability of default p. To be consistent with the interpretation of higher credit supply leading to more buoyant conditions, the function $g(.)$ is decreasing. Figure 7.4 superimposes the function $g(.)$ on Figure 7.3. Now consider a shock to the supply of credit illustrated in Figure 7.5, which illustrates a rightward shift in the supply of credit curve. The new intersection point is to the

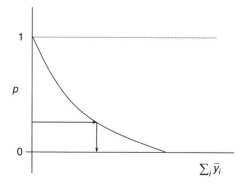

Figure 7.3: Aggregate lending is decreasing in p

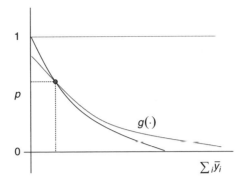

Figure 7.4: Initial point

bottom right-hand side of the initial point, associated with a lower probability of default p and greater total lending to the end-user sector.

Although there are no explicit dynamics in our framework (it is a static model), it is illuminating to trace out the step-wise adjustment resulting from the one-off shift in the supply curve for credit. The initial shift is a rightward shift in the credit supply curve, which results in higher aggregate lending for a fixed p. However, the macro feedback effect of greater loan supply then kicks in, resulting in a decrease in the probability of default. This adjustment is depicted by the first downward sloping arrow in Figure 7.5. However, the fall in p results in greater lending according to the argument for Proposition 9. Greater lending then feeds in to lower p, and so on. The new settling point given in Figure 7.5 is associated with a substantially lower probability of default, as well as with a large stock of lending.

At the cost of some additional complexity, it would be possible to incorporate subprime lending into the story. Suppose that the population of prime borrowers

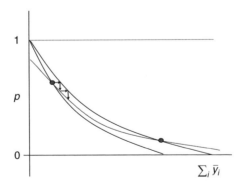

Figure 7.5: Lending boom

is small relative to the expansion of total lending as implied by the new crossing point between the credit supply curve and the macro feedback function $g(.)$ in Figure 7.5. Then, once all the prime borrowers have been granted a mortgage, the banking system has to find additional means of creating assets. One way would be for the banks to lend to each other. However, as discussed earlier, the aggregate lending of the banking system to mortgage borrowers must equal the sum of the equity and the borrowing from outside creditors. Since it is the borrowing from the outside creditors which is increasing, the funding must ultimately find its way to an end-user borrower.

Once all the prime borrowers in the population have a mortgage, the banks must find new borrowers in order to expand their balance sheets. The only way they can do this is to lower their lending standards. Subprime borrowers will then start to receive funding. The mechanical nature of our framework, in which banks simply choose their balance sheet size, masks important questions concerning the short-termist nature of such lending to subprime borrowers. The answer as to why banks would lower their lending standards in order to lend to subprime borrowers must appeal to other frictions within the banking institutions that allow such short-termism. Distorted incentives and shortened decisions horizons induced by agency problems within the bank would be part of the overall story. See Rajan (2005) and Kashyap, Rajan, and Stein (2008) for discussion of such incentives.

As balance sheets expand, new borrowers must be found. When all prime borrowers have a mortgage, but still balance sheets need to expand, then banks have to lower their lending standards in order to lend to subprime borrowers. The seeds of the subsequent downturn in the credit cycle are thus sown.

When the downturn arrives, the bad loans are either sitting on the balance sheets of the large financial intermediaries, or they are in special purpose vehicles (SPVs) that are sponsored by them. This is so, since the bad loans were taken on precisely in order to utilize the slack on their balance sheets. Although final investors such as pension funds and insurance companies will suffer losses, too, the large financial intermediaries are more exposed in the sense that they face the danger of seeing their capital wiped out. The severity of the credit crisis of 2007 and 2008 lies precisely in the fact that the bad loans were *not* all passed on to final investors. Instead, the "hot potato" sits inside the financial system, on the balance sheet of the largest, and most sophisticated, financial intermediaries.

7.4 GLOBAL IMBALANCES

Aggregate lending to end-user borrowers by the banking system must be financed either by the equity in the banking system or by borrowing from creditors outside the banking system. The empirical counterpart to the sector described as the "banking system" is the whole of the leveraged financial sector, which includes the traditional commercial banking system, but also encompasses the market-based financial system that plays a role in extending credit to banks and non-banks by borrowing from outside creditors. In this sense, the leveraged financial sector should be conceived broadly to include all leveraged institutions, such as investment banks, hedge funds and (in the US especially) the government-sponsored enterprises (GSEs) such as Fannie Mae and Freddie Mac.

Insights can be gained into the increased supply of credit to the end-user borrowers by looking at the liabilities side of financial intermediary balance sheets. The reasoning can be summarized in Figure 7.2, which we have seen already. Here, we focus on what happens to the liabilities side of the balance sheet as it expands. In order to fund the new lending to end-user borrowers, it must find sources of financing. Picture a balloon that is expanding. In order to expand, the balloon needs air. Similarly, when bank balance sheets expand, it must find sources of financing for its new lending. As the bank's balance sheet expands, it sucks in funding from new sources. Some of the funding will come from abroad. Indeed, as we will see shortly, foreigners (especially foreign central banks) have been an important funding source for residential mortgage lending in the United States in the period running up to the global financial crisis of 2007 and 2008.

A complete disaggregation of the funding source for the leveraged financial sector is not possible due to the lack of detailed breakdowns in the data between funding from leveraged and unleveraged creditors. A partial picture can be obtained, however, by examining the holding of US agency and GSE-backed securities. Figure 7.6 plots the total holding of US agency and GSE-backed securities broken down into the identity of the creditor from March 1980 to the

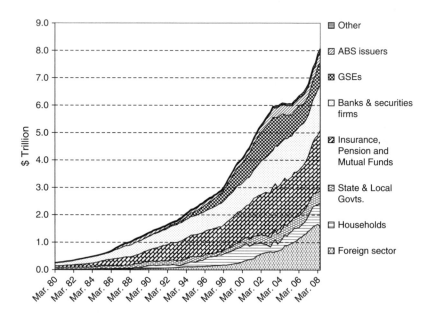

Figure 7.6: Holders of US agency and GSE securities

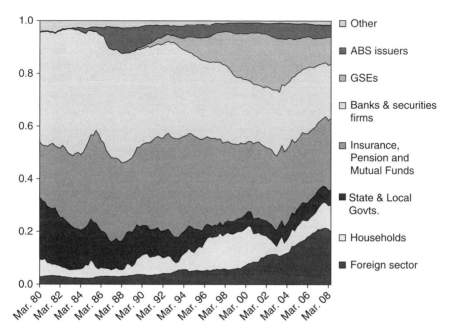

Figure 7.7: Percentage holdings of US agency and GSE securities

beginning of 2008. The data are from the US Flow of Funds accounts compiled by the Federal Reserve (table L.210). Figure 7.7 charts the holders by percentage holdings. We see the rapid increase in the holding of GSE securities by foreigners, both in absolute terms (in Figure 7.6), as well as in proportional terms (Figure 7.7).

The key series for our purposes is the proportion held by other leveraged financial institutions. We see that US leveraged institutions have been holding a declining proportion of the total. There is a consequent increase in the funding provided by the non-leveraged sector (Figure 7.8). In terms of the accounting framework presented in the previous chapter, the increased funding from the non-leveraged sector translates into an overall increase in the supply of credit to end-user borrowers in the economy. Especially notable is the holdings in the "rest of the world" category, which more than tripled from $504 billion at the end of 2001 to $1,540 billion at the end of 2007. A closer look at the role of foreign funding of mortgage debt in the United States reveals some interesting lessons.

7.5 FOREIGN HOLDING OF US DEBT SECURITIES

The US Treasury takes a survey of foreign holdings of US securities at the end of June each year, and then the results are published in April of the following year.

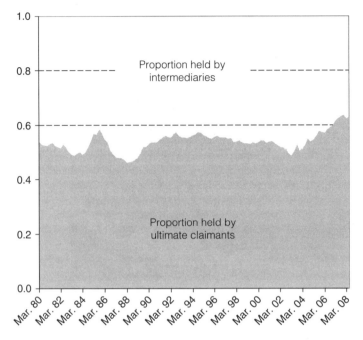

Figure 7.8: Proportion of agency and GSE securities held by non-leveraged holders

Although the survey first started in the 1970s, a breakdown of the identity of the borrowing sector is available only from 2002. Figure 7.9 shows the total holding of US debt securities broken down by the identity of the borrowing sector of the US economy.

As can be seen in Figure 7.9, the largest component is the holding of US Treasury securities and Agency debt securities. The non-financial non-government series aggregates the debt securities issued by manufacturing, retail, mining and other non-financial sectors. We can see that the size of the non-financial, non-government component is somewhat small. The financial sectors account for the bulk of the private-sector debt held by non-US holders.

To get a better picture of the relative speeds at which each of these sectors has grown, Figure 7.10 charts the normalized series where the value at 2002 is set equal to 1. The vertical axis is in log scale. The noteworthy series in Figure 7.10 is the "capital market" series, which has increased by a factor close to 30 in the five years from 2002 to 2007. Such a growth rate is very large compared to the total (which increased 2.6 times). Even other financial sectors, such as the commercial bank sector, saw their foreign debt liabilities increase at a similar pace (rising 3.14 times in the interval). The other financials sector saw much more modest increases in foreign debt liabilities.

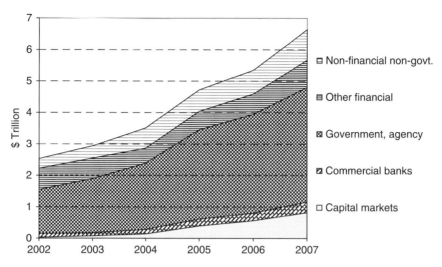

Figure 7.9: Foreign holding of US debt securities by borrowing sector

Since the GSE-backed securities are included in the "government and agency" category, the capital market series includes mainly the liabilities of the private label securitization vehicles. In other words, the capital market series includes the asset-backed securities issued by the ABS issuer sector of the economy. The largest component of the asset-backed securities series in recent years before the crisis

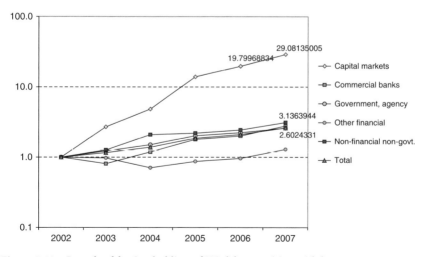

Figure 7.10: Growth of foreign holding of US debt securities, with base year 2002

was the securities backed by subprime mortgage assets (such as the collateralized debt obligations (CDOs) based on subprime mortgages).

These findings throw additional light on the "savings glut" hypothesis advanced by Bernanke (2005), Caballero et al. (2008) and others. One version of the "savings glut" view holds that it is the shortage of high quality assets in developing countries that has increased the demand for US securities as a vehicle for saving. For both Bernanke and Caballero et al., the increased foreign holdings of US debt securities are seen from a "demand pull" perspective. The greater demand for US securities pulls US securities out of the US and into foreign hands.

However, we see from Figure 7.10 that the greatest increase in foreign holdings of US debt securities has been the asset-backed securities issued by private label securitization vehicles. The bulk of these securities were asset-backed securities, the largest part of which were built on subprime mortgages. It is difficult to see why foreigners in search of high quality assets were expressing such a strong preference for securities backed by subprime mortgages—enough that the "capital market" series in Figure 7.10 increased almost 30 times in the space of five years.

Figure 7.10 points to the need to complement the "savings glut" hypothesis with a supply response from US debtors. The "savings glut" hypothesis is built around an accounting identity, and so does a poor job of indicating the underlying economic mechanism that explains the changes in aggregate quantities. However, the way that the savings glut hypothesis has been exposited is to see it as a "demand pull" phenomenon in which the greater demand for US debt securities by foreigners pull US securities out of the US and into foreign hands. In the popular press, such an account can easily turn into a blame game in which foreign investors are blamed for causing the asset price bubble in the US.[2]

The trade surpluses of the Asian emerging market economies and the oil-producing countries provide a potential source of funding for US debt securities, but it is difficult to extract the economic mechanisms from the accounting identities alone. Indeed, as argued by Genberg et al. (2005), the caricature of the "Asian mercantilist" economic policy where Asian exporters manipulate their exchange rates in order to build up reserves is not a persuasive story when the sources of the build-up reserves are examined more carefully.

Our discussion suggests that the "savings glut" hypothesis for global imbalances must be complemented with a supply response on the part of the debtor sectors in the US. Any account of the global imbalances must account for the fact that the largest increases in debt securities held by foreigners are for securities issued by private label mortgage pools, the bulk of which contain low quality subprime assets.

Indeed, there is an alternative "supply push" perspective in which greater holding of US debt securities is explained by the momentum of rapidly growing balance sheets in the residential mortgage sector which searches for funding

---

[2] See, for instance, "The Reckoning: Chinese Savings Helped Inflate American Bubble", *New York Times*, December 26, 2008 <http://www.nytimes.com/2008/12/26/world/asia/26addiction.html>.

sources. Under this alternative story, the US current account deficit in the period before the global financial crisis is explained by the US housing boom and the imperative to increase leverage of the financial system as a whole. Under this alternative story, the bursting of the US housing bubble will lead to the shrinking of global imbalances. As boom has turned to bust, this prediction will soon be put to the test.

7.6 RELATED LITERATURE

The idea that the changes in the lender's balance sheet is important in determining the supply of credit has also figured in an earlier literature that has emphasized the liquidity structure of the banks' balance sheets (Bernanke and Blinder 1988; Kashyap and Stein 2000), or the cushioning effect of the banks' regulatory capital (Van den Heuvel 2002).

The supply-side mechanism for the growth of credit should be distinguished from the larger literature on the fluctuations in credit due to shifts in the *demand* for credit, as emphasized, for instance, by Bernanke and Gertler (1989) and Kiyotaki and Moore (1997, 2005). The key to the demand-side explanations of the fluctuation of credit is the changing strength of the borrower's balance sheet and the resulting change in the creditworthiness of the borrower. The mechanism proposed here for the origin of the subprime crisis has more in common with the supply-side explanation. The greater risk-taking capacity of the shadow banking system leads to an increased demand for new assets to fill the expanding balance sheets, and an increase in leverage.

Gete (2008) shows that current account deficits are closely related to housing booms. Capital flows between Western European countries also follow housing booms, even though the Bernanke (2005) savings glut hypothesis seems less plausible between countries in Western Europe that are at a similar level of development. Gete (2008) shows that European countries such as Spain who have larger housing booms are also those with larger current account deficits.

8

Case of Northern Rock

Many of the themes explored so far can be illustrated in the case of Northern Rock, the UK bank that failed in 2007. In September 2007, television viewers around the world witnessed the spectacle of what seemed like an old-fashioned bank run—of depositors queuing outside the branch offices of the UK bank, Northern Rock, to withdraw their money. The current generation of economists who study bank runs in their theoretical models have had few opportunities to experience what they study, unless it was in Christmas movies by Jimmy Stewart or in *Mary Poppins*.

The last bank run in the UK before Northern Rock was in 1866 (with Overend Guerney). Runs were more common in the US in the 1930s, but they have been rare since. For economists, the run on Northern Rock seemed to offer a rare opportunity to study at close quarters all the elements involved in their theoretical models—the futility of public statements of reassurance, the mutually reinforcing anxiety of depositors, as well as the power of the media in galvanizing and channeling that anxiety through the power of television images.

However, appearances are deceptive. Retail depositors started queuing outside the branch offices only after the Bank of England announced its emergency liquidity support for Northern Rock on the morning of Friday, September 14. On the previous evening, the BBC's evening television news broadcast first broke the news that Northern Rock had sought the Bank of England's support.

The damage had been done well before the run by its retail depositors. Even as early as July 2007, ominous signs were developing in short-term funding markets that the subprime crisis was beginning to exert stresses on the balance sheets of banks and the off-balance sheet entities they sponsored. But the demise of Northern Rock dates from August 9, when the short-term funding market and interbank lending all but froze. The triggering event on the day was the news that BNP Paribas was closing three off-balance sheet investment vehicles with exposures to US subprime mortgage assets, but in the days leading up to the August 9 watershed, other investment vehicles that tapped short-term financing had begun experiencing difficulties in rolling over their short-tem borrowing. On August 9, the European Central Bank intervened by injecting 94 billion euros into Europe's banking system.

Northern Rock was unusual among UK mortgage banks in its heavy reliance on non-retail funding. By the summer of 2007, only 23% of its liabilities were in the form of retail deposits. The rest of its funding came from short-term borrowing in the capital markets, or through securitized notes and other longer-term funding sources, as we discuss in more detail below. The dating of the beginning of the credit crisis can be seen in Figure 8.1, which charts the weekly series on the outstanding amounts of asset-backed commercial paper (ABCP), obtained from the Federal Reserve's website. Asset-backed commercial paper was the favored means for off-balance sheet vehicles to fund their holdings of long-dated mortgage-related assets, and as such, served as the barometer for the appetite for short-term lending against mortgage assets. The weekly series shows a sharp break between August 8 to August 15. Although Northern Rock did not sponsor off-balance sheet vehicles that used asset-backed commercial paper, it was nevertheless fishing from the same pool of short-term funding, as we will see shortly.

The managers of Northern Rock had informed its regulators, the Financial Services Authority (FSA), as early as August 13 of Northern Rock's funding problems. The Bank of England was informed on August 14. From that time until the fateful announcement on September 14 that triggered the depositor run (i.e. for a full month), the FSA and Bank of England sought to resolve the crisis behind the scenes, possibly arranging a takeover by another UK bank. However, the unfolding credit crisis and the reluctance of the authorities to commit public funds was not a promising backdrop for persuading other private sector institutions to take over a troubled bank. Having failed to find a buyer for Northern

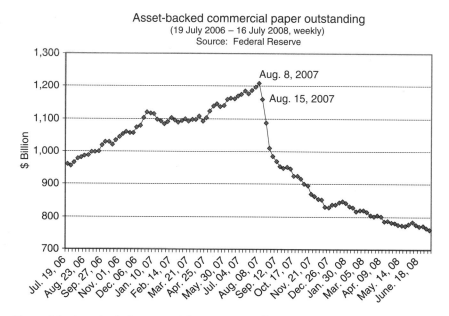

Figure 8.1: Asset-backed commercial paper outstanding
Source: Federal Reserve.

Rock, the public announcement by the Bank of England on September 14 was recognition that Northern Rock's predicament had reached the point where only central bank support could avoid bank failure. The depositor run, although dramatic on television, was an event in the *aftermath* of the liquidity crisis at Northern Rock, rather than the event that triggered its liquidity crisis. In this sense, the run on Northern Rock was not an old-fashioned bank run of the sort we see in the movies.

The irony of the television images is that retail deposit funding is perhaps the most stable form of funding available to a bank. Although retail deposits can be withdrawn on demand, their effective duration is much longer, with bankers joking that a depositor is more likely to get divorced than switch banks. Indeed, a stable deposit base figures prominently when valuing banks in terms of their franchise value. The textbook bank run model in which retail depositors rush to the bank to withdraw their money, fearing that others are going to, therefore paints an overly pessimistic view of the fragility of the capital structure of a deposit-funded bank.

So, the real question raised by the Northern Rock episode is not so much why retail depositors are so prone to running, but instead why the plentiful short-term funding that Northern Rock enjoyed before August of 2007 suddenly dried up. To turn the question around, the issue is why sophisticated lenders who operate in the capital markets and the interbank credit market chose suddenly to deny lending to another bank with an apparently solid asset book, with virtually no subprime lending. Northern Rock was in the business of prime mortgage lending to UK households. The asset quality of any mortgage bank is vulnerable to a sharp decline in house prices and rising unemployment. However, 2007 was the Indian summer of the housing boom in the UK and there were no outward signs of seriously deteriorating loan quality.

The answers to these questions reveal much about the nature of banking in the age of securitization and capital markets. The conventional distinctions between a bank-based financial system and a market-based financial system turn out to be less relevant in the securitization era, and the most important lesson from the Northern Rock case is that modern banking cannot be viewed separately from capital market developments.

In this chapter, we outline the salient features of the Northern Rock crisis, expose the relevant facts for scrutiny, and compare the features of the Northern Rock case to the textbook bank run model of a run by its depositors, and argue that the traditional models come up short. We will see many of the themes discussed so far at play. Rather than the classic coordination failure view of bank runs, a better perspective on Northern Rock can be gained by looking at the pressures on the creditors to Northern Rock. The creditors to Northern Rock were sophisticated investors that tailor their risk-taking strategy to unfolding events. When measured risks are low—that is, in boom times—balance sheets expand, and funding is easy to obtain. But when a crisis strikes, exposures are cut in response. Doing so is dictated by prudent risk management, and regulators have also encouraged such behavior. However, prudent cutting of exposures by the creditors of Northern

Rock is a withdrawal of funding from the point of view of Northern Rock. The Northern Rock case raises a number of important policy issues, not least how banking regulation should be formulated in the age of securitization and capital markets. There are also important issues for the theoretical analysis of banking crises and the role of the bank capital structure in welfare analysis.

8.1 BACKGROUND

Northern Rock was a building society (i.e. a mutually owned savings and mortgage bank) until its decision to go public and float its shares on the stock market in 1997. As with other building societies in the UK, Northern Rock traced its origin to the mutual movement of the 19th century, arising out of the merger of the Northern Counties Permanent Building Society (established in 1850) and the Rock Building Society (established in 1865). Even its name, "Northern Rock" conjured up associations of dour solidity, which seemed appropriate for a savings and mortgage bank.

As with other UK building societies, Northern Rock started life as a regionally based institution, serving its local clientele. In Northern Rock's case, its base was the North East of England, around the city of Newcastle upon Tyne. Northern Rock's successes as a bank made it emblematic of the revitalization of the North East region following the decline of traditional industries, such as coal mining and shipbuilding. Northern Rock funded a highly visible charitable trust, and becoming the main sponsor to the local football team, Newcastle United, known for its loyal fan base. For all these reasons, Northern Rock commanded fierce loyalty in its local base.

In spite of its modest origins, Northern Rock had larger ambitions. In the nine years from June 1998 (the first year after demutualization) to June 2007 (on the eve of its crisis), Northern Rock's total assets grew from 17.4 billion pounds to 113.5 billion pounds. This growth in assets corresponds to a constant equivalent annual growth rate of 23.2%, a very rapid rate of growth by any standards. By the eve of its crisis, Northern Rock was the fifth largest bank in the UK by mortgage assets.

Northern Rock's liabilities reflect both the funding constraints it faced, as well as the way it overcame those constraints. Figure 8.2 charts the composition of Northern Rock's liabilities from June 1998 to June 2007. The first notable feature is how quickly Northern Rock's total balance sheet size outstripped its traditional funding base of retail deposits. Even as total assets grew by a factor of 6.5 in this period, retail deposits only grew from 10.4 billion pounds to 24 billion pounds. As a result, retail funding fell to 23% of total liabilities on the eve of the crisis (and much further after the run). Even in the case of retail deposits, we will see later that only a small proportion consisted of the traditional branch-based deposits. The bulk of the retail deposits were non-branch-based deposits such as postal and telephone accounts. It was these non-branch retail deposits that proved most vulnerable to withdrawal in the aftermath of the run on Northern Rock.

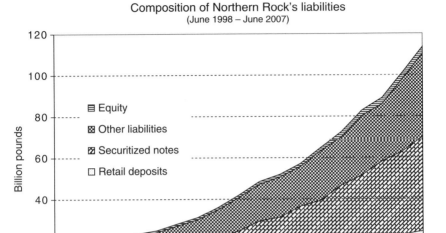

Figure 8.2: Composition of Northern Rock's liabilities

The gap in funding was made up by securitized notes and other forms of non-retail funding, such as interbank deposits and covered bonds. Given the importance of securitized notes for the Northern Rock story, we postpone a discussion of securitized notes until later. Covered bonds are long-term liabilities written against segregated mortgage assets. We will have more to say about covered bonds in another context in a later chapter. Covered bonds are liabilities that are illiquid and long-term in nature, and so were not implicated in the run. However, other short-run wholesale funding was more closely implicated in the run on Northern Rock, as we will see shortly.

Before examining the components of Northern Rock's liabilities more closely, it is worthy of note that Northern Rock was not unique among UK banks in making growing use of non-retail funding, although the extent to which it relied on non-retail funding made it an outlier. Figure 8.3, taken from the Bank of England's Financial Stability Report (Bank of England, 2008) charts the trend in the use of non-retail funding among large UK banks since 2000 as given by the time plot of the cross-section median, and the cross-section interquartile range. The median UK bank's non-retail funding started at 27.8% in December 2000, but had almost doubled to 47.8% by December 2007. Thus, Northern Rock was not unique among UK banks in making use of non-retail funding, but what set it aside from others was the extent to which it relied on such funding.

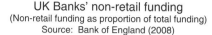

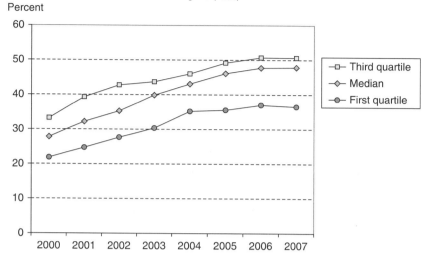

Figure 8.3: UK banks' non-retail funding
Source: Bank of England (2008).

8.2 SECURITIZATION PROCESS

The role played by securitized notes has received considerable scrutiny in the Northern Rock episode. It has become the received wisdom that such securitized notes made Northern Rock's business model unusual, its balance sheet less traditional, and that securitization was somehow responsible for Northern Rock's downfall. However, the role of securitization seems to be more subtle than suggested by the received wisdom.

Northern Rock's securitized notes were of medium to long-term maturity, with an average maturity of over one year. It assigned portions of its mortgage assets to a trust—Granite Finance Trustees, which then entered into an agreement with special purpose entities (SPEs) called "Funding" and "Funding 2". In turn, these SPEs entered into loan agreements with a separate note-issuing company, who were the ultimate note issuers. Figure 8.4 is drawn from the offer documentation for a particular bond offering—in this case, the Granite Master Issuer series 2005-2. Table 8.1 lists the full series of offerings taken from Northern Rock's annual reports.

The notes issued by Granite were floating rate "controlled amortization notes" that paid out according to set redemption dates spread over several years. The notes were ranked according to seniority, with Class A notes being more senior

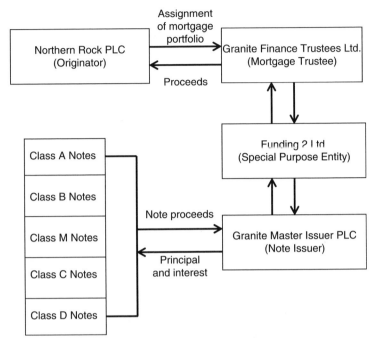

Figure 8.4: Northern Rock's securitization process

(paying 4 basis points above LIBOR) and Class D notes being the most junior (paying 50 basis points above LIBOR). Unlike the US securitization process, where the special purpose entities are off-balance sheet vehicles, Northern Rock kept a residual interest in the securitized assets, and hence the SPEs were consolidated on Northern Rock's main balance sheet. In this respect, the rapid growth of Northern Rock's balance sheet reflects the accounting regime, as much as the flow of new loans originated.

There is another contrast between Northern Rock and the US and European banks caught up in the subprime crisis. The latter banks sponsored off-balance sheet entities such as conduits and SIVs (structured investment vehicles) that held subprime mortgage assets funded with very short-term liabilities such as asset-backed commercial paper (ABCPs), which were at the heart of the subprime crisis.

In contrast, the notes issued by Granite were much longer term. The relatively longer maturity of the Granite notes, as compared to the notes issued by SIVs and conduits, can be seen in Table 8.1, which lists the series of securitization offerings from Northern Rock's annual reports. Take the last column. The last column lists the redemptions during 2006 as given by the difference between the amounts outstanding at the end of 2006 and the amounts outstanding at the end of 2005.

Table 8.1: Northern Rock's Securitization Issues

Securitization vehicle	Issue date	Outstanding end 2007 (A)	Outstanding end 2006 (B)	Outstanding end 2005 (C)	2007 Redemptions (B–A)	2006 Redemptions (C–B)
Granite Mortgages 00-1 plc 1	Mar. 00	0.00	170.60	213.10	170.60	42.50
Granite Mortgages 00-2 plc 25	Sep. 00	0.00	265.90	375.50	265.90	109.60
Granite Mortgages 01-1 plc 26	Mar. 01	424.10	507.90	641.10	83.80	133.20
Granite Mortgages 01-2 plc 28	Sep. 01	0.00	0.00	713.20	0.00	713.20
Granite Mortgages 02-1 plc 20	Mar. 02	0.00	1,123.60	1,366.30	1,123.60	242.70
Granite Mortgages 02-2 plc 23	Sep. 02	1,068.60	1,302.60	1,677.60	234.00	375.00
Granite Mortgages 03-1 plc 27	Jan. 03	1,644.90	1,718.80	1,981.30	73.90	262.50
Granite Mortgages 03-2 plc 21	May. 03	962.70	1,129.00	1,468.90	166.30	339.90
Granite Mortgages 03-3 plc 24	Sep. 03	876.90	1,058.90	1,372.30	182.00	313.40
Granite Mortgages 04-1 plc 28	Jan. 04	1,485.80	1,802.50	2,364.80	316.70	562.30
Granite Mortgages 04-2 plc 26	May. 04	1,694.90	2,044.60	2,587.10	349.70	542.50
Granite Mortgages 04-3 plc 22	Sep. 04	1,962.10	2,378.10	3,112.70	416.00	734.60
Granite Master Issuer plc—Series 05-1	Jan. 05	2,795.10	3,254.60	4,000.40	459.50	745.80
Granite Master Issuer plc—Series 05-2	May. 05	2,413.60	2,880.10	3,762.10	466.50	882.00
Granite Master Issuer plc—Series 05-3	Aug. 05	503.80	511.10	582.20	7.30	71.10
Granite Master Issuer plc—Series 05-4	Sep. 05	2,383.30	2,840.60	3,891.30	457.30	1,050.70
Granite Master Issuer plc—Series 06-1	Jan. 06	4,423.80	5,048.10		624.30	
Granite Master Issuer plc—Series 06-2	May. 06	2,460.40	2,786.10		325.70	
Granite Master Issuer plc—Series 06-3	Sep. 06	4,761.50	5,400.30		638.80	
Granite Master Issuer plc—Series 06-4	Nov. 06	2,787.30	3,206.20		418.90	
Granite Master Issuer plc—Series 07-1	Jan. 07	5,607.00				
Granite Master Issuer plc—Series 07-2	May. 07	4,570.80				
Granite Master Issuer plc—Series 07-3	Sep. 07	5,074.10				
Total (million pounds)					6,780.80	7,121.00

The total redemptions during 2006 of notes outstanding at the beginning of the year were 7.12 billion pounds. At the end of 2005, there were 31.1 billion pounds' worth of notes outstanding. So, only a small fraction (23%) of the notes outstanding were redeemed over the following year. This is in sharp contrast to the off-balance sheet vehicles that roll over their liabilities several times during the year.

There is one instance where securitization did play a role in Northern Rock's downfall. This has to do with the Granite Master Issue 07-3, listed in the bottom row in the table in Table 8.1. The notes were due to be issued in September of 2007, but the crisis intervened before the notes could be sold. None of the notes as placed with investors, and the whole issue of notes—around 5 billion pounds at face value—were taken back onto Northern Rock's balance sheet. In this instance, the problem was that the planned sale of notes did not proceed, depriving Northern Rock of cash, rather than there being a problem with the rolling over of existing liabilities.

When these factors are taken together, the lesson to emerge from Northern Rock's securitization process is that the role played by Granite in Northern Rock's downfall is somewhat more subtle than is often portrayed by financial commentators in the press. Commentators have emphasized the non-standard business model of Northern Rock as being to blame for the run. At least for the securitized notes of Northern Rock, they were not directly culpable. The Northern Rock case was therefore different from the outwardly similar downfalls of SIVs and conduits sponsored by other European banks, such as BNP Paribas or 1KB, the German bank that suffered a liquidity crisis in August 2007. We return to this issue later.

8.3 THE RUN ON NORTHERN ROCK

A snapshot of the run on Northern Rock can be gained by comparing the composition of its liabilities before the run and after the run. The comparison is given in Figure 8.5, taken from the 2007 annual report of Northern Rock. The left-hand bar gives a snapshot of the main components of Northern Rock's liabilities as of the end of June 2007 (i.e. before the run), while the right-hand bar is a snapshot at the end of the year, after its run and after the liquidity support from the Bank of England.

The most glaring difference is the liability to the Bank of England after its liquidity support to Northern Rock, which stood at 28.5 billion pounds at the end of 2007. However, covered bonds and securitized notes are seen to be relatively stable across the two dates. In fact, covered bonds increase from 8.1 billion in June to 8.9 billion in December. Securitized notes fall only slightly from 45.7 billion to 43 billion.

The largest falls are for retail deposits, and for wholesale liabilities, with the latter falling from 26.7 billion pounds in June to 11.5 billion pounds in December. The wholesale funding in this chart refers to the non-retail funding that does not

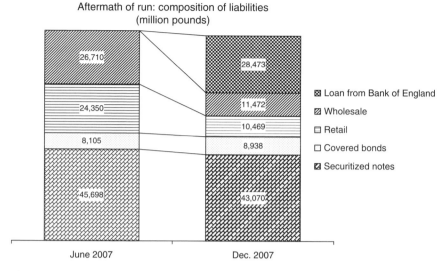

Figure 8.5: Composition of liabilities before and after run

fall under either covered bonds or securitized notes. Although a detailed break-down of the wholesale funding is not disclosed in the annual reports, they do contain some clues on the maturity and sourcing of the funding. The 2006 annual report (p. 41) states that wholesale funding consists of a "balanced mixture of short and medium term funding with increasing diversification of our global investor". Medium-term funding refers to term funding of six months or longer, while short-term funding has maturity of less than six months. The 2006 annual report (p. 41) states:

Following substantial inflows from securitisation during the first half, we repaid net £2.3 billion, mainly short term funds. In the second half we raised a net £5.2 billion, leading to a full year net funding of £2.9 billion. During the year, we raised £3.2 billion medium term wholesale funds from a variety of globally spread sources, with specific emphasis on the US, Europe, Asia and Australia. This included two transactions sold to domestic US investors totalling US$3.5 billion. In January 2007, we raised a further US$2.0 billion under our US MTN [medium term notes] programme. Key developments during 2006 included the establishment of an Australian debt programme, raising A$1.2 billion from our inaugural issue. This transaction was the largest debut deal in that market for a single A rated financial institution targeted at both domestic Australian investors and the Far East.

It is clear from this description that Northern Rock's short-term wholesale funding shared many similarities with the short-term funding raised by off-balance sheet vehicles such as SIVs and conduits, aimed at institutional investors. As such, Northern Rock was fishing from the same pool as the SIVs and conduits. This type of funding was more short term (less than one year; frequently much shorter), and more vulnerable to the liquidity crisis that hit the capital markets in August 2007.

The 2007 annual report (p. 31) states that, although Northern Rock managed to raise a net 2.5 billion pounds of wholesale funding in the first half of the year, the second half saw "substantial outflows of wholesale funds, as maturing loans and deposits were not renewed. This resulted in a full year net outflow of £11.7 billion."

This is the true run on Northern Rock. Maturing loans and deposits were not renewed by the investors in Northern Rock short- and medium-term paper. The timing coincides with the kink in the ABCP series shown in Figure 8.1. Thus, it was the wholesale funding that was unrelated to the securitized notes or covered bonds that was at the heart of the crisis.

A closer look at the retail deposits of Northern also reveals that there is more to the Northern Rock story than meets the eye. Figure 8.6 charts the change in the composition of retail deposits of Northern Rock from December 2006 to December 2007. There is a large fall in the total, as one would expect from there having been a depositor run in the meantime. Total retail funding falls from 26.7 billion to 11.5 billion. However, what is noteworthy is how little of the deposit funding is attributable to the conventional, branch-based customer deposits. Branch-based customer deposits fall from 5.6 billion to 3 billion. In contrast, postal account deposits, offshore deposits, and telephone and internet

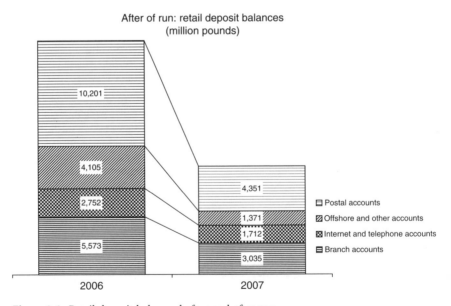

Figure 8.6: Retail deposit balances before and after run

deposits saw much more substantial falls. Evidently, not all retail deposits had the same stickiness. The irony of the television images of depositors queuing at the branch offices was that it was the branch deposits that were the most stable.

8.4 REASSESSING THE RUN ON NORTHERN ROCK

Drawing together the main strands of the discussion so far, we are faced with the following facts. First, although the television images of retail depositors outside branch offices were dramatic, they were not the immediate cause of the liquidity crisis at Northern Rock. Neither were the investors in covered bonds or in the securitized notes. Instead, it was the short-term and medium-term creditors who had previously bought Northern Rock paper but who withdrew from the market that caused the liquidity crisis at Northern Rock.

Although these creditors were not retail depositors, it is still pertinent to ask whether the classic coordination failure model of bank runs could be the best description of the events. According to the coordination failure model, such as in Bryant (1980) and Diamond and Dybvig (1983), an individual depositor runs for fear that others will run, leaving no assets in place for those who do not run.

Although some element of coordination clearly played a role in the credit crisis of August 2007, the important fact to bear in mind is that the withdrawal of credit hit the whole market, not simply a subset of the institutions. Figure 8.1 on the evolution of the asset-backed commercial paper stock shows the dramatic nature of the withdrawal of funding from the whole market. Thus, if there was a run driven by a coordination failure, then it was a run from all the institutions that relied on short-term funding of this type, rather than from Northern Rock in particular.

A better perspective on the crisis can be gained by looking at the pressures on the creditors to Northern Rock. In the coordination failure model of bank runs, the creditors are individual consumers who rationally choose whether to run or not, based on their beliefs about what other depositors do. They are not themselves constrained in any way by other considerations.

However, many of the creditors to Northern Rock would have been sophisticated investors that tailor their risk-taking strategy to unfolding events. When measured risks are low, risk constraints on capital do not bind, and such investors will be able to expand balance sheets, meaning that they are willing to lend and are looking for borrowers. However, when a crisis strikes, risk constraints bind and lenders cut back their exposures in response. This will be the case especially if the investor is leveraged. For a leveraged institution, prudent risk management dictates the cutting back of exposures when market turmoil strikes. However, the prudent cutting of exposures by the creditors to Northern Rock will look like a run from the point of view of Northern Rock itself.

The key is to recognize that the creditors themselves face constraints in their decisions. They do not conform to the picture of the unconstrained household depositor whose only decision is whether to run or not. The constrained creditor has less discretion in the face of market developments. The run on Northern Rock may be better seen as the tightening of constraints on the creditors of Northern Rock, rather than as a coordination failure among them.

One way we can understand the fluctuations in funding conditions is to look at the implicit maximum leverage that is permitted in collateralized borrowing transactions such as repurchase agreements (repos). The discussion of repurchase agreements is instructive in thinking about leverage and funding more generally, even though Northern Rock did not make substantial use of repos in its own funding.

In a repurchase agreement, the borrower sells a security today for a price below the current market price on the understanding that it will buy it back in the future at a pre-agreed price. The difference between the current market price of the security and the price at which it is sold is called the "haircut" in the repo, and fluctuates together with funding conditions in the market.

The fluctuations in the haircut largely determine the degree of funding available to a leveraged institution. The reason is that the haircut determines the maximum permissible leverage achieved by the borrower. If the haircut is 2%, the borrower can borrow $98 for $100 worth of securities pledged. Then, to hold $100 worth of securities, the borrower must come up with $2 of equity. Thus, if the repo haircut is 2%, the maximum permissible leverage (ratio of assets to equity) is 50.

Suppose that the borrower leverages up the maximum permitted level. Such an action would be consistent with the objective of maximizing the return on equity, since leverage magnifies return on equity. The borrower thus has a highly leveraged balance sheet with leverage of 50. If at this time, a shock to the financial system raises the market haircut, then the borrower faces a predicament. Suppose that the haircut rises to 4%. Then, the permitted leverage halves to 25, from 50. The borrower then faces a hard choice. Either it must raise new equity so that its equity doubles from its previous level, or it must sell half its assets, or some combination of both.

Times of financial stress are associated with sharply higher haircuts, necessitating substantial reductions in leverage through asset disposals or raising of new equity. Table 8.2 is a table of repo haircuts taken from the October 2008 issue of the *Global Financial Stability Report* of the International Monetary Fund (IMF 2008), and shows the haircuts in secured lending transactions at two dates—in April 2007 before the financial crisis and in August 2008 in the midst of the crisis. Haircuts are substantially higher during the crises than before. The increase in haircuts depicted in Table 8.2 entails very substantial reductions in leverage, necessitating asset disposals or raising of new equity. For instance, a borrower holding AAA-rated residential mortgage-backed securities would have seen a ten-fold increase in haircuts, meaning that its leverage must fall from 50 to just 5.

Raising new equity or cutting assets entails painful adjustments for the borrower. Raising new equity is notoriously difficult in distressed market conditions. But selling assets in a depressed market is not much better. The evidence points to

Table 8.2: Haircuts on repo agreements (%)

Securities	April 2007	August 2008
US treasuries	0.25	3
Investment-grade bonds	0–3	8–12
High-yield bonds	10–15	25–40
Equities	15	20
Senior leveraged loans	10–12	15–20
Mezzanine leveraged loans	18–25	35 +
Prime MBS	2–4	10–20
ABS	3–5	50–60

borrowers adjusting leverage through adjustments in the size of the balance sheet, leaving equity unchanged, rather than through changes in equity directly (see Adrian and Shin 2007 forthcoming).

To the extent that the financial system as a whole holds long-term, illiquid assets, financed by short-term liabilities, any tensions resulting from a sharp decrease in permitted leverage will show up somewhere in the system. Even if most institutions can adjust down their balance sheets flexibly in response to the greater stress, there will be some pinch points in the system that will be exposed by the deleveraging. The pinch points will be those institutions that are highly leveraged, but who hold long-term illiquid assets financed with short-term debt. When the short-term funding runs away, the financial institution holding the long-term illiquid assets will face a liquidity crisis. Arguably, this is exactly what happened to Northern Rock.

The scenario painted above becomes more compelling when we examine the leverage of Northern Rock. Leverage is defined as the ratio of total assets to equity. Figure 8.7 plots the leverage series from June 1998 to December 2007 according to three different measures of equity.

In the early years of Northern Rock's operation as a public limited company (PLC), there was no distinction between total equity, shareholder equity and common equity. All equity was just common equity. However, beginning in 2005, the three series start to diverge sharply. In 2005, the total equity series included for the first time 736.5 million pounds' worth of subordinated debt, as well as 299.3 million pounds' worth of reserve notes. Both of these items had been issued much earlier (in 2001), but they were included in the equity series in the annual report for the first time in 2005. The inclusion of these subordinated debt items introduced a jump up in the equity series for Northern Rock, and accounts for the sharp jump down in the leverage series in June 2005 in Figure 8.7. However, as we can also see from Figure 8.7, when the subordinated debt items are excluded, and equity is construed just as shareholder equity, the equity series continues to climb in 2005.

Subordinated debt is classed as a capital buffer under the Basel rules but their economic significance for the purpose of computing permitted leverage is

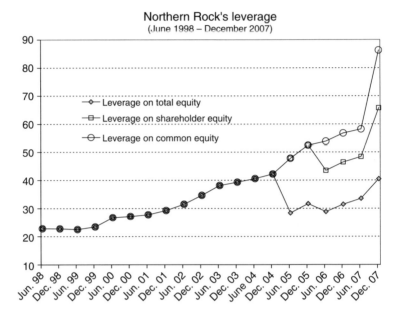

Figure 8.7: Northern Rock's leverage

unclear. Under the Basel rules, subordinated debt is junior debt relative to the other creditors, and so has elements of a buffer. This is the reason why it is seen as capital under the Basel rules.

However, subordinated debt holders are just another class of creditor to the bank. They do not have control of the bank's operations as the common equity holders do. For the purpose of calculating the permissible leverage in a moral hazard context, where the must have sufficient equity at stake so as to prevent them from engaging in moral hazard, it is common equity that matters, rather than the equity enhanced by subordinated debt. This is because common equity holders will take account of the possible losses that result from their portfolio decisions, rather than the interests of the subordinated debt holders. Adrian and Shin (2008b) discuss the theoretical basis for fluctuating leverage based on such a feature.

In 2006, Northern Rock issued 396.4 million pounds' worth of preference shares, which is counted as shareholder equity. This issuance of new preference shares accounts for the jump down in the leverage series with respect to shareholder equity in June 2006. However, the economic meaning of preference shares for the determination of permissible leverage depends crucially on the degree to which the common equity holders who exercised control would have subscribed to the preference shares. If the preference shareholders did not exercise control, then the moral hazard argument and the necessity of the minimum stake implies that the maximum permissible leverage should be calculated on the basis of common equity alone.

When leverage is interpreted strictly as the ratio of total assets to common equity, then we can see from Figure 8.7 that Northern Rock's leverage continued to climb throughout its history as a public company, rising from 22.8 in June 1998, just after its floatation, to 58.2 in June 2007, on the eve of its liquidity crisis. This is a very large number, even by the standards of US investment banks, who hold very liquid and short-term assets. Of course, Northern Rock's leverage jumped even higher in December 2007 after its run, following the depletion of its common equity from losses suffered in the second half of 2007. The leverage on common equity at the end of 2007 was 86.3.

When a bank is so highly leveraged, even a small increase in the implicit haircut on its borrowing will entail a withdrawal of funding from that bank. Thus, although most of the discussion above has focused on the constraints facing the leveraged creditors to Northern Rock, many of the points will apply also to non-leveraged creditors to Northern Rock—such as money market mutual funds, or insurance companies.

When a borrower is as highly leveraged as Northern Rock, small fluctuations in implied haircuts can cause large shifts in funding. In this sense, the run on Northern Rock was just a matter of when the next pull back in funding conditions would arrive. When the tide eventually turned, institutions with balance sheet mismatches were left on the beach. Northern Rock was not the only one to find itself beached, but it lacked the liquidity support of a larger sponsor—apart, that is, from the Bank of England.

The Northern Rock episode gives us an opportunity to revisit some of the economic principles behind the use of short-term debt to finance long-term assets. As argued above, when the financial system as a whole finances long-term, illiquid assets with short-term liabilities, not everyone can be perfectly hedged in terms of their maturity profile. Pinch points will emerge somewhere in the system. Northern Rock could be seen as precisely such a "pinch point" in the financial system where the tensions would finally be manifested.

There are well-known arguments for the desirability of short-term debt in disciplining managers. Calomiris and Kahn (1991) have argued that demand deposits for banking arose naturally as a response by the bank's owners and managers to commit not to engage in actions that dissipate the value of the assets, under pain of triggering a depositor run.

Diamond and Rajan (2001) have developed this argument further, and have argued that the coordination problem inherent in a depositor run serves as a commitment device on the part of the depositors not to renegotiate in the face of opportunistic actions by the managers. When the bank has the right quantity of deposits outstanding, any attempt by the banker to extort a rent from depositors will be met by a run, which drives the banker's rents to zero. Foreseeing this, the banker will not attempt to extort rents. In a world of certainty, the bank maximizes the amount of credit it can offer by financing with a rigid and fragile all deposit capital structure

However, in both Calomiris and Kahn (1991) and Diamond and Rajan (2001), the relationship between the bank and the depositors is seen as being self-contained. In particular, the depositors are unconstrained. Under these conditions, the economic rationale for short-term debt is compelling. Short-term debt has desirable incentive effects, and the fragility of the balance sheet has an economic rationale. However, the lesson from Northern Rock is that sometimes creditors are subject to external constraints, and may have to take actions that are the consequence of factors outside the immediate principal-agent relationship with the bank.

Take the following simple example, illustrated by Figure 8.8, taken from Morris and Shin (2008). Bank 1 has borrowed from bank 2. Bank 2 has other assets, as well as its loans to bank 1. Suppose that bank 2 suffers credit losses on these other loans, but that the creditworthiness of bank 1 remains unchanged. The loss suffered by bank 2 depletes its equity capital. In the face of such a shock, a prudent course of action by bank 2 is to reduce its overall exposure, so that its asset book is trimmed to a size that can be carried comfortably with the smaller equity capital. From the point of view of bank 2, the imperative is to reduce its overall lending, including its lending to bank 1. By reducing its lending, bank 2 achieves its micro-prudential objective of reducing its risk exposure. However, from bank 1's perspective, the reduction of lending by bank 2 is a withdrawal of funding. Unless bank 1 can find alternative sources of funding, it will have to reduce its own asset holdings, either by curtailing its lending, or by selling marketable assets.

In the case where we have the combination of (i) bank 1 not having alternative sources of funding, (ii) the reduction in bank 2's lending being severe, and (iii) bank 1's assets being so illiquid that they can only be sold at fire-sale prices, then the withdrawal of lending by bank 2 will feel like a run from the point of view of bank 1. In other words, a prudent shedding of exposures from the point of view of bank 2 is a run from the point of view of bank 1. Arguably, this type of run is one element of what happened to Northern Rock.

Questions of overall economic welfare cannot be addressed without the system perspective that incorporates all spillover effects and externalities. The example given in Figure 8.8 illustrates the externalities that are generated by bank 2 on bank 1 as the former tries to follow a prudent course of action that reduces its exposures.

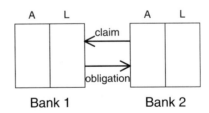

Figure 8.8: Run on bank 1 by bank 2

When evaluated from a system perspective, maturity mismatch on the balance sheet is double-edged. In spite of the incentive effects that make a fragile balance sheet desirable from the point of view of incentives, the spillover effects from outside the principal-agent relationship will generate countervailing inefficiencies. The relative strengths of the desirable and undesirable consequences of balance sheet fragility will determine the overall economic rationale for maturity mismatch on a bank's balance sheet. In the case of Northern Rock, its demise is a lesson in the possible downside costs in the overall welfare calculation.

8.5 IMPLICATIONS FOR FINANCIAL REGULATION

Traditionally, capital requirements have been the cornerstone of the regulation of banks. The rationale for capital requirements lies in maintaining the solvency of the regulated institution. By ensuring solvency, the interests of creditors—especially retail depositors—can be protected. A creditor who has the ability to monitor the firm can protect his interests through the enforcement of covenants and other checks on the actions of the firm's managers. However, in the case of a traditional deposit-funded bank, the creditors are small retail depositors. Small depositors face a coordination problem in achieving the monitoring and other checks that large creditors are able to put in place. The purpose of bank regulation has been seen as the protection of the interests of depositors by putting into place through regulation the restrictions on the manager's actions that would arise in normal creditor–debtor relationships.

The traditional rationale for capital regulation leads naturally to the conclusion that the key determinant of the size of the regulatory capital buffer should be the riskiness of the assets. If the purpose of regulation is ensuring solvency, then the riskiness of assets determines the size of the regulatory capital buffer required. This is because the degree to which solvency can be ensured depends on the likelihood that the realized value of assets falls below the notional value of the creditors' claim. The original Basel capital accord of 1988 introduced coarse risk buckets into which assets could be classified, but the Basel II rules have taken the idea much further, by refining the gradations of the riskiness of the assets, and fine-tuning the regulatory capital to the risks of the assets held by the bank.

However, the fall of Northern Rock and the turmoil in the financial system more generally in the 2007/8 financial crisis pose a challenge to the traditional view of regulation. The traditional capital buffer view of financial regulation misses the importance of externalities generated by the actions of one financial institution that impact on the interests of others. In particular, the balance sheet maturity mismatch, when embedded in a system context, generates stresses that result as a consequence of unintended actions. The prudent reduction of exposures by the creditors of Northern Rock, Bear Stearns or Lehman Brothers was a run from the point of view of these institutions.

There are two specific proposals that deserve closer attention. The first is some type of liquidity regulation that imposes constraints on the composition of assets, rather than a quantitative restriction on the relative size of total assets relative to equity (which is the more traditional capital regulation). The second is a limit on the raw leverage ratio, rather than on risk-weighted assets.

The rationale for liquidity regulation is to put in place some restrictions on the composition of assets. The ideas are discussed in more detail in Morris and Shin (2008, 2009). The rationale is that a bank can survive a run if (1) it has sufficient liquid assets and cash or (2) it has sufficiently stable (i.e. illiquid) liabilities, such as long-term debt.

Moreover, the liquidity requirement may not be too onerous if the requirement is adhered to widely in the financial system. The idea is that when small liquidity buffers are distributed widely in the financial system, spillover effects can be mitigated by amplifying the buffer effects, just as the absence of liquidity buffers will tend to amplify shocks that reverberate inside the system.

The theme of leverage constraints is taken up in more detail in the next chapter. The argument for a raw leverage constraint is that it can act as a binding constraint "on the way up" when banks increase leverage on the back of permissive funding conditions. The build-up of excessive leverage makes the system vulnerable to a shock that raises the implicit haircuts, and hence lowers the permitted leverage. By preventing the build-up of leverage during good times, the leverage constraint could act as a dampener in the financial system.

The leverage constraint works at the level of both the debtor, as well as the creditor. Refer to the example in Figure 8.8 again. From the point of view of bank 1 (the debtor), the leverage constraint will prevent bank 1 building up excessive leverage, thereby making bank 1 less susceptible to a tick-up in the implied haircut. From the point of view of bank 2 (the creditor), the leverage constraint binds "on the way up", so that when eventually the tide turns, there is slack in the balance sheet capacity of bank 2. Hence, its lending to bank 1 will suffer a smaller shock to any rise in implied haircuts. Thus, for both the lender and the borrower, the leverage constraint binds during boom times so that the imperative to reduce leverage is less strong in the bust. Indeed, the bust may be averted altogether, as the initial boom is dampened.

The most commonly encountered criticism of a raw leverage constraint is that it does not take account of the riskiness of the assets. Basel II rules specify a very finely graduated capital requirement that depends on minute shifts in measured risks of the asset portfolio. A simple leverage ratio is seen as throwing away all the finely calibrated calculations of asset risk. However, when viewed through the lens of systemic stability, the leverage ratio constraint has desirable properties that cannot be replicated by risk-based capital ratios alone.

Northern Rock was a victim of its earlier success. The rapid growth of its balance on the back of benign credit conditions propelled it to being the most innovative and celebrated bank in the UK, winning numerous prizes along the way from industry sponsors and generally being the toast of the UK banking industry. However, the high implied leverage that was built up during the boom times was vulnerable to a reversal in the permitted leverage implicit in market haircuts. When, eventually, the tide turned, the balance sheet maturity mismatch of Northern Rock's balance sheet proved to be its undoing.

The Northern Rock episode raises many profound questions on the economic rationale for maturity mismatch on banks' balance sheets, and the potential role of financial regulation to mitigate the inefficiencies. A liquidity requirement combined with a raw leverage ratio may have some role to play in mitigating the system-wide externalities generated by one financial institution that impact on the interests of others. Financial regulation then has the role of imposing the appropriate Pigovian taxes that internalize the externalities as much as possible. The Pigovian tax perspective is likely to yield better insights into system stability than the traditional risk-based capital requirements under the Basel process.

9

Securitization and the Financial System

The global financial crisis that erupted in the summer of 2007 has the distinction of being the first post-securitization crisis in which banking and capital market developments have been closely intertwined. Historically, banks have always reacted to changes in the external environment, expanding and contracting lending in reaction to shifts in economic conditions. However, in a market-based financial system built on securitization, banking and capital market developments are inseparable, and the recent crisis is a live illustration of the potency of the interaction between the two.

Securitization was meant to disperse credit risk to deep-pocketed investors who were well-placed to share in any losses from defaults. But in the financial crisis, the risks appear to have been concentrated in the financial intermediary sector itself, rather than with the deep-pocketed final investors. To understand the true role played by securitization in the financial crisis, we need to dispose of two pieces of received wisdom concerning securitization—one old and one new. The old view, now discredited, emphasized the positive role played by securitization in dispersing credit risk, thereby enhancing the resilience of the financial system to defaults by borrowers.

But having disposed of this old conventional wisdom, the new fashion is to emphasize the chain of unscrupulous operators who passed on bad loans to the greater fool next in the chain. We could dub this less charitable view the "hot potato" hypothesis, and it has figured frequently in speeches given by policy makers on the credit crisis. The motto would be that there is always a greater fool next in the securitization chain who will buy the bad loan. At the end of the chain, according to this view, is the hapless final investor who ends up holding the hot potato and suffers the eventual loss. A celebrated anonymous cartoon strip has circulated widely on the internet,[1] depicting a hapless official from a Norwegian municipality in conversation with his broker after suffering losses on subprime mortgage securities. There is mounting empirical evidence that lending standards had been lowered progressively in the run-up to the credit crisis of 2007 (see Demyanyk and van Hemert 2007; Keys et al. 2007; and Mian and Sufi 2007).

But the new conventional wisdom is just as flawed as the old one. Not only does it fall foul of the fact that securitization worked well for thirty years before the subprime crisis, it fails to distinguish between *selling* a bad loan down the chain and *issuing liabilities* backed by bad loans. By selling a bad loan, you get rid

---

[1] For instance <http://bigpicture.typepad.com/comments/2008/02/how-subprime-re.html>.

of the bad loan and it's someone else's problem. In this sense, the hot potato is passed down the chain to the greater fool next in the chain. However, by issuing liabilities against bad loans, you do not get rid of the bad loan. The hot potato is sitting on your balance sheet or on the books of the special purpose vehicles that you are sponsoring. Thus, far from passing the hot potato down the chain, you end up keeping the hot potato. In effect, the large financial intermediaries are the last in the chain. While the investors who buy your securities end up losing money, the financial intermediaries that have issued the securities are in danger of larger losses. Since the intermediaries are leveraged, they are in danger of having their equity wiped out, as some have found to their cost.

Indeed, Greenlaw, et al. (2008) report that of the approximately $1.4 trillion total exposure to subprime mortgages, around half of the potential losses were borne by US leveraged financial institutions, such as commercial banks, securities firms, and hedge funds. When foreign leveraged institutions are included, the total exposure of leveraged financial institutions rises to two-thirds (see Table 9.1). Far from passing on the bad loans to the greater fool next in the chain, the most sophisticated financial institutions amassed the largest exposures to the bad assets. Gorton (2008) also argues against the hot potato hypothesis by noting that financial intermediaries have borne a large share of the total losses. In the game of passing the hot potato to the greater fool next in the chain, the largest and most sophisticated financial institutions were the last in the chain—they were the greatest fools. How can this fact be explained?

To get at the answer to this puzzle, it is useful to review some historical background. Securitization has played a crucial role in the growth of residential mortgage lending in the last thirty years or so, especially in the United States. Figure 9.1 plots the total outstanding US home mortgage assets held by various classes of financial institutions from 1980. Even as recently as the early 1980s, banks and savings institutions held the bulk of home mortgages. Since then, the

Table 9.1: Subprime Exposures by Type of Institution

	Total reported sub-prime exposure (US$bn)	Percent of reported exposure
Investment banks	75	5
Commercial banks	418	31
GSEs	112	8
Hedge funds	291	21
Insurance companies	319	23
Finance companies	95	7
Mutual and pension funds	57	4
Leveraged sector	896	66
Unleveraged sector	472	34
Total	1,368	100

Source: Greenlaw et al. (2008).

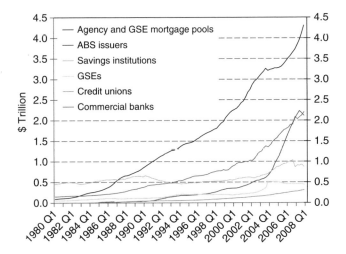

Figure 9.1: US home mortgage assets (1980 Q1 – 2008 Q1)
Source: US Federal Reserve, Flow of Funds.

mortgage pools of the government-sponsored enterprises (GSEs) such as Fannie Mae and Freddie Mac have become the largest holders of residential mortgages. Also noticeable are the securitization vehicles classified under asset-backed securities (ABS) issuers. ABS issuers hold mortgages that do not conform to GSE standards, and hence they hold subprime mortgages as well as large mortgages ("jumbo" mortgages) that exceed the upper threshold on the GSE guaranteed mortgages.

Figure 9.2 is an aggregate series that distinguishes the "bank-based" holdings of residential mortgages from the "market-based" holdings. The latter is the sum of the holdings of the government-sponsored enterprises, the GSE mortgage pools, and the private label ABS issuers. The bank-based series is the sum of the remaining three categories. We can see that the market-based series overtook the bank-based series in 1990, and now accounts for two-thirds of the nearly $11 trillion worth of residential mortgages outstanding.

The changing nature of mortgage lending toward market-based institutions has meant that the nature of financial intermediation has undergone far-reaching changes. A characteristic feature of financial intermediation based on the US-style securitization system is the long chains of financial intermediaries involved in channeling funds from ultimate creditors to ultimate borrowers. The difference can be illustrated in the contrast between short and long intermediation chains seen in an earlier chapter in Figures 6.6 and 6.7.

In the illustration of the long intermediation chain in Figure 6.7, the mortgage asset is held in a mortgage pool—a passive firm whose sole role is to hold mortgage assets and issue liabilities (mortgage-backed securities, MBSs) against

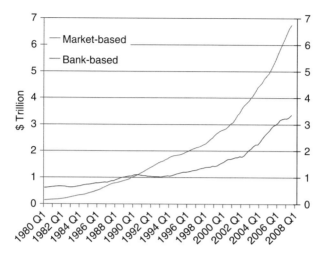

Figure 9.2: Bank-based and market-based home mortgage holdings (1980 Q1 – 2008 Q1)
Source: US Federal Reserve, flow of Funds.

those assets. The mortgage-backed securities might then be owned by an asset-backed security (ABS) issuer who pools and tranches the MBSs into another layer of claims, such as collateralized debt obligations (CDOs). Then, a securities firm (a Wall Street bank, say) might hold CDOs on their own books for their yield, but finances such assets by collateralized borrowing through repurchase agreements (repos) with a larger commercial bank. In turn, the commercial bank would fund its lending to the securities firm by issuing short-term liabilities, such as financial commercial paper. Money market mutual funds would be natural buyers of such short-term paper, and ultimately the money market fund would complete the circle, since household savers would own shares in these funds. Martin Hellwig (1994, 1995) has been one of the early voices to comment on the trend of lengthening intermediation chains and the possible consequences of such lengthening chains for financial stability.

What is noticeable from the institutions involved in Figure 6.7 is that they were precisely those institutions that were at the sharp end of the financial crisis of 2007 and 2008. Subprime mortgages cropped up in this chain, and the failure of Bear Stearns and Lehman Brothers was owing to problems in the smooth function of this chain. This realization begs the question of what advantages can be gained by such long intermediation chains.

One possible argument might be that securitization enables the disperson of credit risk to those who can best bear losses. We have already commented on the apparent failure of this particular mechanism, but we will return to examine it more closely below. Leaving that to one side, another possible justification for long intermediation chains is that there is an inherent need for maturity transformation in the financial system because ultimate creditors demand short-term claims, and that the process of stringing together long lending relationships makes it easier to perforin the overall maturity transformation role.

There are well-known arguments in favor of the desirability of short-term debt for incentive reasons—in particular, in disciplining managers. We have already encountered the arguments of Calomiris and Kahn (1991) and Diamond and Rajan (2001) that demand deposits for banking arose naturally as a response by the bank's owners and managers to commit not to engage in actions that dissipate the value of the assets, under pain of triggering a depositor run.

However, in both Calomiris and Kahn (1991) and Diamond and Rajan (2001), the focus is on traditional bank deposits, where the creditors are not financial intermediaries themselves. What is notable about the financial boom and bust cycle witnessed recently is that the largest fluctuations in ultra-short-term debt have not been associated with liabilities to retail depositors, but rather with liabilities to other financial intermediaries. Adrian and Shin (2009) compare the stock of repurchase agreements of US primary dealers plus the stock of financial commercial paper (CP) expressed as a proportion of the M2 stock. M2 includes the bulk of retail deposits and holdings in money market mutual funds, and so is a good proxy for the total stock of liquid claims held by ultimate creditors against the financial intermediary sector as a whole. As recently as the early 1990s, repos and financial CP were only a quarter of the size of M2. However, the total rose rapidly, reaching over 80% of M2 by the eve of the financial crisis in August 2007, only to collapse with the onset of the crisis.

The ultra-short-term nature of financial intermediaries obligations to each other can be better seen when plotting the overnight repos component of the overall repo series. Figure 9.3 plots the size of the overnight repo stock, financial commercial paper and M2, normalized to be equal to 1 on July 6, 1994 (the data on overnight repos are not available before that date). The stock of M2 has grown by a factor of around 2.4 since 1994, but the stock of overnight repos grew almost seven-fold up to March 2008. Brunnermeier (2009) has noted that the use of overnight repos became so prevalent that, at its peak, the Wall Street investment banks were rolling over a quarter of their balance sheets every night. What is evident from Figure 9.3 is that the rapid growth and subsequent collapse of the overnight repos cannot be easily explained by the demand for short-term liquid claims of retail depositors.

A more promising route to explaining the boom and bust is to appeal to the consequences of balance sheet management in an era when measured risks are low. As balance sheets expand, new borrowers must be found. *Someone* has to be on the receiving end of the new loans. When all prime borrowers already have a mortgage, but balance sheets still need to expand, then banks have to lower their lending standards in order to lend to subprime borrowers.

When the downturn arrives, the bad loans are either sitting on the balance sheets of the large financial intermediaries, or they are in special purpose vehicles (SPVs) that are sponsored by them. This is so, since the bad loans were taken on precisely in order to utilize the slack on their balance sheets created by the

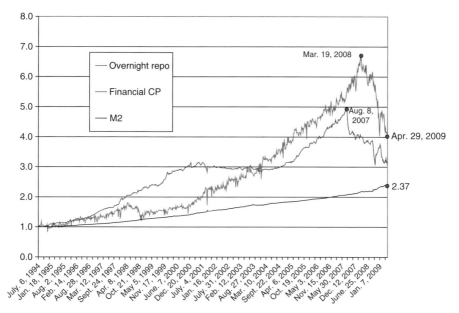

Figure 9.3: Overnight repos, financial commercial paper, and M2 (normalized to 1 on July 6, 1994)

apparent lull in measured risks. Although final investors such as pension funds and insurance companies will suffer losses, too, the large financial intermediaries are more exposed in the sense that they face the danger of seeing their capital wiped out. The reason for the severity of the recent credit crisis lies precisely in the fact that the bad loans were *not* all passed on to final investors. Instead, the "hot potato" was sitting inside the financial system, on the balance sheet of the largest, and most sophisticated, financial intermediaries.

9.1 ACCOUNTING FRAMEWORK REVISITED

In order to have a framework to think about securitization and its impact on the workings of the financial system as a whole, it is useful to revisit the accounting identities for the financial system examined earlier in Chapter 6. We will use the same notation as we did then. Denote by Yi the market value of the claims held by bank i on the ultimate borrowers, such as household mortgages or consumer loans. For our purposes, it does not matter much whether y_i is in face values or market values. However, in what follows, it is useful to interpret all quantities as being in market values, since the comparative statics take on additional richness due to valuation effects.

As well as claims on ultimate borrowers, the banks hold claims against each other. Denote by x_i the total value of the liabilities of bank i, by x_{ij} the value of bank i's liabilities held by bank j and by π_{ij} the share of bank i's liabilities that are held by bank j. Denoting by e_i the value of equity of bank i, the balance sheet of bank i is

Assets	Liabilities	
y_i	e_i	(9.1)
$\sum_{j=1}^{n} x_j \pi_{ji}$	x_i	

The balance sheet identity of bank i is:

$$y_i + \sum_j x_j \pi_{ji} = e_i + x_i \qquad (9.2)$$

The left-hand side is the value of assets and the right-hand side is the sum of debt (x_i) and equity (e_i). The matrix of claims and obligations between banks can then be depicted as below. The (i, j)th entry in the table is the debt owed by bank i to bank j. Then, the ith row of the matrix can be summed to give the total value of debt of bank i, while the ith column of the matrix can be summed to give the total assets of bank i. We can give the index $n+1$ to the outside creditor sector (households, pension funds, mutual funds etc.), so that $x_{i,n+1}$ denotes bank i's liabilities to outside claimholders. Deposits would be the prime example of a liability that a bank has directly to outside creditors.

	bank 1	bank 2	$\cdots$	bank n	outside	debt
bank 1	0	x_{12}	$\cdots$	x_{1n}	$x_{1,n+1}$	x_1
bank 2	x_{21}	0	$\cdots$	x_{2n}	$x_{2,n+1}$	x_2
$\vdots$	$\vdots$	$\vdots$	$\ddots$	$\vdots$	$\vdots$	
bank n	x_{n1}	x_{n2}	$\cdots$	0	$x_{n,n+1}$	x_n
end-user loans	y_1	y_2	$\cdots$	y_n		
total assets	a_1	a_2		a_n		

Following our earlier argument in Chapter 6, the total lending to end-user borrowers $\sum_i y_i$ can be written as:

$$\sum_{i=1}^{n} y_i = \sum_{i=1}^{n} e_i z_i (\lambda_i - 1) + \sum_{i=1}^{n} e_i \qquad (9.3)$$

Equation (9.3) is the key balance-sheet identity for the financial sector as a whole, where all the claims and obligations between banks have been netted out.

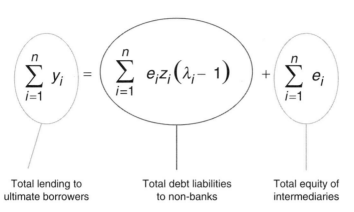

Figure 9.4: Aggregate balance sheet identity

The left-hand side is the total lending to end-user borrowers. The second term on the right-hand side of (9.3) is the total equity of the banking system, and the first term is the total funding to the banking sector provided by the *outside* claim-holders (note that the second term can be written as $\sum_{i=1}^{n} x_i z_i$). Ultimately, credit supply to end-users must come either from the equity of the banking system, or from the funding provided by non-banks.

The total debt liabilities of the banking sector to the household creditors can be expected to be sticky, and will be related to total household assets. Thus, the expression in the balloon in Figure 9.4 labelled "total debt liabilities to non-banks" will be slow-moving, in line with shifts in the total household holding of debt claims on the banking sector. For the purposes of short-term comparative statics, we could treat it as being approximately constant. If we treat the expression in the central balloon as a constant, we learn much about the impact of various shifts in the parameters on the configuration of the financial system. We now examine two scenarios.

9.2 BOOM SCENARIO

Consider a boom scenario where the marked-to-market equity of the banks are healthy such (the profile of equity $\{e_i\}$ is strong) and the decline in measured risks leads to an increase in leverage $\{\lambda_i\}$. In order for the expression in the central balloon to remain roughly constant, there must be an overall decline in $\{z_i\}$, the proportion of funding coming from outside claimholders. In other words, banks must lend more to each other in order to achieve their desired risk-taking profile and leverage, given their strong capital position. In such a scenario, banks take on more of each other's debts and the intertwining of claims and liabilities becomes more far-reaching. The image is of an increasingly elaborate edifice built on the same narrow foundation, so that the structure becomes more and more precarious. The systemic risks therefore increase during the boom scenario. Adrian and Brunnermeier (2009), IMF (2009), and Andy Haldane (2009) have highlighted the heightened nature of the interwoven risks in the financial system.

Our accounting identity above shows why such closely interconnected balance sheets are a necessary feature of a boom scenario when banks have strong capital positions and measured risks are low. For any fixed pool of funding to be drawn from the household sector, any substantial increase in balance-sheet size of the financial intermediaries can be achieved only by *borrowing and lending to each other*. The key variables are the $\{z_i\}$, which gives the proportion of funding obtained from outside the intermediary sector. In order to increase the profile of leverage $\{\lambda_i\}$ within the intermediary sector, the banks must lower the funding profile $\{z_i\}$, since they are competing for the same limited pool of outside funding. The banks can raise their risk exposure to their desired level only by borrowing and lending between themselves, since outside funding is inadequate to meet their growing needs.

An architectural analogy is appropriate. In order to build additional rooms in a house whose footprint is limited by shortage of land, the only way is to build upward—like a skyscraper in Manhattan. The lower is the funding profile $\{z_i\}$ the taller is the skyscraper. However, even this analogy is somewhat misleading, in that the Manhattan skyscraper would be planned in advance and built as a coherent whole. An interconnected financial system that builds upward is much less coordinated, and hence is liable to result in greater unintended spillover effects. It would be as if additional floors are built on top of existing ones, where the architects of the lower floors did not anticipate further building on top.[2]

Shortening of maturities would be a natural counterpart to the lengthening intermediation chains. In order for each link in the chain to be a profitable leveraged transaction, the funding leg of the transaction must be at a lower interest rate. When the yield curve is upward-sloping, this would entail funding with shorter and shorter maturities at each step in the chain. The prevalence of the overnight repo as the dominant funding choice for securities firms before the current crisis can be understood in this context. The use of ultra-short-term debt is part and parcel of long intermediation chains.

The importance of the short-term interest rate in determining the size and fragility of the financial system can be seen from the above line of reasoning. A period of sustained low short-term interest rates (with the assurance of continued low short rates by the central bank) is a highly favorable environment for the taking on of such short-term bets. Adrian and Shin (2008c) show that the Fed Funds rate is an important determinant of the growth of securities firms'

[2] Architecturally, the closest example would be the Sutyagin house in Archangel, Russia, reported in the *Daily Telegraph* of March 7, 2007. The 13-floor 144 feet wooden structure is described as "a jumble of planking" and the "eighth wonder of the world". A Google image search for "Sutyagin House" yields dozens of photos of the structure.

balance sheets, which in turn has significant effects on the real economy. Thus, there is a monetary policy angle to the increasing length of intermediation chains.

9.3 BUST SCENARIO

Now consider the reversal of the boom scenario whereby perceptions of heightened risk raise Value-at-Risk and induce deleveraging of the financial system, leading to lower $\{\lambda_i\}$. In addition, falls in asset prices and possible credit losses eat into the marked-to-market equity levels $\{e_i\}$. This is a double whammy for the financial system as a whole, since in order for the expression in the middle balloon in Figure 9.4 to stay roughly constant, there have to be substantial *increases* in $\{z_i\}$. The increase in z_i means that a greater proportion of the funding comes from outside claimholders—that is, the funding that banks had granted to each other must now be withdrawn. This is a classic run scenario where banks run on other banks. The runs on Northern Rock, Bear Stearns, and Lehman Brothers are all instances of such a run.

The direct manifestation of a run of this type can be given a simpler depiction in the following two bank examples examined earlier in Figure 8.8. From the point of view of bank 2, the imperative is to reduce its overall lending, including its lending to bank 1. By reducing its lending, bank 2 achieves its micro-prudential objective of reducing its risk exposure. However, from bank 1's perspective, the reduction of lending by bank 2 is a withdrawal of funding. Unless bank 1 can find alternative sources of funding, it will have to reduce its own asset holdings, either by curtailing its lending, or by selling marketable assets.

In the case where we have a combination of (i) bank 1 not having alternative sources of funding, (ii) the reduction in bank 2's lending being severe, and (iii) bank 1's assets being so illiquid that they can only be sold at fire-sale prices, then the withdrawal of lending by bank 2 will feel like a run from the point of view of bank 1. In other words, a prudent shedding of exposures from the point of view of bank 2 is a run from the point of view of bank 1. Arguably, this type of run is one element of what happened to Northern Rock, Bear Stearns, and Lehman Brothers.

9.4 PRESCRIPTIONS

The prescriptions for moderating the flucutations associated with the boom and busts scenarios can also be understood in terms of the aggregate balance-sheet identity (9.3). We discuss three in particular—regulatory interventions, various forms of forward-looking provisioning, and the reform of the institutions involved in financial intermediation.

Approach 1: Regulatory Intervention

The first approach is to moderate the fluctuations in leverage and balance-sheet size through capital regulation with an explicit countercyclical element, such as the countercyclical capital targets advocated in the recent Geneva Report (Brunnermeier et al. 2009) and the Squam Lake Working Group's memo on capital requirements (Squam Lake Working Group 2009). The leverage cap introduced in Switzerland recently (Hildebrand 2008) can also be understood in this connection.

Leverage caps or countercyclical capital targets aim at restraining the growth of leverage $\{\lambda_i\}$ in boom times so that the corresponding bust phase of the financial cycle is less damaging, or can be avoided altogether. In the aggregate balance-sheet identity depicted in Figure 9.4, moderating the fluctuations in $\{\lambda_i\}$ implies that the marked-to-market equity values $\{e_i\}$ and the outside financing proportions $\{z_i\}$ can also be kept within moderate bounds, so as to prevent the rapid build-up of cross-exposures which are then subsequently unwound in a disorderly way as runs against other banks.

A closely related set of proposals are those that address the *composition* of assets, rather than the capital ratio. The idea is to impose liquidity requirements on the banks so as to limit the externalities in the bust phase of the cycle. Cifuentes, Ferrucci, and Shin (2004) is an early statement of the proposal, subsequently incorporated in the Bank of England's RAMSI frarnework for systemic risk.[3]

Morris and Shin (2008, 2009) describe the rationale for liquidity requirements and provide an analysis of the mechanisms invoked. The idea is to take those elements that are responsible for the vicious circle of distress and self-reinforcing runs and then harness them to create a *virtuous circle* of beliefs, leading to a stable outcome. Liquidity requirements mandate a cushion of cash assets over some interval of time, such as requiring banks to maintain reserves at the central bank over some fixed maintenance period. Such liquidity requirements can moderate the externalities involved in a run by influencing the risks of spillovers across financial intermediaries. When a borrower bank has a high level of liquidity, then the withdrawal of funding by its creditor banks can be met (at least partly) by its liquid resources, which makes the debtor bank less likely to run on other banks.

For creditor banks, there are two effects. First, knowing that the debtor bank is less vulnerable to runs reduces the incentive to run that arises purely from a coordination motive. In addition, when each creditor bank realizes that other creditor banks have higher liquidity levels, the coordination problem among the creditor banks becomes less sensitive to strategic risk—making them less jittery when faced with a run scenario. The more relaxed attitudes of creditors and debtors are mutually reinforcing, just in the same way that distress and concerns about others' viability can be self-reinforcing. In this way, the same forces that

---

[3] The Bank of England's RAMSI framework is described in the recent issue of the IMF's *Global Financial Stability Report* (2009, chapter 2).

lead to the vicious circle of run psychology can be harnessed and channeled to generate a *virtuous circle* of stability.

Approach 2: Forward-Looking Provisioning

A second way to moderate the fluctuations of the boom-bust cycle is to operate directly on the equity $\{e_i\}$ of the banks. The forward-looking statistical provisioning scheme that has operated in Spain is a good example of such a method. By imposing a provisioning charge when new loans are made, there is a corresponding diminution of the equity level of the bank making the loan. In the aggregate balance-sheet identity depicted in Figure 9.4, we see that for any given desired leverage of the bank, a lower equity level means lower total assets, hence restraining the rapid growth of balance sheets.

The Spanish pre-provisioning scheme highlights one of the important lessons in a boom.[4] Under a boom scenario, the problem is that there is *too much equity* in the banking system. There is overcapacity in the sense that the level of aggregate capital is too high. Capital is higher than is consistent with only prudent loans being made. Overcapacity leads to the chasing of yields and the lowering of credit standards.

In the Geneva Report (Brunnermeier et al. 2009), the authors discuss the merits of a variant of the Spanish pre-provisioning scheme called the Pigovian tax. The idea is that rather than reducing equity through a forward-looking provision, equity can also be lowered in a boom through an explicit centralized tax. The tax has the potential to enhance the efficiency of the overall financial system in the same way as a congestion charge would improve traffic in a city. By counteracting an existing inefficiency through a tax, one can counteract the harmful externality. Just as with a traffic congestion charge, the revenue raised in the tax is not an essential component of the scheme. However, if the revenue raised through the Pigovian tax could be put into a separate bank resolution fund, then the scheme would not imply a net transfer away from the banking sector.

Approach 3: Structural Reform of Intermediation

A third approach is more long term, and is aimed at influencing the market structure of the financial intermediary sector as a whole. The idea is to restrain the lengthening of intermediation chains, and encourage the formation of shorter intermediation chains.

In terms of the aggregate balance-sheet identity depicted in Figure 9.4, the objective is to operate directly on the mode of financial intermediation so that the funding profile $\{z_i\}$ is maintained at high levels, thereby limiting the number of intermediaries n and moderating the fluctuations in leverage and total assets.

---

[4] For a description of the Spanish pre-provisioning system, see the Bank of Spain working paper by Fernandez et al. (2000).

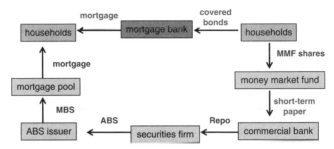

Figure 9.5: Shortening the intermediation chain through covered bonds

The idea is to induce a shortening of the financial intermediation chain by linking ultimate borrowers and ultimate lenders more directly.

One potential way to induce such shortening of the intermediation chain would be through the encouragement of the issuance of covered bonds—bonds issued against segregated assets on a bank's balance sheet, with recourse against the issuing bank itself. Figure 9.5 illustrates.

The intermediation chain associated with a covered bond is short, since the bank holds mortgage claims against ultimate borrowers, and issues covered bonds that could be sold directly to households or to long-only institutions such as mutual funds or pension funds. The bonds offer longer duration that matches the duration of the assets. The longer duration of the liabilities has two advantages. First, the duration matching between assets and liabilities means that the issuing bank does not engage in maturity transformation in funding. Rigorous application of marking to market makes less sense when loans are segregated to back such liabilties. In the Geneva Report, the authors have argued that the accounting treatment of such assets can take account of what the banks are *capable* of holding, rather than simply appealing to their *intentions*, as is the rule under the current mark-to-market accounting rules.

Second, the fact that liabilities have long duration means that the short-term funding that is prevalent in the long intermediation chains will be less likely to be employed, provided that the covered bonds are held directly by households or by long-only institutions such as pension funds and mutual funds. The long duration of such securities would be a natural source of sought-after duration for pension funds that wish to match the long duration of their pension liabilities. We saw in Chapter 5 the value of such long duration assets to pension funds that wish to hedge against the fluctuations in the market value of their pension liabilities. Household savers would also find such products a good substitute for government bond funds. The shortening of the intermediation chain in this way will have important benefits in terms of mitigating the fluctuations in leverage and balance-sheet size in the financial boom-bust cycle.

Covered bonds have been a familiar feature of many European countries, especially in Denmark (with its mortgage bonds) and Germany (with its *pfandbriefe*).

But to date, over twenty countries in Europe have some form of covered bonds backed by laws that underpin their role in the financial system. Packer, Stever, and Upper (2007), in a recent overview of the covered bond system, report that as of mid-2007 the outstanding amount of covered bonds reached 1.7 trillion euros.

Covered bonds are securities issued by a bank and backed by a dedicated, segregated group of loans known as a "cover pool". The bondholders have two safeguards in their holding of covered bonds. First, the bonds are backed by the cover pool over which the bondholders have senior claims in case of bankruptcy. Second, because the covered bonds are the obligations of the issuing bank, the bondholders have recourse to the bank if the cover pool is insufficient to meet the bond obligations. In this second sense, covered bonds differ from the US-style mortgage-backed security, which are obligations of the special purpose vehicle— a passive company whose sole purpose is to hold assets and issue liabilities against those assets. The loans backing the covered bonds stay on the balance sheet of the bank, eliminating one step in the intermediation chain, and also guarding against potential incentive problems in the "originate to distribute" model of securitization in which the originating bank can sell the loan and take it off its balance sheet altogether.

The double protection offered by covered bonds distinguishes them both from senior unsecured debt and asset-backed securities (ABSs). In contrast to ABSs, the cover pool serves mainly as credit enhancement and not as a means to obtain exposure to the underlying assets. Also, cover pools tend to be dynamic in the sense that issuers are allowed to replace assets that have either lost some quality or have been repaid early. These features imply that covered bonds are seen not so much as an instrument to obtain exposure to credit risk, but rather as a higher-yielding alternative to government securities.

These payoff attributes of covered bonds are reflected in the identity of the investors who hold them. The identity of the investors are critical in determining the funding profile $\{z_i\}$ of the intermediation sector. The objective of achieving a higher funding profile is achieved if the investors are either household savers or non-bank institutions such as pension funds and mutual funds. A survey of the investors in covered bonds was released in May 2009 by the European Covered Bond Dealers Association (SIFMA 2009), and is reproduced in Figure 9.6. We see that the bulk of the investors in covered bonds are non-banks, with the largest category being asset management firms. Leveraged institutions and intermediaries constitute only around one-third of the total. Even within the intermediary sector, institutions such as private banks are closer to asset management firms in character than intermediaries such as broker dealers who lengthen the intermediation chain.

Even among covered bonds, the Danish system of mortgage bonds has attracted considerable attention recently as a resilient institutional framework for household mortgage finance due to the added feature that household mortgage borrowers can redeem their debt by purchasing the relevant issue of the mortgage bonds at the prevailing market price (see Boyce 2008). By being able to extinguish debt obligations at market prices, household borrowers participate

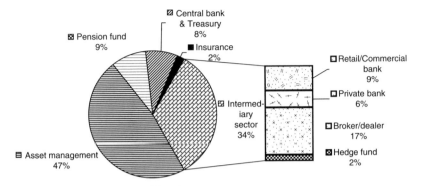

Figure 9.6: Investors in covered bonds
Source: SIFMA (2009).

as purchasers in the market for mortgage debt, and prevent the type of collapse in mortgage-backed securities seen in the United Slates in the financial crisis of 2007 and 2008.

The legislation required to underpin the operation of a covered bond system is more developed in some regions than others. Europe leads the world in this respect. In the European Union, covered bonds are defined by the Capital Requirements Directive (CRD), which limits the range of accepted collateral maximum loan-to-value ratios. While the CRD only recognizes securities issued under special legislation as covered bonds, market participants tend to work with a more general definition that also includes bonds issued under private contractual arrangements, using elements from structured finance. There have been a number of such "structured covered bonds", primarily in countries without covered bond legislation (e.g. the United Kingdom, the Netherlands, and the United States) (see Packer et al. 2007).

Indeed, one of the main barrier against the widespread introduction of a covered bond system has been the legal hurdle of introducing a class of claimholders for the cover pool that are senior to the deposit insurance agency, and hence the general depositors of the bank. The larger is the cover pool for covered bonds, the smaller is the general pool of assets that are accessible to the deposit insurance agency. In the United States, the FDIC has issued a statement on the treatment of covered bonds, limiting the size of covered bonds to 4% of total liabilities after issuance.[5] Given the benefits associated with the shortening of the intermediation chain, there are legitimate questions vex how much political will can be mustered in order to amend the relavant laws to allow the operation of the covered bond system.

A possible alternative legal approach would be to permit specialist "narrow" banks whose liabilities are restricted to covered bonds only, and hence whose

---

[5] The FDIC's statement on covered bonds is at <http://www.fdic.gov/news/news/financial/2008/fil08073.html>.

liabilities are not insured by the deposit insurance agency. Such narrow banks would be akin to Danish mortgage banks, whose liabilities match the duration of the assets perfectly and whose equity provides a cushion for bond holders. There is a need to focus on the overall systemic impact of long versus short intermediation chains. Long intermediation chains have been associated with the rapid development of the securitized, market-based financial system in the United States. I have argued that long intermediation chains carry costs in terms of greater amplitude of fluctuations in the boom-bust cycle of leverage and balance-sheet size. Shorter intermediation chains carry benefits for stability of the financial system.

9.5 SIZE OF BANKING SECTOR

What determines the size of the banking sector relative to the real economy? The total size of the banking sector in gross terms can be written as the sum of all bank assets, given by $\sum_{i=1}^{n} a_i$. A closely related measure would be the aggregate value of all bank debt, given by $\sum_{i=1}^{n} x_i$. However, we have seen that the aggregate size of the banking sector does not tell us how much credit flows to the ultimate borrowers, unless we have more information on the extent of double-counting involved when adding balance-sheet quantities across banks. However, since aggregate balance-sheet statistics incorporate such double-counting, it is useful to have a framework that relates aggregate balance-sheet numbers to net credit to ultimate borrowers.

To address the extent of double-counting, begin with the definition of leverage λ_i, the ratio of total assets to equity of bank i. Leverage is given by

$$\lambda_i = \frac{a_i}{a_i - x_i} \tag{9.4}$$

Then, solving for x_i and using the notation $\delta_i = 1 - \frac{1}{\lambda_i}$, we have

$$x_i = \delta_i \left(y_i + \sum_j x_j \pi_{ji} \right)$$

$$= \delta_i y_i + [x_1 \cdots x_n] \begin{bmatrix} \delta_i \pi_{1i} \\ \vdots \\ \delta_i \pi_{ni} \end{bmatrix} \tag{9.5}$$

Let $x = [x_1 \cdots x_n]$, $y = [y_1 \cdots y_n]$, and define the diagonal matrix Δ as follows.

$$\Delta = \begin{bmatrix} \delta_1 & & \\ & \ddots & \\ & & \delta_n \end{bmatrix} \tag{9.6}$$

Then we can write (9.5) in vector form as:

$$x = y\Delta + x\Pi\Delta$$

Solving for x,

$$
\begin{aligned}
x &= y\Delta(I - \Pi\Delta)^{-1} \\
&= y\Delta\left(I + \Pi\Delta + (\Pi\Delta)^2 + (\Pi\Delta)^3 + \cdots\right)
\end{aligned}
\tag{9.7}
$$

The matrix $\Pi\Delta$ is given by

$$
\Pi\Delta =
\begin{bmatrix}
0 & \delta_2\pi_{12} & \cdots & \delta_n\pi_{1n} \\
\delta_1\pi_{21} & 0 & & \delta_n\pi_{2n} \\
\vdots & & \ddots & \vdots \\
\delta_1\pi_{n1} & \delta_2\pi_{n2} & \cdots & 0
\end{bmatrix}
\tag{9.8}
$$

The infinite series in (9.7) converges since the rows of $\Pi\Delta$ sum to a number strictly less than 1, so that the inverse $(I - \Pi\Delta)^{-1}$ is well-defined.

Equation (9.7) gives us a clue as to what to look for when gauging the extent of the double-counting of lending to ultimate borrowers that results from heavy use of funding raised from other financial intermediaries. The comparison is between y, which is the profile of lending to the ultimate borrowers in the economy and x, which is the profile of debt values across all banks which give a gross measure of balance-sheet size. The factor that relates the two is the matrix:

$$\Delta\left(I + \Pi\Delta + (\Pi\Delta)^2 + (\Pi\Delta)^3 + \cdots\right)$$

This matrix has a finite norm, since the infinite series $I + \Pi\Delta + (\Pi\Delta)^2 + (\Pi\Delta)^3 + \cdots$ converges to $(I - \Pi\Delta)^{-1}$. However, for a financial system where leverage is high and banks are tightly interwoven, the norm can grow without bound. This is because as leverage becomes large, $\delta_i \to 1$, so that Δ tends to the identity matrix. Moreover, as the extent of interconnections between banks become large, the norm of the matrix Π converges to 1, since then each row of Π will sum to a number that converges to 1. In the limit as $\Delta \to I$ and $\|\Pi\| \to 1$, the norm of the matrix $\Delta\ (I + \Pi\Delta + (\Pi\Delta)^2 + (\Pi\Delta)^3 + \cdots)$ grows without bound.

The consequence of this result is that the size of the financial intermediation sector relative to the size of the economy as a whole can vary hugely over the financial cycle. We can illustrate this phenomenon with Figures 9.7 and 9.8, which show the growth of four sectors in the United States from 1954. The four sectors are (i) the non-financial corporate sector, (ii) the household sector, (iii) the commercial banking sector, and (iv) the security broker-dealer sector. The data are taken from the Federal Reserve's Flow of Funds accounts. The series are normalized so that the size in Q1 1954 is set equal to 1. Three of the four sectors grew to roughly 80 times their size in 1954, but the broker-dealer sector grew to

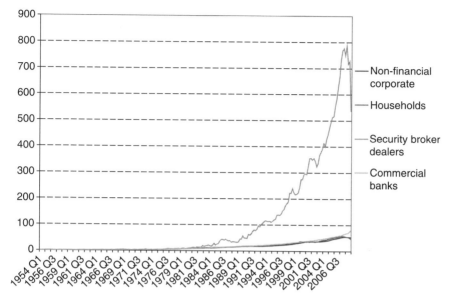

Figure 9.7: Growth of four US sectors (1954 Q1=1)
Source: Federal Reserve, Flow of Funds.

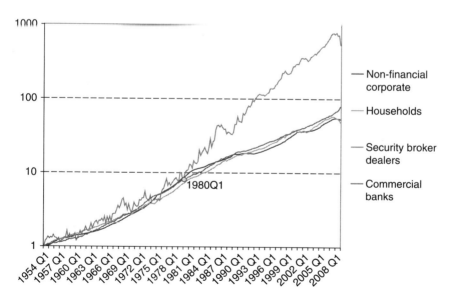

Figure 9.8: Growth of four US sectors (1954 Q1 = 1) (in log scale)
Source: Federal Reserve, Flow of Funds.

around 800 times its 1954 level at the height of the boom, before collapsing in the recent crisis.

Figure 9.8 is the same chart, but in log scale. The greater detail afforded by the chart in log scale reveals that the securities sector kept pace with the rest of the economy until around 1980, but then started a growth spurt that outstripped the other sectors. On the eve of the crisis, the securities sector had grown to around ten times its size relative to the other sectors in the economy. Clearly, such a pace of growth could not go on forever. Even on an optimstic scenario, the growth of the securities sector would have tapered off to a more sustainable pace to keep in step with the rest of the economy.

The relative size of the securities sector can be seen as a mirror of the lengthening intermediation chains in the market-based system of financial intermediation. One could reasonably conclude that some of the baroque flourishes that appeared in the Indian summer of the expansion of the securities sector (such as the growth of exotic asset-backed securities such as CDO-squared) have gone for good, and are unlikely to feature in a steady state of the securities sector.

Overall, it would be reasonable to speculate that the securities sector that emerges from the current crisis in sustainable form will be smaller, with shorter intermediation chains, perhaps less profitable in aggregate, and with less maturity transformation. The backdrop to this development will be the regulatory checks and balances that are aimed at moderating the fluctuations in leverage and balance-sheet size that were instrumental in making the current financial crisis the most severe since the Great Depression.

10

A Fresh Start

In May 2001, a group at the Financial Markets Group (FMG) of the London School of Economics convened a conference to discuss the proposals from the Basel Committee on Banking Supervision on the new Basel II bank capital regulation proposals. The discussions at the conference resulted in a paper (Danielsson et al. 2001) that was submitted to the Basel Committee in response to their call for comments on the initial Basel II proposals. Three conclusions of the report were summarized in the report's executive summary in the following terms.

- The proposed regulations fail to consider the fact that risk is endogenous. Value-at-Risk can destabilise and induce crashes when they would not otherwise occur.

- Heavy reliance on credit rating agencies for the standard approach to credit risk is misguided as they have been shown to provide conflicting and inconsistent forecasts of individual clients' creditworthiness. They are unregulated and the quality of their risk estimates is largely unobservable.

- Financial regulation is inherently procyclical. Our view is that this set of proposals will, overall, exacerbate this tendency significantly. In so far as the purpose of financial regulation is to reduce the likelihood of systemic crisis, these proposals will actually tend to negate, not promote this useful purpose. (Danielsson et al. 2001, executive summary)

Eight years later, these conclusions still have resonance. But back in 2001, the group's proposals must have been as welcome as Banquo's ghost at Macbeth's banquet. The submission presumably failed the test of being "constructive", and it is hardly surprising that our comments did not have much impact on the ultimate direction of the Basel II process.

Realistically, none of us imagined that the submission would have a fundamental impact, although in our more optimistic moments we hoped that our arguments might have some marginal impact on the shape of the latest bell or whistle to be attached to the overall rules.

The Basel II rules could hardly be faulted for lack of *quantity* of financial regulation, if quantity is measured in terms of thickness of the rule books. The Basel II rules famously generated reams of paper, all the while sapping the energy and patience of the hapless cadre of officials debating the exact value to be attached to some parameter in the credit risk model. The flaw with Basel II lay rather in its twin assumptions—that the purpose of regulation is to ensure the soundness of individual institutions against the risk of loss on their assets, and that ensuring the soundness of each individual institution ensures the soundness of the system as a whole.

The Basel II process illustrates how changes in regulation are typically achieved incrementally. Incremental change has the strength that it builds on accumulated wisdom. But it is possible for such an incremental, and generally reactive, process to migrate over time in wrong, or just inferior, directions. It is a revealing piece of sociology on the intellectual underpinnings of the subject of economics and of the bureaucratic process. It is only with wrenching economic crises, such as the Great Depression, that there is a general willingness to review the fundamental tenets of the regulatory framework. With the global financial crisis that began in 2007, we may be experiencing another comparable shift in the collective willingness to review the foundations of regulation.

The financial crisis has generated a flurry of activity from numerous groupings with their own sets of proposals. The accumulated set of reports has some common themes, such as the importance of countering the procyclical nature of risk taking, and have sought to counter such trends by augmenting the existing set of rules.

The Geneva Report on the World Economy (Brunnermeier et al. 2009) argues for a fundamental reappraisal of the basis for financial regulation and sets out a proposal on how the existing Basel II regulations should be modified to incorporate macro-prudential goals—in particular, how the existing Basel II capital requirements ought to be modified by the multiplication by a systemic impact coefficient that depends on indicators of potential spillovers. The Squam Lake Working Group (2009) and Achrya and Richardson (2009) have also proposed changes in the rules governing bank capital that share the same purpose of curtailing the procyclical nature of the financial system, especially in the down-phase of the financial cycle when banks are close to insolvency. The resolution of problem banks has risen to the top of the agenda following the turmoil caused in the financial markets in 2008 and 2009. Appendix 1 of the report by the Committee on Capital Markets Regulation (CCMR 2009) gives a useful table listing the various reports that have been issued up to May 2009, and cross-listing the various proposals against each report.

However, as desirable as such regulatory changes are, they are almost certainly inadequate by themselves to meeting the challenge of the next boom-bust cycle. As seen in these lectures, the main culprit for the boom-bust cycle is the underpricing of risk in the boom phase of the cycle. To summarize Andrew Crockett once more, risks increase in booms, and are only manifested in busts.

The question is how well one can meet the underpricing of risks just with blunt regulatory tools that have to be codified and enforced as laws or regulations. Even if a new set of rules and laws can be put in place that would have been effective in preventing yesterday's crisis, there is little guarantee that they will continue to be effective against new crises, riding on the back of as yet unimagined innovations designed to circumvent the rules. Some commentators have taken the possibility of avoidance as a case against relying on countercyclical regulation altogether, in favor of private insurance schemes that have an automatic element (see Kashyap et al. 2008).

Many would part company with a sweeping rejection of the role of counter-cyclical regulation. Clearly, any regulation will be subject to constant probing for potential avenues for circumvention. But a leaky bucket is surely better than no bucket at all—all the more so, since any proposals for an automatic mechanisms for contingent capital and plans for orderly unwinding are fully consistent with an overlay of countercyclical capital regulation. But the skceptics do have a point on the effectiveness of an approach that relies solely on financial regulation, while everything else goes back to business as usual. Top of the list is monetary policy.

The dominant theme in central banking in recent years has been a narrow interpretation of the principle that the sole role of the central bank is to focus on stable consumer price inflation and stable output over some fixed horizon. The Tinbergen separation principle is often invoked to argue that the central bank's role is just to look after price stability, and that financial stability is the lot of a specialist regulatory agency. This narrow view of monetary policy has driven many of the institutional reforms around the world, exemplified by the institutional reforms that set up the UK's Financial Services Authority. No doubt, this trend is partly attributable to the dominant intellectual strands in macroeconomics ruling in academia and in central banks. The argument is laid out clearly in an often-cited speech by Ben Bernanke from 2002, when he was a governor of the Federal Reserve.[1]

My suggested framework for Fed policy regarding asset-market instability can be summarized by the adage, *Use the right tool for the job.*

As you know, the Fed has two broad sets of responsibilities. First, the Fed has a mandate from the Congress to promote a healthy economy—specifically, maximum sustainable employment, stable prices, and moderate long-term interest rates. Second, since its founding the Fed has been entrusted with the responsibility of helping to ensure the stability of the financial system. The Fed likewise has two broad sets of policy tools: It makes monetary policy, which today we think of primarily in terms of the setting of the overnight interest rate, the federal funds rate. And, second, the Fed has a range of powers with respect to financial institutions, including rule-making powers, supervisory oversight, and a lender-of-last resort function made operational by the Fed's ability to lend through its discount window. *By using the right tool for the job, I mean that, as a general rule, the Fed will do best by focusing its monetary policy instruments on achieving its macro goals—price stability and maximum sustainable employment—while using its regulatory, supervisory, and lender-of-last resort powers to help ensure financial stability.* (Emphasis added)

Here, Bernanke is enunciating a principle that would have commanded almost universal support when he gave the speech. Indeed, in spite of the financial crisis, the Tinbergen separation of monetary policy from policies toward financial stability is still the dominant intellectual strain within central banks. For those

---

[1] Bernanke (2002) <http://www.federalreserve.gov/boarddocs/speeches/2002/20021015/default.htm>.

who espouse the Tinbergen principle, the new activist proposals for financial supervision and regulation are an opportunity to go back to business as usual, focusing monetary policy on the narrow issues of consumer price inflation and the output gap, leaving the messy and unglamorous business of supervising banks and ensuring financial stability to others—perhaps in another part of the central bank, separated from the core of the organization that conducts monetary policy.

Thus, the greatest dangers of a consensus on the need for countercyclical regulation arise from not only from circumvention of the rules, but also from the opportunities that the consensus will present to unreformed central banks to repeat their mistakes by taking a blinkered attitude to the financial system.

As we have seen in this book, financial stability is about regulating the price of risk, and monetary policy is inextricably linked to the pricing of risk. Changes to financial regulation will be for nothing if the intellectual landscape at the institution at the core of the financial system (the central bank) does not change. If the central bank is unaware of the importance of financial stability, then changes in institutional arrangements, however far reaching, will have been for nothing.

Bernanke's 2002 speech is a revealing window on the mainstream thinking at the time about how far monetary policy should take account of financial stability goals. Indeed, the debate itself is posed narrowly as whether central banks should "prick" asset price bubbles. The suggested answer is "no" for the following reasons.

- Identifying a bubble is difficult.
- Even if there were a bubble, monetary policy is not the right policy tool in addressing the problem. An asset price bubble will not respond to small changes in interest rates. Only a drastic increase in interest rates will prick the bubble.
- However, such a drastic increase in interest rates will cause more harm than good to the economy in terms of future output and output volatility.

The claim that an asset price bubble will not respond to a small change in interest rates has mostly been argued in the context of the stock market, where the proposition is indeed plausible. However, the stock market is not the best context in which to discuss the financial stability role of monetary policy, as stocks are held mostly by unlevered investors such as mutual funds. As we have seen in this book, much more central is the credit market and the financial intermediary sector, especially when backed by residential or commercial real estate. A difference of a quarter or a half percent in the funding cost may make all the difference between a profitable venture and a loss-making one for leveraged financial intermediaries. Adrian and Shin (2008c) present evidence that bears on this issue.

Focusing on the pricing of risk and the conduct of financial intermediaries is a better way to think about financial stability since it helps us to ask the right questions. Concretely, consider the following pair of questions.

Question 1. Do you know for sure there is a bubble in real estate prices?
Question 2. Could the current benign funding conditions reverse abruptly with adverse consequences for the economy?

One can answer "yes" to the second question even if one answers "no" to the first. This is because we know more about the script followed by financial intermediaries and how they set the price of risk in equilibrium (and then react to changes in the price of risk) than we do about what the "fundamental" value of a house is, and whether the current market price exceeds that value.

In any case, for a central banker, it is the second question which is more immediately relevant. Even if the central banker were convinced that the higher price of housing is fully justified by long-run secular trends in population, household size, rising living standards, and so on, policy intervention would be justified if he also believed that, if left unchecked, the virtuous circle of benign funding conditions and higher housing prices will go too far, and reverse abruptly with adverse consequences for the economy.

Following the trauma of the financial crisis, the climate of opinion has become more receptive to change. Some central bankers are at last beginning to redress the balance between monetary policy and policies toward financial stability that has been missing in recent years. But the window of opportunity for reform will not be open for long. Failure to seize this opportunity to put monetary policy and financial regulation on more secure conceptual foundations would be a lost opportunity. Future generations will bear the cost if we fail to seize this opportunity.

References

Acharya, Viral and Matthew Richardson (2009), *Restoring Financial Stability: How to Repair a Failed System*, New York University Stern School of Business, New York: John Wiley & Sons.

—— Hyun Song Shin, and Tanju Yorulmazer (2008), "A Theory of Slow Moving Capital and Contagion", working paper, NYU (New York University) Stern School of Business

Adrian, Tobias and Markus Brunnermeier (2009), "CoVaR", Federal Reserve Bank of New York Staff Reports, 348, September.

—— and Hyun Song Shin (2008a), "Liquidity and Financial Contagion", *Banque de France Financial Stability Review*, 11: 1–8.

—— —— (2008b), "Financial Intermediary Leverage and Value at Risk", Federal Reserve Bank of New York Staff Reports 338, July.

—— —— (2008c), "Financial Intermediaries, Financial Stability and Monetary Policy", Proceedings of the Federal Reserve Bank of Kansas City Symposium at Jackson Hole.

—— —— (2009), "Money, Liquidity and Monetary Policy", *American Economic Review*. 99(2): 600–4.

—— —— (forthcoming), "Liquidity and Leverage", *Journal of Financial Intermediation*.

—— Erkko Etula, and Hyun Song Shin (2009), "Risk Appetite and Exchange Rates", Federal Reserve Bank of New York Staff Reports 361, January.

—— Emanuel Moench, and Hyun Song Shin (2009), "Financial Intermediation, Asset Prices and Macroeconomic Dynamics", working paper.

Afonso, Gara and Hyun Song Shin (2008), "Systemic Risk and Liquidity in Payment Systems", Federal Reserve Bank of New York Staff Reports, 352.

Alizalde, A. and R. Repullo (2006), "Economic and Regulatory Capital in Banking: What is the Difference?", CEMFI working paper.

Allen, F. and D. Gale (2004), "Financial Intermediaries and Markets", *Econometrica*, 72: 1023–61.

—— —— (2006), *Understanding Financial Crises*, Clarendon Lectures in Finance, Oxford: Oxford University Press.

Ashcraft, A. and T. Schuermann (2008), "Understanding the Securitisation of Subprime Mortgage Credit", Staff Report 318, Federal Reserve Bank of New York <http://www.newyorkfed.org/research/staff_reports/sr318.pdf>.

Bank for International Settlements (2008), *78th Annual Report*, Basel, Switzerland.

Bank of England (2004), *Financial Stability Review*, December, Bank of England.

—— (2008), *Financial Stability Report*, April, Bank of England.

Bernanke, Ben S. (2002), "Asset-Price 'Bubbles' and Monetary Policy" <http://www.federalreserve.gov/boarddocs/speeches/2002/20021015/default.htm>.

—— (2005), "The Global Savings Glut and the U.S. Current Account Deficit" <http://www.federalreserve.gov/boarddocs/speeches/2005/200503102/default.htm>.

—— and A. Blinder (1988), "Credit, Money and Aggregate Demand", *American Economic Review*, 78: 435–9.

—— and M. Gertler (1989), "Agency Costs, Net Worth, and Business Fluctuations", *American Economic Review*, 79: 14–31.

Black, Fischer and Myron Scholes (1973), "The Pricing of Options and Corporate Liabilities", *Journal of Political Economy*, 81–3.

Bookstaber, Richard (2007), *A Demon of Our Own Design: Markets, Hedge Funds, and the Perils of Financial Innovation*, New York: Wiley.

Borio, Claudio and Philip Lowe (2002), "Asset Prices, Financial and Monetary Stability: Exploring the Nexus", Bank for International Settlements Working Paper 114.

—— and Kostas Tsatsaronis (2004), "Accounting, Prudential Regulation and Financial Stability: Elements of a Synthesis", *Journal of Financial Stability*, 1: 111–35.

—— and William White (2003), "Whither Monetary and Financial Stability? The Implications of Evolving Policy Regimes", Proceedings of the Federal Reserve Bank of Kansas City Symposium at Jackson Hole 2003 <http://www.kc.frb.org/publicat/sympos/2003/sym03prg.htm>.

—— and Haibin Zhou (2008), "Capital Regulation, Risk-Taking and Monetary Policy: A Missing Link in the Transmission Mechanism?" Bank for International Settlements Working Paper 268.

Boyce, Alan (2008), "Covered Bonds vs. Securitisation Transparency vs. Opacity: Which is the Right Question", working paper, Absalon <https://www.ibm.com/developerworks/blogs/resources/adler/20090325_1.pdf>.

Brady, N. (1988), *Report of the Presidential Task Force on Market Mechanisms*, Washington, DC: Government Printing Office.

Brealey, Richard, Stewart Myers, and Franklin Allen (2008), *Principles of Corporate Finance*, 8th edn., New York: McGraw-Hill.

Brunnermeier, Markus (2009), "De-Ciphering the Credit Crisis of 2007", *Journal of Economic Perspectives*, 23(1): 77–100.

—— and Lasse Pedersen (2009), "Market Liquidity and Funding Liquidity", *Review of Financial Studies*, 22: 2201–38.

—— and Yuliy Sannikov (2009), "A Macroeconomic Model with a Financial Sector", Princeton University working paper.

—— Andrew Crockett, Charles Goodhart, Avi Persaud, and Hyun Song Shin (2009), "The Fundamental Principles of Financial Regulation", Geneva Report on the World Economy 11.

Bryant, John (1980), "A Model of Reserves, Bank Runs and Deposit Insurance", *Journal of Banking and Finance*, 4: 335–44.

Caballero, Ricardo J., Emmanuel Farhi, and Pierre-Olivier Gourinchas (2008), "An Equilibrium Model of 'Global Imbalances' and Low Interest Rates", *American Economic Review*, 98: 358–93.

Calomiris, Charles and Charles Kahn (1991), "The Role of Demandable Debt in Structuring Optimal Banking Arrangements", *American Economic Review*, 81: 497–513.

Cassidy, John (2009), *How Markets Fail: The Logic of Economic Calamities*, New York: Strauss and Giroux.

Cifuentes, Rodrigo, Gianluigi Ferrucci, and Hyun Song Shin (2004), "Liquidity Risk and Contagion", Bank of England working paper 264; short version published in *Journal of the European Economic Association* (2005), 3: 556 66.

Committee on Capital Markets Regulation (2009), "The Global Financial Crisis: A Plan for Regulatory Reform" <http://www.capmktsreg.org/pdfs/TGFC_CCMR_Report_(5-26-09).pdf>.

Crockett, Andrew (2000), "Marrying the Micro- and Macro-prudential Dimensions of Financial Stability", Remarks before the Eleventh International Conference of Banking Supervisors, Basel, September 20–21 <http://www.bis.org/speeches/sp000921.htm>.

Crouhy Michel, Dan Galai, and Robert Mark (2001), *The Essentials of Risk Management*, New York: McGraw-Hill.

Danielsson, Jon, Paul Embrechts, Charles Goodhart, Felix Muennich, Con Keating, Olivier Renault, and Hyun Song Shin (2001), "An Academic Response to Basel II", Financial Markets Group Special Paper 130 <http://hyunsongshin.org/www/basel2.pdf>.

—— and Hyun Song Shin (2003), "Endogenous Risk", in Peter Field (ed.), *Modern Risk Management: A History*, London: Risk Books.

—— —— and Jean-Pierre Zigrand (2004), "The Impact of Risk Regulation on Price Dynamics", *Journal of Banking and Finance*, 28: 1069–87.

—— —— —— (2009), "Risk Appetite and Endogenous Risk", working paper.

—— and Jean-Pierre Zigrand (2008), "Equilibrium Asset Pricing with Systemic Risk", *Economic Theory*, 35: 293–319.

Demyanyk, Y. and O. van Hemert (2007), "Understanding the Subprime Mortgage Crisis", Stern School of Business, New York University working paper.

Diamond, Douglas and Philip Dybvig (1983), "Bank Runs, Deposit Insurance, and Liquidity", *Journal of Political Economy*, 91: 401–19.

—— and Raghuram Rajan (2001), "Liquidity Risk, Liquidity Creation, and Financial Fragility: A Theory of Banking", *Journal of Political Economy*, 109: 287–327.

Dimsdale, Nicholas (2008), "The International Banking Crisis and British Experience", Oxford University working paper.

Dowd Kevin (2005), *Measuring Market Risk*, New York: John Wiley & Sons.

Eisenberg, L. and T. H. Noe (2001), "Systemic Risk in Financial Systems", *Management Science*, 47: 236–49.

Elsinger, Helmut, Alfred Lehar, and Martin Summer (2006a), "Using Market Information for Banking System Risk Assessment", *International Journal of Central Banking*, 2(1): 137–65.

—— —— —— (2006b), "Systemically Important Banks", *International Economics and Economic Policy*, 3(1): 73–89.

—— —— —— (2006c), "Risk Assessment for Banking Systems" *Management Science*, 52 (9): 1301–14.

Embrechts, Paul, Alexander McNeil, and Daniel Straumann (2002), "Correlation and Dependence in Risk Management: Properties and Pitfalls", in M. Dempster (ed.), *Risk Management: Value at Risk and Beyond*, Cambridge: Cambridge University Press, 176–223.

Etula, Erkko (2009), "Risk Appetite and Commodity Returns", Federal Reserve Bank of New York working paper.

Fernandez, S., J. Pages, and J. Saurina (2000), "Credit Growth, Problem Loans and Credit Risk Provisioning in Spain", Bank of Spain working paper 18.

Fisher, Irving (1930), *The Theory of Interest*, New Haven: Yale University Press.

Garleanu, Nicolae and Lasse Heje Pedersen (2009), "Margin-Based Asset Pricing and Deviations from the Law of One Price", working paper.

Geanakoplos, John (1997), "Promises, Promises", in W. B. Arthur, S. Durlauf and D. Lane (eds.), *The Economy as an Evolving Complex System, II*, Reading, MA: Addison-Wesley, 285–320.

—— (forthcoming), "The Leverage Cycle", *2009 NBER Macroeconomics Annual*.

Genberg, Hans, Robert McCauley, Yung Chul Park, and Avinash Persaud (2005). *Official Reserves and Currency Management in Asia: Myth, Reality and the Future*, Geneva Report on the World Economy 7, London: Centre for Economic Policy Research.

Genotte, Gerard and Hayne Leland (1990), "Hedging and Crashes", *American Economic Review*, 999–1021.

Gete, Pedro (2008), "Housing Markets and Current Account Dynamics", Georgetown University working paper.

Gorton, G (2008), "The Panic of 2007", Proceedings of the Federal Reserve Bank of Kansas City Symposium at Jackson Hole.

—— and N. Souleles (2006), "Special Purpose Vehicles and Securitisation", in R. Stulz and M. Carey (eds.), *The Risks of Financial Institutions*, Chicago: University of Chicago Press.

Greenlaw, D., J. Hatzius, A. Kashyap, and H. S. Shin (2008), "Leveraged Losses: Lessons from the Mortgage Market Meltdown", US Monetary Policy Forum Report 2 <http://research.chicagogsb.edu/igm/events/docs/MPFReport-final.pdf>.

Gromb, Denis and Dimitri Vayanos (2002), "Equilibrium and Welfare in Markets with Financially Constrained Arbitrageurs", *Journal of Financial Economics*, 66: 361–407.

Gurley, John G, and E. S. Shaw (1955), "Financial Aspects of Economic Development", *American Economic Review*, 45(4): 515–38.

Haldane, Andrew (2009), "Rethinking Financial Networks", Speech delivered at Financial Student Association in Amsterdam, April 28.

He, Zhiguo and Arvind Krishnamurthy (2007), "Intermediary Asset Pricing", Northwestern University working paper.

Hellwig, Martin (1994), "Banking and Finance at the End of the Twentieth Century", University of Basel WWZ discussion paper 9426.

Hellwig, Martin (1995), "Systemic Aspects of Risk Management in Banking and Finance", *Swiss Journal of Economics and Statistics*, 131(4/2): 723–37.

Hildebrand, Philipp (2008), "Is Basel II Enough? The Benefits of a Leverage Ratio", Financial Markets Group Lecture <www.bis.org/review/r081216d.pdf>.

Holmstrom B. and J. Tirole (1997), "Financial Intermediation, Loanable Funds, and the Real Sector", *Quarterly Journal of Economics*, 112. 663–92.

Holmstrom, Bengt, and Jean Tirole (1998), "Private and Public Supply of Liquidity", *Journal of Political Economy*, 106: 1–40.

Holton, Glyn (2003), *Value-at-Risk: Theory and Practice*, San Diego, CA: Academic Press.

Hull, John (2009), *Options, Futures and Other Derivatives*, 7th edn., New York: Prentice-Hall.

International Monetary Fund (1998), "World Economic Outlook and International Capital Markets: Interim Assessment" <http://www.imf.org/external/pubs/ft/weo/weol298/index.htm>.

—— (2008), *Global Financial Stability Report*, April, Washington, DC.

—— (2009), *Global Financial Stability Report*, April, Washington, DC.

Jorin, Philippe (2006), *Value at Risk: The New Benchmark for Managing Financial Risk*, 3rd edn., New York: McGraw-Hill.

Kashyap, A., R. Rajan, and J. Stein (2008), "Rethinking Capital Regulation", paper for the Federal Reserve Bank of Kansas City Symposium at Jackson Hole.

—— and J. Stein (2000), "What do a Million Observations on Banks Say about the Transmission of Monetary Policy?", *American Economic Review*, 90: 407–28.

Keys, Benjamin, Tanmoy Mukherjee, Amit Seru, and Vikrant Vig (2007), "Did Securitisation Lead to Lax Screening? Evidence From Subprime Loans", University of Chicago GSB working paper.

Kiyotaki, Nobuhiro, and John Moore (1997), "Credit Cycles", *Journal of Political Economy*, 105: 211–48.

Kiyotaki, Nobuhiro, and John Moore (2005), "Liquidity and Asset Prices", *International Economic Review*, 46: 317–49.

Khandani, Amir and Andrew W. Lo (2007), "What Happened to the Quants in August 2007?", MIT working paper.

Klemperer, Paul (2002), "How (Not) to Run Auctions: The European 3G Telecom Auctions", *European Economic Review*, 46(4–5): 829–45.

Kyle, A. S. and Xiong, Wei (2001), "Contagion as a Wealth Effect", *Journal of Finance*, 56: 1401–40.

Lowenstein, Roger (2000), *When Genius Failed*, New York: Random House.

Mayes, David and Geoffrey Wood (2008), "Lessons from the Northern Rock Episode", University of Auckland and Cass Business School working paper.

McNeil, Alexander, Rüdiger Frey, and Paul Embrechts (2005), *Quantitative Risk Management: Concepts Techniques and Tools*, Princeton: Princeton University Press.

Mian, Atif and Amir Sufi (2007), "The Consequences of Mortgage Credit Expansion: Evidence from the 2007 Mortgage Default Crisis", University of Chicago GSB working paper.

Michael, Ian (2004), "Accounting and Financial Stability", *Financial Stability Review*, June, Bank of England, 118–28.

Milgrom, Paul and John Roberts (1990), "Rationalizability, Learning, and Equilibrium in Games with Strategic Complementarities", *Econometrica*, 58/6, November: 1255–77.

—— —— (1994), "Comparing Equilibria", *American Economic Review*, 84: 441–59.

Milne, Alistair and Geoffrey Wood (2008), "Shattered on the Rock? British Financial Stability from 1866 to 2007", Cass Business School working paper.

Minsky, Hyman (1975), *Stabilizing an Unstable Economy*, New Haven: Yale University Press.

Morris, Stephen and Hyun Song Shin (1998), "Unique Equilibrium in a Model of Self-Fulfilling Currency Attacks", *American Economic Review*, 88: 587–97; reprinted in *New Research in Financial Markets*, edited by B. Biais and M. Pagano, Oxford: Oxford University Press (2002); reprinted in *Credit, Intermediation and the Macroeconomy*, edited by S. Bhattacharya, A. Boot, and A. Thakor, Oxford: Oxford University Press (2004).

—— —— (1999), "Risk Management with Interdependent Choice", *Oxford Review of Economic Policy*, 15 Autumn; 52–62, reprinted in the *Financial Stability Review*, Bank of England, November 1999.

—— —— (2004), "Liquidity Black Holes", *Review of Finance*, 8: 1–18.

—— —— (2008), "Financial Regulation in a System Context", *Brookings Papers on Economic Activity*, Fall: 229–74.

—— —— (2009), "Illiquidity Component of Credit Risk", Princeton University working paper.

Oehmke, Martin (2008), "Liquidating Illiquid Collateral", Columbia University GSB working paper.

Packer, F., R. Stever, and C. Upper (2007), "The Covered Bond Market", *BIS Quarterly Review*, September: 43–55.

Persaud, Avinash (2001), "Liquidity Black Holes", working paper, State Street Bant <www.statestreet.com/knowledge/research/liquidity_black_holes.pdf>.

Plantin, Guillaume, Haresh Sapra, and Hyun Song Shin (2005), "Marking to Market, Liquidity and Financial Stability", *Proceedings of the 12th International Conference*, Bank of Japan.

—— —— —— (2008) "Marking to Market: Panacea or Pandora's Box?", *Journal of Accounting Research*, 46: 435–60.

Rajan, R. (2005), "Has Financial Development Made the World Riskier?", Proceedings of the Federal Reserve Bank of Kansas City Symposium at Jackson Hole <http://www.kc.frb.org/publicat/sympos/2005/sym05prg.htm>.

Repullo, Rafael and Javier Suarez (2008), "The Procyclical Effects of Basel II", CEMFI working paper.

Schnabel, Isabel and Hyun Song Shin (2004), "Liquidity and Contagion: the Crisis of 1763", *Journal of the European Economic Association*, 2(6): 929–68.

Shin, Hyun Song (2005a), "Financial System Liquidity, Asset Prices and Monetary Policy", Proceedings of the 2005 Reserve Bank of Australia Annual Conference <http://www.rba.gov.au/PublicationsAndResearch/Conferences/2005/shin.pdf>.

—— (2005b), "Commentary: Has Financial Development Made the World Riskier?", Proceedings of the Federal Reserve Bank of Kansas City Symposium it Jackson Hole <http://www.kc.frb.org/publicat/sympos/2005/sym05prg.htm>.

—— (2008), "Risk and Liquidity in a System Context", *Journal of Financial Intermediation*, 17: 315–29.

—— (2009a), "Securitisation and Financial Stability", *Economic Journal*, 119: 309–32.

—— (2009b), "Reflections on Northern Rock: The Bank Run that Heralded the Global Financial Crisis", *Journal of Economic Perspectives*.

Shleifer, Andrei and Robert Vishny (1992), "Liquidation Values and Debt Capacity: A Market Equilibrium Approach", *Journal of Finance*, 47: 1343–66.

—— —— (1997), "The Limits of Arbitrage", *Journal of Finance*, 52: 35–55.

SIFMA (2009) First European Covered Bond Investors' Survey, European Covered Bond Dealers Association, May <http://europe.sifma.org/ecbda.shtml>.

Squam Lake Working Group (2009), "Reforming Capital Requirements for Financial Institutions", policy memo <http://www.squamlakeworkinggroup.org>.

Tarski, A. (FA3), "A Lattice-Theoretical Fix-Point Theorem and its Applications", *Pacific Journal of Mathematics*, 5: 229–31.

Topkis, Donald M. (1978), "Minimizing a Submodular Function on a Lattice", *Operations Research*, 26(2), March–April: 305–21.

Van den Heuvel, S. (2002), "The Bank Capital Channel of Monetary Policy", Wharton, School, University of Pennsylvania working paper <http://www3.hi.is/~ajousson/kennsla2005/Bank_channel.pdf>.

Vasicek, O. (2002), "The Distribution of Loan Portfolio Value" <http://www.moodyskmv.com/conf04/pdf/papers/dist_loan_port_val.pdf>.

Wong, Elaine (2008), *The Impact of Market Prices on Valuation: A Case Study on the European 3G License Allocation Process*, undergraduate senior thesis, Princeton University, April.

Xiong, Wei (2001), "Convergence Trading with Wealth Effects: An Amplification Mechanism in Financial Markets", *Journal of Financial Economics*, 62: 247–92.

Yorulmazer, T. (2008), "Liquidity, Bank Runs and Bailouts: Spillover Effects During the Northern Rock Episode", Federal Reserve Bank of New York working paper.

Index

inhibitor + incentive

Les: sycophantic

actions of short

write pour

trade

see mom ask - sell h'l

which cuts our risk

Actionable
info

search
for
yield

Risk
underwater
x
misprice